THE HOLLYWOOD PROFESSIONALS

Volume One:

Michael Curtiz
Raoul Walsh
Henry Hathaway

by
Kingsley Canham

This new series spotlights the work of the many professional directors at work in Hollywood during its heyday—talents who might otherwise be ignored by film students and historians. Kingsley Canham has contributed monographs and very detailed filmographies of Michael Curtiz, Raoul Walsh, and Henry Hathaway, who between them made scores of familiar movies with a c[illegible]tence and a gloss now rarely seen in the cir[illegible]

In the same series, produced by THE TANTIVY PRESS and edited by Peter Cowie:

THE MARX BROTHERS Their World of Comedy by Allen Eyles
FRENCH CINEMA SINCE 1946 (Vol. 1: The Great Tradition)
(Vol. 2: The Personal Style) by Roy Armes
HITCHCOCK'S FILMS by Robin Wood
BUSTER KEATON by J. P. Lebel
HORROR IN THE CINEMA by Ivan Butler
THE CINEMA OF JOSEPH LOSEY by James Leahy
SUSPENSE IN THE CINEMA by Gordon Gow
THE CINEMA OF ALAIN RESNAIS by Roy Armes
4 GREAT COMEDIANS Chaplin, Lloyd,
Keaton, Langdon by Donald W. McCaffrey
HOLLYWOOD IN THE TWENTIES by David Robinson
HOLLYWOOD IN THE THIRTIES by John Baxter
HOLLYWOOD IN THE FORTIES by Charles Higham and Joel Greenberg
HOLLYWOOD IN THE FIFTIES by Gordon Gow
HOLLYWOOD IN THE SIXTIES by John Baxter
HOLLYWOOD TODAY by Allen Eyles and Pat Billings
RELIGION IN THE CINEMA by Ivan Butler
THE CINEMA OF FRITZ LANG by Paul M. Jensen
THE CINEMA OF JOHN FRANKENHEIMER by Gerald Pratley
SCIENCE FICTION IN THE CINEMA by John Baxter
THE CINEMA OF FRANÇOIS TRUFFAUT by Graham Petrie
THE CINEMA OF ROMAN POLANSKI by Ivan Butler
EARLY AMERICAN CINEMA by Anthony Slide
GRIFFITH & THE RISE OF HOLLYWOOD by Paul O'Dell
THE CINEMA OF CARL DREYER by Tom Milne
THE CINEMA OF JOHN FORD by John Baxter
THE CINEMA OF OTTO PREMINGER by Gerald Pratley

The Hollywood Professionals

MICHAEL CURTIZ
RAOUL WALSH
HENRY HATHAWAY

by

Kingsley Canham

THE TANTIVY PRESS, LONDON
A. S. BARNES & CO., NEW YORK

Acknowledgements

I would like to express my thanks to the following for their aid in the publication of this book:

My wife Jean; Peter Cowie, Felix Bucher, Allen Eyles in whose magazine *Focus on Film* the Hathaway material previously appeared in an abridged form; Robert Holton; Brenda Davies and her staff at the British Film Institute Information Library.

Stills appear by courtesy of Chris Wicking; Barrie Pattison; Barbara De Lord of 20th Century-Fox; Elizabeth Anderson of Paramount; and the British Film Institute Stills Library. Permission to use extracts from *Hollywood Cameramen* with the courtesy of Martin Secker and Warburg (G.B.), and the Indiana University Press (U.S.A.); from *Monthly Film Bulletin* with the courtesy of Jan Dawson of the British Film Institute; from *Films in Review* with the courtesy of Henry Hart, and from *Hollywood in the Thirties* with the courtesy of The Tantivy Press (G.B.) and A. S. Barnes & Co. (U.S.A.).

Cover Design by Stefan Dreja

FIRST PUBLISHED 1973

Library of Congress Catalogue Card No. 72-1786
SBN 90073058 7 (U.K.)
SBN 498-01204-2 (U.S.A.)

Printed in the United States of America

Contents

To my wife
Jean

Curtiz talks to William Powell on the set of LIFE WITH FATHER

Author's Introduction

This book is intended as the first in a series examining the careers of a number of Hollywood directors, who for various reasons, have been underestimated in the host of film books published in recent years. It does not attempt to be a definitive study, partly through lack of space, but more because it is intended as a guide to these particular directors and the conditions in which they made their films. Thus I have outlined their careers, choosing a dozen or so films for particular attention, while providing as full as possible filmographies relating to their *American* work, in the hope that it creates some interest or stimulates existing interest in both the casual reader and the more specialised reader. Credits on the early films are not always consistent, but without seeing the films themselves, there is little hope of achieving total consistency. Although the book is not seen in terms of *auteur* criticism, it should hopefully extend the reader's awareness of a director's role in shaping a film, for I have tried to stress the technical skill and ability which has gone into the work of these men, and their range; they have little in common, other than the fact that they all entered the cinema in its earliest years to emerge after they had completed their initial groundwork as highly skilled professionals with a particular knack for making polished action films.

KINGSLEY CANHAM

George O'Brien woos Dolores Costello in a somewhat unusual setting in Curtiz's NOAH'S ARK

Curtiz: Cynicism, Cinema and Casablanca.

The American film industry, in the silent days, proved to be one of the most adaptable media in which the variety of ethnic immigrant groups in the United States could function on equal terms with the native inhabitants. Initially the cinema attracted shrewd, hard-working men from these groups with a head for business; they bickered and quarrelled, but gradually organised production and distribution monopolies, and emerged as the first movie moguls. The American government laid down statutory laws, further legalising the industry, as well as stabilising it.

As public interest in the cinema grew, and European films were imported to supplement the range of material available, the moguls sensed the public admiration of the skill and originality of some of these foreign works, so they sent talent scouts and agents abroad to lure stars and technicians to work for them in America. Thus new blood constantly stimulated the American studios, and the competition ensured that everyone on the studio payroll gave of their utmost ability. The Warner Brothers, Sam, Harry and Jack, were a typical example. Former butchers, they had entered the industry in 1920; but they found the competition fierce, and were struggling by 1925 with Rin-Tin-Tin and John Barrymore as their sole assets when they took over Vitagraph, an early company with an impressive roster of players and directors. Sam, who handled the majority of policy decisions, took a gamble, and made an agreement with Western Electric to use their equipment in an attempt to introduce talking pictures. The idea was restricted to synchronised soundtracks at first, but they recorded some words of dialogue, spoken by Al Jolson in *The Jazz Singer* (1927), and the public response was overwhelmingly in favour of talkies. Sam Warner died on the eve of his success, but his brothers continued to capitalise on his gamble, as well as continuing the policy of importing foreign talent.

When Jack Warner saw a film entitled *Moon of Israel* (1927), made in Austria by a Hungarian director named Mikhaly Kertesz, he signed him up, thus launching the highly successful and prolific American career of Michael Curtiz. Curtiz had entered his native film industry in its infancy, and is rumoured to have been the director of the first feature film made in Hungary. He spent some time in Denmark at Nordisk studios learning the techniques involved in professional film-making, before returning home to put his acquired skill into practice. He served briefly in the infantry during the First World War, but was returned to civilian life in 1915, ostensibly to serve as a newsreel cameraman; but he was soon making feature films again, many starring his wife Lucy Dorraine and later a girl named Mary Kidd. A few of the latter reached America in the early Twenties, but made no immediate impression. Curtiz had fled Hungary in 1918, when Béla Kun's Communist *régime* had nationalised the film industry. Rumour has it that he worked in both France and Germany, before signing a contract with Sascha Films in Austria, but there is no concrete evidence to support these claims.

★ ★ ★

Curtiz was a hard, efficient and fast worker. A manic-depressive by nature, he seldom allowed himself the luxury of any social contact, and often expressed contempt for those who worked to live, as opposed to one such as himself who lived to work. His ruthless approach to work, his arrogance and temperament combined with his speed and technical ability, made him a perfect craftsman in the eyes of the Warner Brothers. The struggle for power had left its mark on them, and the studio attained a unique reputation for parsimony, through their contract policy, which was master-minded by Harry Warner. Long-term contracts were designed to milk every possible iota of talent from the contractees, without making any adjustment to their salary during the period of the contract; a clause allowed Warner Brothers the option of cancelling the contract at the end of each year but made no such allowance to the contractee, while any breach of contract (i.e. refusal to take a role etc.) meant a suspension until an alternative performer was found and the finished film in the can. A suspension would be added to the end of the contract, so that a troublesome star could find that his contract was almost indefinite in length. Bogart, Cagney, Bette Davis and Olivia De Havilland among others spent so much time on suspension that it is amazing that they worked as frequently as they did for the studio. The latter two ladies both fought court cases to amend the terms of their respective contracts, with Bette Davis losing and Olivia De Havilland eventually winning her case, and altering all Hollywood studio contracts as a result.

Curtiz, however, gave Warner Brothers little bother in this respect, turning out a staggering total of forty-four features between 1930 and 1939. His first big success was the film Jack Warner had in mind for him when he originally signed him up, *Noah's Ark* (1928), a spectacular split-level vehicle paralleling a Biblical story with a First World War love affair. It was his second film to contain dialogue scenes, but his first important work came in 1930, when he made *Mammy* starring Al Jolson. A simple story of love and friendship in a touring minstrel show with several of the production numbers shot in two-tone Technicolor, it was well received by public and the critics:

"*Mammy* is undoubtedly the most effective drama in which Al Jolson has yet appeared . . . color scenes are most effective . . . the simplicity of the story constitutes the great appeal of the film . . . the settings of the minstrel show are very effective, and the gradual expansion with the tide of prosperity is cleverly suggested." (National Film Theatre programme note).

Re-seen today, Jolson's hamming mars the film, but the atmosphere is exceptionally well drawn, considering Curtiz was a Mittel European only four years away from home. Possibly only Fritz Lang and Alfred Hitchcock have adapted themselves to the mores of an alien culture so rapidly, while most foreign directors eased themselves in more gently, or like Mauritz Stiller and Paul Fejos were never able to adapt themselves to the Hollywood system. It is even more remarkable in the case of Curtiz, considering the propensity for malapropisms with which his command of the English language was enhanced! In fact many of the lines which legend has attributed to Samuel Goldwyn erroneously, stemmed from Curtiz. The year 1930 also marked the start of his famous feuds with actors, and Olivia De Havilland in a recent lecture when asked about working with him, replied that until the latter years of his career, he was always "an angry man." The successful Flynn-De Havilland-Curtiz working combination was eventually broken up by the mutual antipathy of the two men for one another.

★ ★ ★

Curtiz was also the first director to film an all colour horror film, *The Mystery of the Wax Museum* (1933). Although derivative in theme from the necrophiliac obsessions of Gothic drama (Paul Leni's *Die Wachsfigurenkabinett*), Curtiz's style owes more to the horror comedies of Benjamin Christensen, with Glenda Farrell as the heroine's friend wise-cracking her way through the film, while Fay Wray as the heroine is mainly required, as in *King Kong*, to register a variety of forms of fear. An element of comedy is also present in the relish with which Lionel Atwill develops his role as a mad sculptor, who moulds wax over corpses and living bodies in order to exhibit them as historical figures in his wax museum.

The dramatic confusion in his mind between flesh and wax enables Curtiz to put across a number of sly, cynical, visual jokes about the sexual satisfaction which he obtains from making these life-like simulacra. It is also notable as one of the earliest examples in his work to touch on a motif of misguided ambition—here in the form of Atwill's obsession.

Taking the career of Curtiz in perspective, the sheer quantity of his output, and the range which he encompassed successfully, outwit any attempt to illustrate his work by means of analysis as an *auteur*. There is no consistent development of ideas or themes, nor are there any specific identifiable trademarks or signatures of style common only to him. Many of his early American works betray the speed with which they were made, and the shallowness of their respective plots or acting. Few, if any, lack pace, and they are representative of the full gamut of the Hollywood "bread and butter" cycle. He worked in nearly every genre, producing films of great merit in each as well as lesser vehicles. For every *Yankee Doodle Dandy* there is an *I'll See You in My Dreams*; for every *Mildred Pierce* there is *The Scarlet Hour*; for every *Dodge City* there is a *Bright Leaf*.

Many of the budding Warner Brothers talents worked with him in the early years; Bette Davis played her first notable Southern bitch, luring, taunting and losing Richard Barthelmess in *Cabin in the Cotton* (1932); while in *20,000 Years in Sing Sing* (1933), she was the tough, faithful, vulnerable moll in love with a big-headed mobster, played by Spencer Tracy. It is an uneven film, attacking—by means of a precise visual semi-documentary reconstruction—the primitive conditions in American prisons in the late Twenties and early Thirties. The ritualised customs and terminology are graphically depicted in terms of both comedy (with the rebellious Tracy refusing to don the oversize uniform with which he has been presented, starting a minor riot by pelting the prison officers with shoes), and drama (the devious scheming of Tracy's lawyer, Louis Calhern, to ensure that he remains behind bars while Calhern attempts to seduce Bette Davis). Midway through the film, the narrative becomes rather confused and the juxtaposing of the action between Tracy and Davis is often haphazard and imbalanced.

There is no confusion in his first film with James Cagney, *Jimmy the Gent* (1934), in which Cagney takes his head as a one-man whirlwind, chewing up the scenery in between rattling out dialogue at a completely incredible rate as a fast-talking, quick-thinking shyster running his business with the same sort of benevolence as George Bancroft in Rowland Brown's superb *Blood Money* (1933), who shares the same weakness—an ambition to climb the social scale. It is one of the very few occasions in which Bette Davis as a heroine is acted off the screen, and completely out-paced. Curtiz's later work with Cagney includes *Angels with Dirty Faces* (1938), and *Yankee Doodle Dandy* (1942). The former is the first of a cycle of crime films featuring a priest as the central figure who successfully combats the detrimental influence of their environment on slum children. In this case, it is Pat O'Brien who finally wins his battle by persuading the vicious killer, Cagney, to feign cowardice as he goes to the electric chair, so that he will lose face in the eyes of the kids, for whom he has become a hero figure. The Cagney pugnacity is combined with a desire to rise above his slum background by taking whatever he wants, regardless of the law or human feelings; a stock characterisation which he was to repeat many times in his career in different guises. Also in a smaller role as a treacherous gangster was Humphrey Bogart, with whom Curtiz was later to work on his enduring masterpiece *Casablanca* (1942).

★ ★ ★

Opposite: Old pals Lowell Sherman and Al Jolson fall out over a girl in Curtiz's MAMMY

The box-office success of the standard Warner films, seven reel melodramas, and the prestige which they had acquired as the pioneers of sound films, had vastly improved their status, and accordingly altered the style and budget of their typical films. While other lesser directors continued to turn out the staple diet of cheap bread and butter films, employing the talents of novice actors or actresses, or second-string players who had a minority appeal, Curtiz was among those directors elevated to handling Warner's prestige products, using the major talents on the lot. His first film in this field was *British Agent* (1934), an adaptation of British diplomat Bruce Lockhart's tale of his attempts to prevent the completion of a Russo-German peace treaty, prior to the outbreak of the Russian Revolution. It was hampered by an excessively heavy and absurdly romantic script; the supporting performances by

John Barrymore exerts his evil charms on hapless Mae Madison in this scene from Curtiz's THE MAD GENIUS

J. Carrol Naish as Trotsky, and Irving Pichel as Stalin are carefully drawn, but the most memorable aspect of the film is Curtiz's visual style: chattering machine-gun bullets raking the mirror-lined salon during an ambassadorial ball; the camera darting and weaving through the panic-stricken flight of civilians as fighting breaks out in the streets; and a telling example of Curtiz's cynical humour, cited by John Baxter in his book, *Hollywood in the Thirties*: "An odd vignette concerning one of the diplomats, who goes out to contact a Russian Army officer. Curtiz cuts promptly to the two men walking through a gate as part of a group. The diplomat, smoking nervously says with a grin, 'Well, Colonel, at least I found you.' The next shot shows them lined up against a wall with the others and executed." (*Hollywood in the Thirties* by John Baxter. Tantivy Press.)

Another star vehicle with Paul Muni, *Black Fury* (1935), casting Muni as a simple-hearted miner being used by racketeering strikebreakers to destroy his union, has not aged well; Muni, who was reputed to be a very difficult actor to handle, overplays excessively. Curtiz was on much surer ground in directing Errol Flynn in *Captain Blood* (1935), and he did so remarkably well considering that Flynn was a virtual novice at the time. Curtiz had used him earlier the same year in a bit role in a Perry Mason mystery entitled *The Case of the Curious Bride,* and had been impressed by his good looks and urge to succeed.

Although Curtiz was no romantic himself, he had made many romantic love stories in Hungary, and he seized the opportunity to utilise his talents in the grandeur and dramatic sweep of Rafael Sabatini's novel of the gentleman pirate. Pirate films had not been in vogue since the silent days with the athletic Douglas Fairbanks swashbuckling his way through *The Black Pirate* (1926, Albert Parker), or its imitators like James Cruze's *Old Ironsides* (1926) with Charles Farrell and George Bancroft, but 1935 saw the release of both *Captain Blood* and *Mutiny on the Bounty*. Ironically it was pure chance that gave Flynn the role which catapulted him to overnight stardom, since the role had been assigned to Robert Donat, but he withdrew owing to poor health.

Captain Blood stands the test of time well, thanks to a concise narrative, capable performances by all the leading players and a remarkable technical collaboration, engineered by Curtiz, including ingenious process photography and miniature work, precise editing and Erich Korngold's outstanding first film score. Flynn was not entirely happy about working with Curtiz, alleging that: "he liked blood so much he insisted the tips be taken off the swords." Flynn's next swashbuckling role as Robin Hood was begun by William Keighley, and second unit director B. Reeves Eason, but after completing most of the sequences in Sherwood Forest in six or seven weeks, Keighley was replaced by the producer Henry Blanke, who felt that his approach was too light-hearted. Curtiz was called in, and shot some additional exterior footage as well as all the interior sequences. The film remains a classic of its type; bedecked with resplendent colours, and a jolly, rousing score by Korngold, including a superbly orchestrated accompaniment to the final sword fight between Flynn and Sir Guy of Gisborne (Basil Rathbone). Flynn's performance is variable, but Rathbone, Claude Rains, Eugene Pallette and Alan Hale are in splendid form. But the final triumph lies with Curtiz's direction and the castle sets by Carl Jules Weyl (for which he won the 1938 Academy Award). As in all her prewar co-starring vehicles, Olivia De Havilland is a sweet, affecting heroine, mainly called upon to look pretty and to be charming or cool to the hero as the situation demands.

In spite of bad feeling between them, Flynn and Curtiz continued working together on *Dodge City* (1939), an elaborate Western about a cattle-man marshal and a lady editor bringing law and order to one of the more lively towns in Kansas, highlighted by a long, exciting and expansive saloon brawl; and *The Private Lives of Elizabeth and Essex* (1939), adapted from a play by Maxwell Anderson, and dominated by the portrayal of Elizabeth by Bette Davis: "Spectacular period costume piece based on the turbulent and tragic romance of middle-aged Queen Elizabeth of England and young, swashbuckling Earl of Essex. Gripping, if uneven, drama springs from the clash of aims, ambitions and personalities—uneven because

... Bette Davis is superb as Elizabeth; she looks the part, and storms, and rants with terrific conviction, and yet at times, shows a tenderer side. She never allows the Queen, ruthless dictator that she is, to conceal the woman ... whose name is vanity. In contrast, Errol Flynn looks magnificent as Essex, but he is no match histrionically for Bette Davis. Superb spectacle ... supports the pageantry." (National Film Theatre programme note.)

Michael Curtiz (bending third from the rear on the ramp) prepares a scene on CAPTAIN BLOOD

Errol Flynn disposes of a pirate adversary in one of the many action scenes in THE SEA HAWK

Virginia City (1940), another Western, dealt with the efforts of a Southern sympathiser (Miriam Hopkins) to run gold from the West to Richmond, and the attempts of a Yankee officer (Flynn) to prevent her. Curtiz feuded with both Flynn and Hopkins during shooting. *The Sea Hawk* (1940) offered Flynn as a privateer, proceeding without royal consent, but in the best interests of Elizabeth, to impede Spanish progress in building an armada which was to attack England; a tale of swashbuckling, suffering, bravado, guile, chicanery, some carnage and a great deal of romance.

The Flynn-Curtiz feud was now reaching serious proportions as the budgets on their films rose. *The Sea Hawk* cost a reputed $1,700,-000, and Warners were forced to take the matter seriously when Flynn's antipathy for Curtiz caused delays in the production of their penultimate film together, *The Santa Fe Trail* (1940). This is a film which deserves consideration at some length, since it is central to the Curtiz approach to film-making. It follows the careers of Jeb Stuart and George Armstrong Custer from their West Point graduation through their first encounter with John Brown and his Abolitionist movement in Kansas to the Harper's Ferry Massacre and Brown's hanging. Although dealing with a liberal subject, it is totally anti-liberal; and it makes very little concession to the historical importance of its subject matter in the annals of American history; concentrating instead in perpetuating the Flynn character (Stuart) as a hero in the later Raoul Walsh style—that of the invincible American hero, overcoming supreme odds to emerge triumphant. The character is presented with the qualities of bravery, a conventional adherence to the ways of his Southern upbringing and an unquestioning loyalty to the Army. In spite of the events in which he participates, and of the influence of those events on the people closest to him, Custer (Ronald Reagan) and the girl they both pursue ardently (Olivia De Havilland), Stuart does not alter at all, or give the slightest indication of developing.

The element of comedy, normally central in the Flynn-Curtiz films, is subjugated to the occasional antics of two cowboys, who attach themselves to Flynn and Reagan, wishing to join the Army; and the prominent intensity of both Raymond Massey as Brown, and Van Heflin as Rader, his treacherous, money-seeking aide thus promotes them to being the most interesting people in the film. Having therefore ignored to a great extent the factual, liberal and historical implications of his film, and doing very little to interest one in the colourless heroes, Curtiz chooses to emphasise the visual aspects and the action sequences, which abound throughout the film.

Accordingly, the recruits train to the rousing movements of Steiner's score; the graduation ceremony is filmed in a soft focus, underlining the romanticism of the occasion for the young men taking part, and the glances the dashing Flynn, and an obviously interested De Havilland, keep exchanging as all sing the Alma Mater; when a Southern villain (Charles Middleton) is shot dead trying to prevent one of John Brown's sons taking some Negro slaves to safety across the State line, the train conductor peevishly insists: "Get him outta the way. Ain't no use spoilin' the carpet with blood."

The religious fervour of John Brown is signified by shooting his meetings on hill-sides at dusk, or against skylines; Massey is invariably lit in high key, or with a single spot on his face, emphasising the demoniacal glitter in his eyes, bulging as he intones one of his biblical prophecies: "The Lord is a Man of War!; we recognise no law but the law of God!" etc. Equally, the depiction of the Negroes responding to his call fits the anti-liberal tone of the film by having them grouped around the barn in which he is addressing them, raising the roof with shouts of Hallelujah when things are going well, only to emerge from their hiding-place in the hay after the Army have put him to flight, professing some doubt as to whether they want his sort of freedom if it means fighting and bloodshed. The primary set pieces are the action sequences with a rapid change in mood as the camera follows the course of a wagon train being guarded by Stuart and Custer; the mood is one of light relief with the two soldiers bantering over their rivalry for De Havilland's hand as the comic relief scouts entertain them with songs; Curtiz cuts abruptly to Brown's prayer meeting as he prepares to attack the wagon train; once more the camera returns to the wagon train while the singing fills the air, only to be replaced by a pulsating rhythm as Brown rides towards the wagons. Both Stuart and Custer register suspicion as "Mr. Smith" and his followers flag them down in order to collect their assignment of "Bibles." As one of the cases breaks open revealing rifles, Brown's men cover the wagon train while a shot from Massey signals a sweeping pan across the hillside as Brown's reinforcements gallop into sight.

When Brown moves out with the rifles, Stuart initiates a reckless chase, filmed to the accompaniment of Steiner's throbbing music in a series of relentlessly edited pans and tracks across the dusty plains and hillocks. This is merely a rehearsal for the final climax, but first comes the arrest of Stuart, while scouting in plain clothes. Rader relishes the moment, mocking him about his probable martyrdom; and Stuart makes a tactical error when confronted with Brown by informing him of the death of one of his sons. This (to Brown) insult—Stuart: "An Absalom died because he feared his father," only strengthens Brown's resolve, and his mad glare is seen to unnerve Stuart momentarily. As the rope is placed around his neck, Stuart whips a revolver from one of his would-be killers' holster, shoots the nearest man, and dashes into a nearby barn, an action more typical of Walsh than of Curtiz.

Brown's men scatter to cover, although it is late evening and fairly dark, while Stuart pins them down. He still continues to hold his own when they encircle the barn, firing from all directions at once, and manage to set the barn alight. Incredibly, as the Army reinforcements arrive in the nick of time, he is still fighting gamely, and has also managed to save the life of several Negroes who were also hiding in the barn. His ammunition supply had been supplemented by the coincidental storage of the stolen rifles and bullets in the barn. Then Brown escapes, and some attention is given to the completion of the railroad; however this attention is very slight in comparison with that of Ford in either *My Darling Clementine* (1946) or *The Man Who Shot Liberty Valance* (1962), where the dialogue outlining the civilising influence of the railroad, and the importance of its role in bringing law and order to the West, is implemented with visual examples of this influence being put into practice—scenes in schools, homes and churches. Nor does Curtiz pay as much attention to the detail of military life, once the West Point scenes are finished, concentrating instead in greater detail on the selected incidents, both dramatic or romantic, in the lives of the leading players.

He does pay fairly close attention to a ball in Washington which Stuart and Custer attend upon their return from Fort Leavenworth, full of the glory of their defeat of John Brown. A scene with Custer preening himself in his new uniform in front of a mirror as he awaits the appearance of Olivia De Havilland suggests the vanity of the man, as Stuart laughingly puts him on, but soon they are involved in romantic scenes until the arrival of Rader, who has deserted Brown's forces because of non-payment of his services. The call to a briefing of the officers is reminiscent of the famous shot in Rouben Mamoulian's *Becky Sharp* (1935), as the uniformed men move across the screen in the blue outfits, draining the black and white contrast from the screen as they leave the image, which dissolves and the camera tracks back from the figure of Rader outlining Brown's plans.

Rader offers to return to act as a spy ("I could not stand by and see my country torn apart by a madman"); here Lincoln is seen briefly in a single scene, reading early news of Brown's attack on the arsenal at Harper's Ferry; but the film moves rapidly on, bringing Stuart to the scene. When Brown, trapped in the arsenal, slams the door in Stuart's face as he attempts to parley under a flag of truce, it is the signal for a superbly orchestrated battle; figures run across the screen shooting, cannons roar, tearing gaping holes in the building as beams and masonry fall in crumbling concert on Brown's men, while the cavalry raise a dusty cloud of earth and sods of grass as they gallop into support. The precise fusillade of destruction continues as Stuart leads men in with battering rams to smash down the shells of the door as Steiner's stirring score sounds the knell of doom for John Brown and his followers, but not before a raging Brown has destroyed a whimpering, cowering Rader, whose treachery has been revealed.

The pitch of the film is immediately altered with the hanging of Brown, foretelling his vision of blood spilt to purge the sins of a guilty land; as Flynn and De Havilland wed on a train speeding away from the scene, the camera pulls back to follow the motion of the wheels as they revolve to the faint, rumbling rhythm of "John Brown's Body" on the soundtrack, finishing the film with yet another of Curtiz's downbeat endings.

Although *Mammy* (1930) had been fairly successful, Curtiz seldom had much to do with films of a musical nature in the earlier years of his career, although he was destined to make six biographies of musical personalities before he died. Warners had embarked on a return to the musical field when the war broke out, after losing their original monopoly in the person of Busby Berkeley who moved to M-G-M to make the highly successful Judy Garland-Mickey Rooney musical comedy series in the late Thirties. That is not to say that Berkeley was the only talented man working on musicals at Warners in the Thirties, but that he was the best-known, the most extravagant and one of the most creative. Each studio set its own set pattern for musicals; Fox musicals revolved around the central theme of the struggling artist achieving success, and letting it go to his head, temporarily forsaking his nice girl for a gold-digging floozie, and hitting rock bottom before seeing the error of his ways; M-G-M made period pieces, exquisitely and lavishly presented or strung together a variety of disparate numbers in a kind of variety show as did Paramount. The latter also made musical comedies with Bing Crosby and Bob Hope, while Warners concentrated on biographies of light composers such as George M. Cohan (*Yankee Doodle Dandy,* 1942); George Gershwin (*Rhapsody in Blue,* 1943); Irving Berlin (*This Is the Army,* 1943) or Cole Porter (*Night and*

Day, 1946). Largely fictionalised, with the emphasis on schmaltz, they were often of greater interest musically than dramatically.

Yankee Doodle Dandy is an exception thanks to the performances of James Cagney (for which he won an Oscar) and Walter Huston as Cohan Snr. It is also notable as the first of Curtiz's Forties films to use ambition as a central motivation, which does recur in differing forms in many of his later films, particularly *Mildred Pierce* and *Young Man with a Horn* (1950). The biography of Cohan was a timely project, considering Cohan's patriotic fervour, and was in many ways a personal project of the Cagney family, with brother William working on the production side, and James Cagney starring with his sister Jeanne in a supporting role. It is a tribute to Cagney's sheer enthusiasm, Huston's professionalism and Curtiz's expertise that they turn out a competent film from the indifferent framework given them by the two writers, Robert Buckner and Edmund Joseph. This involves a full cycle of flashbacks, opening with Cohan being summoned to an early morning interview with the President, whom he is impersonating in a come-back just prior to America's entering the Second World War. The President expounds on his love of country, and Cohan explains that it originated at the moment of his birth on the Fourth of July; his father (Walter Huston) had just finished a theatrical performance when the news came that his baby was being born. Rushing into the streets, thronged with merry-makers watching an Independence Day parade, Huston commandeers a Civil War gun carriage to take him to the hospital, placing an American flag on his baby boy, and signalling the revellers to fire a one gun salute in tribute to the event.

Not surprisingly, young George grows up to be a very self-centred youth, and his cocky performance in "Peck's Bad Boy" so inflames other youngsters in the audience that they wait outside the stage door and beat him up. The experience has very little effect on him, and ten years later (now played by Cagney), in a typical Curtiz

James Cagney stuns his family by offering them half of his future earnings and royalties in Curtiz's YANKEE DOODLE DANDY. Left to right: Richard Whorf, Cagney, Walter Huston, Joan Leslie, Rosemary De Camp, Jeanne Cagney

joke, he cons an aspiring young actress (Joan Leslie) with words of fatherly advice, dressed in his stage make-up as an octogenarian, and then shocks the life out of her by bursting into a frantic dance, peeling off his fake appearance as he does so! He promotes her career with as much intensity as he does his own, succeeding only in getting her fired from her first job, and himself black-listed for fighting the manager. His family and Leslie loyally support him, but his pride cannot bear this and so he goes solo, conning a rich backer who wants to back a girlie show from giving any heed to an earnest author (Richard Whorf). As soon as he has sewn up a deal for himself, he goodheartedly takes the bemused playwright into partnership. Their first show, "Little Johnnie Jones," is a big hit, and reunites the family, with Cohan promising to write a song especially for Leslie. He does, but cannot resist luring a big Broadway star (Irene Manning) into his next show; she feels his work is not in the right class for her, so he gains her interest by writing a new song while she is on-stage during the first act of her current hit.

Whorf gives her "Mary," the song which Cagney had written for Leslie, much to Cagney's indignation, and she is hooked. This leaves Cagney no option but to propose to Leslie, who had guessed what would happen, and is glad to accept. Ambition in the Curtiz sense always leads to characters involving themselves so deeply in their work that they do not have time for or grow apart from those they love, but like Cagney or Joan Crawford in *Mildred Pierce,* their intentions are for the best and are not self-centred as were those of Lana Turner in Douglas Sirk's *Imitation of Life* (1961), where her efforts to be a great actress totally estranged her from her daughter, and severed the possibility of any affection or love developing.

Cohan becomes the toast of Broadway, with a number of his shows running consecutively, rivalled in popularity only by Eddie Foy. A meeting between them motivates Cohan's desire to include his love of pomp, military ceremony and patriotism in his shows, and is another example of Curtiz's humour—each trying to out-smart the other verbally with Foy just gaining the edge by using his stage impersonation to slobber and spit in the irate Cohan's face as they converse. His jibes about Cohan's patriotism spur Cohan into launching "The Red, White and Blue," which comprises some of the most blatant flag-waving ever seen on any stage or screen. Soon afterwards, the elder Cohan and his wife retire to a little farm, receiving a present of half shares in all George's past, present and future deals; while his sister quits to marry (much to George's indignation). He has his first flop, a straight play, as the Great War breaks out, and he is deemed ineligible for combat, so he writes popular nationalistic songs instead, such as "Over There." When his father dies, he and Whorf split up and go their separate ways, with Cohan retiring restlessly into obscurity until he is asked to portray the President. He is overwhelmed to discover that he has been summoned to receive the Congressional Medal of Honour for his patriotic services, and ends the film being further touched to find his marching songs being sung by the troops marching off to the Second World War.

Apart from the leads, most of the players in *Yankee Doodle Dandy* were second-string performers or character actors of varying quality. So it is a tribute to the expertise of Curtiz in handling players that the film maintains a consistency in its acting as well as in the evocation of the period in some detail. He had a particular eye for locations, many of which had to be painstakingly re-created on the Warner Brothers shooting stages since location filming was comparatively rare in the Thirties. More often the director, or a second unit, would be sent to a location to film stock material, and then the director would rely on the skill of his studio's special effects department to simulate accurately whatever exteriors were needed involving scenes with the principal players. This was the case with a gentle family drama, *Daughters Courageous* (1939), saved from sentimental banality by the adroit direction, holding together the pace and a number of excellent performances against an accurate small town background, superbly lit in soft focus by James Wong Howe.

The basic plot, that of the disruption of a family, is central to the lore of American culture, but the treatment by which the strongest performances come from the more unpleasant, or rather irresponsible characters, is strongly representative of Curtiz. The performance of Claude Rains as the father who walked out twenty years before the period of the film rather than face his responsibilities, and now returns cunningly to win over the sympathy of his daughters, while

The four daughters give their erring father an unexpected birthday present ("We took care of the first payment"). Left to right: Lola Lane, Priscilla Lane, Gail Page, Claude Rains and Rosemary Lane in Curtiz's FOUR DAUGHTERS

at the same time ridiculing the conventional, pipe-smoking suitor their mother is about to marry, is mockingly wry and contemptuous. Rains acts with a similar relish to that of Lionel Atwill in *The Mystery of the Wax Museum,* while John Garfield as the poorly educated, semi-delinquent with a permanent chip on his shoulder against society, who has successfully captured the affection of the youngest girl (Priscilla Lane) gives his first and best performance of a role in which he became type-cast throughout his Warner career. It relates to the modern day youth/family generation gap in this respect although there is currently a greater emphasis on personal psychology and life-style, and some of the pure, girlish antics of the Lane sisters seem very gauche.

★ ★ ★

Directors in the Forties injected new life and style into the thrillers and the dramas, with urbane, hard-boiled cynicism replacing the more obvious verbal humour; society was observed with a baleful eye that cast itself time and again on the violence, corruption and pessimism, spewing from the facade of middle-class suburban life; bored, greedy or frustrated women planned and schemed murder and mayhem, or gave tough "loner" heroes the come-on. Roots

Harry Carey and Edward G. Robinson are feeling the strain as they second for Wayne Morris in Curtiz's KID GALAHAD

and ties were seen as a hindrance; sentimentality was a weakness, and the weak were bound to perish in the garish neon jungle, or in some dingy alley or back-street, left to lie rotting with the garbage. Public transport or seedy hotel rooms became the place of assignation for the blackmailer, the seducer or his victim, the professional killer, the stool pigeon or the private eye; while bar-rooms, theatre foyers and night clubs reflected countless threats and fights in their wall-length mirrors. Low-key photography ruled the day, chilling the blood with its association of shadow and menace; glistening rain represented cold fear or impending doom. Such films held a cold, pristine romanticism, visually more realistic and exciting than reality; theirs was an enclosed but enthralling fantasy world, dominated by the harsh, resonant sounds of the night: feet echoing on pavements and wooden staircases, the screech of police sirens or car brakes, the bellow of factory sirens or the boom of fog-horns, the shrill, impersonal voices of the people. It was a type of film which bore a strong resemblance to Gothic drama and romanticism; thus it is not surprising that it was best conveyed by *émigré* directors like Lang, Siodmak, Preminger, Wilder and Curtiz.

Historians have tended to isolate varieties of films from this period under headings such as the *film noir* and the melodrama, incorporating the private eye stories with their particular underworld vernacular coined from the books of Dashiell Hammett, Raymond Chandler and Philip MacDonald, as well as the tales of suburban housewives led into crime or corruption in urban business organisations, but it is more difficult to isolate the contributions of Curtiz into one bracket exclusively. *Mildred Pierce* is definitely melodrama, but *Casablanca* is variously one or a number of combinations of wartime propaganda; romantic drama and an examination of existential philosophy; or just sentimental kitsch. *The Unsuspected* (1947) is a blend of the *film noir* and melodrama.

While John Huston was responsible for initiating the Bogart

legend by casting him as a hero in *The Maltese Falcon* (1941), it was Curtiz who created the archetype of the Bogart hero as a loner, believing in nothing and making his own private deals with destiny. For in *The Maltese Falcon* Bogart is motivated by the desire to avenge the death of his partner, no matter how half-heartedly he admits it to himself, while in Walsh's *High Sierra* (1941), as "Mad Dog" Roy Earle, he is driven to his final mountain showdown with the police by the shallow, insensitive behaviour of the lame girl (Joan Leslie), in whom he has taken a romantic and protective interest. Yet in *Casablanca*, his affair with Bergman is long over before the film starts; he is living in North Africa quite contentedly, running his business until she returns, and he spends a good deal of the time being converted to the realisation that he must take sides. Curtiz gave full rein to his jaded, worldly-wise cynical appeal which Bogart wore like a glove in portraying the bitter lover with little faith in the general good. The look of derision that sprung so easily to his battered features; his aggressive manner of kissing a girl, at the same time grasping her throat in a slightly menacing manner; or the cold hard stare, unblinking, into a foe's eyes; or the equally disturbing mannerism of tugging at the lobe of his ear, with a mockingly bemused expression in his eyes as his mouth slid automatically into a vacant half-grin. These and many other typical gestures project an extremely capable, confident man; a man who knew no fear, and could look after himself in any situation—the perfect hero, in spite of his lack of normal good looks, and what is generally considered to be charm.

As Bette Davis implied, during a recent John Player Lecture at The National Film Theatre, the pressure on directors such as Curtiz, Lloyd Bacon and Raoul Walsh to finish each film on schedule, often restricted any artistic intent which they had towards the material. But in the Forties his pressure was relaxed somewhat by external factors, so that on *Casablanca* the characterisation of Bogart as a liberal figure could be reasonably achieved by bringing in Howard Koch as a specialist writer, solely to work on Bogie's dialogue.

Casablanca is a very tightly constructed film, holding one's attention from start to finish as it relentlessly builds up atmosphere, and weaves its way through a score of neatly drawn sub-plots, without ever losing the thread of the central story. The opening sequence of a global map, spinning around to come to rest on North Africa, as an off-screen narrator sets the scene and itemises the escape route from Occupied France with all roads leading finally to Casablanca, moves easily into a montage sequence illustrating the commentary. This is the main contribution of Don Siegel and James Leicester, although some of their work is also evident in a later flashback of the Germans occupying Paris. Pace dominates the film as Curtiz rapidly links the global metaphor to the thronging populace on a crowded Casablanca street. The danger and excitement of everyday life is illustrated by means of two overlapping sequences; firstly of a professional pickpocket lifting the wallet of a gullible Englishman, while he watches the second event taking place nearby. This is the murder of two German couriers. Police cars seal off the district, their sirens wailing as they tear along the densely crowded streets, scattering pedestrians, braking wildly with a screech of tyres and unloading armed men to seek out and arrest suspects. A Free French member is shot down under a poster of Pétain as he tries vainly to escape when the police identify his papers as being forged. Automatically, all eyes lift hopefully towards the Lisbon plane, seen landing at the airport near "Rick's Café Americain," for many people are waiting hopefully in Casablanca until they can raise the money for an exit visa to take them on their next step to freedom.

The plane contains Colonel Strasser (Conrad Veidt), a typically scarred Gestapo officer, sporting a monocle, who listens imperiously to the French police chief, Captain Renault (Claude Rains), as he promises to arrest the fugitive killer of the couriers that night at Rick's Café. Both studiously ignore the efforts of their Italian counterpart to introduce himself, as the scene changes to evening at Rick's. A long pan across the room once more underlines the international populace; nervous fugitives, sly wheelers and dealers, desperate gamblers hocking their possessions, furtive men and women forever planning and scheming. A gradual build-up introduces Rick (Bogart); a waiter tells a customer that Rick never drinks with customers, and this is repeated several times in later scenes; the camera tracks in to a shot of his hand signing a bill,

A reunion between Humphrey Bogart and Ingrid Bergman, with Claude Rains as the police chief and Paul Henreid as the husband in Curtiz's CASABLANCA

finally pulling up to reveal an aggressive, scowling Rick, as he deals with Bugati (Peter Lorre, in a characteristic, fidgety performance) as the fugitive killer. Bugati is trying to sell the letters of transit, which he has stolen from his victims, but Rick is scornful: "I don't mind a parasite, but I object to a cut rate one." Rick agrees to look after the letters, however, until Bugati can make a deal later that night, hiding them in his Negro pianist's instrument before crossing swords with rival café owner, Señor Ferrari (the bulky Sydney Greenstreet: "Isolationism is no longer a practical policy, my dear Rick"), whom he despises since Ferrari is involved in the white slave traffic ("How extravagant, throwing away women, Ferrari; one day they may be scarce!"). The script cynically pokes fun at each character, while establishing them in sharply drawn cameos. Thus Bogart, when quizzed on his reasons for coming to Casablanca, retorts: "I came for the waters." Ferrari: "But we are in the middle of the desert!" Rick: "I was misinformed."

The stage has been set for the development of the main plot, which is introduced during a conversation between Renault and Rick. Renault is played as a cool, wily lecher with a swift nose for appreciating which side of the fence to choose, swapping over with deft amiability and charm as the situation demands; his mocking tone and gestures are shown in an attractive and sympathetic light, as opposed to the dry, languid cynicism of a George Sanders cad, while one is never allowed to forget that beneath his pose he can be a dangerous man. He warns Rick not to get involved in helping Bugati or another fugitive, Victor Laszlo (Paul Henreid); Rick asserts that he sticks his neck for nobody, but displays an admiration for Laszlo: "He's succeeded in impressing half the world." They make a bet as to whether Laszlo will escape from Casablanca, as Renault reveals that Strasser has been sent to stop him (Renault: "Make it ten thousand, Rick. I'm only a *poor* corrupt official").

Renault also refers to Rick's previous record of gun-running in Ethiopia, and fighting for the Loyalists in the Spanish Civil War, pointing out that he always chose the under-dog.

Renault's deftness is emphasised as he and Strasser watch the arrest of a screaming Peter Lorre while Rick stands grimly by, ignoring his appeals for aid. Strasser picks on the way in which the Third Reich is referred to in conversation; ". . . as if you expected there to be *others*." Renault retorts quickly that he serves whomever leads. The arrival of Laszlo, and his mistress, Ilsa Lund (Ingrid Bergman), creates a stir; they make contact with an underground agent, who vanishes when Renault joins the conversation, introducing Strasser. Laszlo coldly acknowledges him, refusing to admit that his country, Czechoslovakia, is now part of Germany ("I have never accepted the *privilege* of citizenship of the Third Reich"), as Ilsa watches fearfully. She recognises Sam (Dooley Wilson), the pianist, and asks him to play some old songs for her, including "As Time Goes By." The music brings Rick over, furious that his orders never to play the song have been ignored, and he is stunned to see Ilsa, whom he has known in the past.

While the emotional impact is played to the hilt (softer focus; tears glistening in Bergman's eyes; Bogart's speechlessness), the narrative moves relentlessly on with Renault's commenting on the precedent of Rick's accepting a drink with a customer, and picking up the bill. In this way Curtiz draws considerable suspense from a pregnant situation, tantalising the audience with memories of the couple's previous meetings in Paris ("The Germans wore grey; you wore blue . . ."), but temporarily shelving the topic as Laszlo leaves with Ilsa, who passes Rick off as an acquaintance. Her fake casualness is given the lie by the next scene in very low-key lighting with Rick and Sam alone in his empty café. Rick is sullen and morose as he drinks steadily, and fights off Sam's efforts to get him to bed, musing to himself ("Of all the gin joints and taverns all over the world, she walks into mine . . . Play it, Sam, you played it for her . . . you can play it for me").

As Sam begins playing, the film fades into a flashback of their idyllic love affair, with the emphasis on soft lighting and sentimental music as "Perfidia" plays over a long kiss, only to be replaced by the dramatic tones of "Deutschland Über Alles" and a montage of war shots as the German advance on Paris is announced. The typical Bogart mannerisms, such as tugging his ear lobe with a quizzical expression as he asks Ilsa to translate a German announcement over the loudspeakers, are interspersed with very carefully manipulated, emotional dialogue exchanges, which involve a complex pattern elaborating and elucidating the psychology of the people with the assistance of a superbly delineated score by Max Steiner. Arthur Edeson's evocative camerawork runs the entire gamut of black-and-white photography in establishing the mood of each scene. Weyl's sets are so perfectly created in their precise detail that one is never aware of the studio setting, and Owen Marks edits hundreds of complicated shots into a cohesive body. Fused together, these elements combine to produce one of the most outstanding works ever to emerge from a Hollywood studio.

Since it is so carefully calculated and cleverly constructed, the emotional impact cannot fail to impress, and scenes such as Bergman's entry into the deserted club; a radiant figure in white, her dress shimmering in a reflected light, as Bogart summons up his memories of Paris, waiting for her in the teeming rain at the station as the last train pulled out before the German invaders arrived, only to receive a note telling him she'll never see him again; or a later scene in which Laszlo orders the café band to strike up the Marseillaise in order to drown out the Horst Wessel Song which Strasser and his cronies are performing, have an effect on modern audiences, untarnished or undiminished by time.

The film continues with Rick's slow realisation that he cannot remain uninvolved ("I'm not much good at being noble, but it doesn't take much to see that the problems of three little people don't amount to a hill of beans in this world"); this awareness comes from understanding the nature of Ilsa's love for Laszlo; from recognising the quiet, sincere courage and dignity which drives Laszlo; and from the incident in which he saves the young Bulgarian girl (Joy Page) from the lecherous designs of Renault by allowing her husband to win enough at roulette to buy two visas, after brutally brushing aside her pleas for advice until he equates their situation with his in Paris. The character of Rick is so subtly drawn and played that an ambiguity exists until the last reel; one is never sure if he realises that Ilsa, in her desperation in offering herself to him in exchange for Laszlo's life, is cheapening their relationship in Paris—but with the purest of motives—or if he believes her change of heart; and it is only clarified at the climax when he forces Renault to assist in their escape with the stolen transit documents, shooting Strasser when the German makes a last minute attempt to foil his plans at the aerodrome. Renault's cynicism is maintained until the last image of the film, since it is he who summoned Strasser to the scene by phone on the pretext of clearing the fugitives' path there. But as the plane takes off with Laszlo and Ilsa safely aboard, with German reinforcements arriving on the scene, Renault saves Rick with a terse order: "Colonel Strasser's been shot. Round up the usual suspects!"

Although the presence of Bogart, and his existential characterisation, represent the primary reason for the popularity of *Casablanca* as a cult film today, one viewing is sufficient to ensure an appreciation of the consistently high quality of all the players; it is difficult to name many other films in which the quality of performances have ranged so far down the cast list. Bergman has never been so attractive or so moving, Henreid has seldom been so believable.

★ ★ ★

The one other Curtiz film that does approach *Casablanca* in consistency of performance is *Mildred Pierce* (1945), although it tends to be seen purely as a Joan Crawford vehicle. Miss Crawford won an Oscar for her performance as the ambitious housewife, who through choice becomes the bread-winner for her two daughters, working her way up the ladder from a waitress to owner of a chain of restaurants, only for her world to crumble about her. Her portrayal of a hard, domineering woman differs from that of Bette Davis in one interesting aspect. Davis women are brittle and selfish in their hardness, often failing because they are too proud or calculating to humble themselves, and even if they do it is with great reluctance, and only as a temporary measure. Crawford's portrayals are often very practical women, who become in a sense subservient through their misapplication of ambition. It is evident in *Mildred Pierce* that of the three men in her life, her ex-husband with whom she begins and ends the film is the least interesting, but the more sordid aspects of her involvements are handled with taste, and the sexual element is carefully underplayed. This is in complete contrast to her later work such as *Female on the Beach* (1955), in which she plays a rich woman who becomes involved with a pair of swindlers, of whom Jeff Chandler is the most brazen in describing the sheer animal attraction with which he uses his body to trap rich, lonely women, without feeling any guilt or even considering the morality of the situation. Obviously censorship played a great part in the restraint of sexual elements in Forties films, but it also led to the more creative directors evolving a network of symbols and planted suggestions which could be more effective than the direct visual image of copulation or any associated act.

Ranald MacDougall, who later was much less effective directing Joan Crawford in films like *Queen Bee* (1955), adapted James M. Cain's novel of *Mildred Pierce* into a screenplay laced with bitterness, cynicism and wry humour, unfolding the story in a series of

Joan Crawford is confronted with the murder weapon by Chief Detective Moroni Olsen as her ex-husband Bruce Bennett (second from right) is charged with the killing in Curtiz's MILDRED PIERCE

developing flashbacks after a brutal opening sequence. Waves flow over the credits washing each group away; the camera picks up a distant beach house and approaches it in a series of takes. Suddenly the calm is shattered by the sound of gun-shots; a rapid cut shows the gun pumping bullets into the sagging body of Berrigan (Zachary Scott), who falls to the floor, mouthing, "Mildred!" as he dies. A dark figure runs out and drives off in a car. The scene changes to a pier, with the camera picking out the figure of Mildred Pierce (Joan Crawford) walking slowly along it toward the sea. Angled shots reveal her distraught state, and the repeated view of her staring at the waves suggests she is contemplating suicide. This is confirmed as she raises her leg toward the barrier, but she is interrupted by a policeman rapping his baton sharply on the railing.

A terse dialogue exchange brings Mildred to her senses, and she wanders into a nearby club, run by a venal, cocksure, lecherous acquaintance named Wally (Jack Carson). On impulse she lures him to her beach house (Carson: "I like good stuff. Maybe this is my lucky day"), and deserts him. He panics on discovering that all the doors are locked, moving from room to room with the low-key lighting emphasising the shadows thrown from the Venetian blinds, and the prison bar motif reflected by decorative railings and spiral staircases. Finally he careers into a lampshade. It falls over—drawing the cold, dead features of Berrigan's corpse into relief. A passing police prowl car is alerted as Wally breaks a French window to escape, only to be trapped in the glare of a spot-light and a hail of bullets.

Up to this point, Curtiz has drawn a red herring across the characterisation of Mildred by appearing to indict her as a callous, unstable murderess, but the mood changes as she arrives at the police station to assist with inquiries. Her apparent calm is thrown off-balance when she finds her manageress and business associate (Eve Arden) present; and Curtiz's emphasis on the monotony of police routine—swilling coffee, chain-smoking, reading papers or filling in forms in complete silence, broken only by the ticking of the station clock—underlines the unnerving effect the wait has on Mildred. When she is eventually called in to see the detective investigating the case, he lulls her nerves by apologising for what has turned out to be an unnecessary wait, since they feel they have solved the case. He expounds at some length on the procedures undertaken to solve crimes, before confronting her with their suspect, her ex-husband (Bruce Bennett). Her breakdown at this point introduces the first flashback as she tells her version of the events in order to clear Bennett.

Although the sets and costumes of *Mildred Pierce* rather belie the social milieu which they are supposed to be representing, the script and direction, with their loving attention to detail, reflect an intimate knowledge of and feeling for the texture of the suburban American life-style. They highlight key points in Mildred's life; wed at seventeen, cooking, washing and having children until her husband breaks up his real estate partnership with Carson; the quarrels over his attention to another woman, and her obsessive attempts to buy the love of her eldest child, Veda (Ann Blyth), which have turned Veda into a spoilt, ungrateful, spiteful brat. Mildred suffers the humiliations of Veda's patronising her ("Good afternoon, Mother. I'm learning a new piece, Valse Brillante. That means Brilliant Waltz"), and complaining about the poor quality of the dress she has slaved to buy for her. She lies in order to keep the truth about her split with her husband from the nosy girl, who knows the reason anyway, and she has to hide the fact that she is working as a waitress from Veda's scorn.

When Veda discovers the truth, she flings her mother's past in her face, and is only pacified by the revelation of Mildred's ambition—to own her own restaurant. With the aid of Wally (Jack Carson), Mildred persuades an indolent local playboy into providing her with the property, in return for a one third share of the profits. He shows more than a passing interest in her ("I do too much of everything. I'm spoilt, but I loaf in a highly decorative and charming manner"), seducing Mildred with soft lights and sweet music. The price she has to pay for her romantic entanglement is high; her younger daughter contracts pneumonia and dies, and this furthers the rupture between her and Bennett. He felt she had neglected Kay, but Mildred defends herself on the grounds that Kay was more demonstrative and nicer, therefore she needed less attention than Veda.

Her inverted or divided loyalty is further shown after the successful opening of the restaurant when Bennett finds her kissing Monty Berrigan, as he comes in to agree to grant her a divorce. Mildred is partially responsible for the instant hostility which develops between the two men. Later as she builds up a chain of restaurants, she recalls, "Everything I touched turned to gold, and I needed it for Veda, a young lady with expensive tastes." Her initial ambition for her daughter is turned into a blind slavery, blind because she is too busy to notice either that Veda and Berrigan are forming an attachment or that between them they are driving her to ruin. It is necessary for Eve Arden to needle her into a realisation of the latter fact, but even though she throws Monty out, she retains little of her early foresight.

Thus she is horrified by Veda's fake pregnancy in order to obtain money and a quick divorce after an ill-considered society marriage. She abandons Veda but cannot cope without her, and so marries Monty in order to provide Veda with the social setting she desires. The business runs to seed, and she is double-crossed by Monty and Wally with the final straw coming as she finds Monty and Veda embracing at his beach house. As she leaves, sickened, a sneering Monty rejects Veda ("You really didn't think I could be in love with a rotten little tramp like you, did you?"). She promptly shoots him. Mildred accepts Veda's claim that the guilt is attributable to both of them, and thus tries to frame Wally. The catalogue of misguided matriarchal feeling ends with Veda being led away to await trial as Mildred and her ex-husband are reunited.

* * *

Opulence and Claude Rains, exercising his special talent for injecting calculated evil into a personality of avuncular whimsicality and weary charm, dominated *The Unsuspected* (1947), a polished murder thriller with a particularly strong visual style. There is more than a suggestion of Gothic imagery in the use of reflections (in low-key) from table tops and record surfaces. The Hitchcockian suspense motif of imposing a shot of a drugged drink in the foreground beside the intended victim is well used by Curtiz; and there are sharp overhead camera positions for dramatic effect. Wit and cynicism rub shoulders in a complex script: a police officer, viewing the corpse of a hatchet murder victim: "No, she's not so small. There's only half of her there!"; or a neurotically jealous wife (Audrey Totter): "Oh, the picture? My husband—in his sober period . . . before he married me." This year, 1947, was a vintage one for Curtiz, since he also made *Life with Father,* a vastly underrated piece of Americana about family life in New York City in the 1880's, which stands up well by comparison with *Meet Me in St. Louis* (1944, Vincente Minnelli) and *I Remember Mama* (1948, George Stevens). But it was also the start of a long period of popular but technically minor musical comedies, many with Doris Day, or second-rate reworkings of previously successful films. Few of the last twenty-nine films made by Curtiz are worth much consideration, even though he continued to work with major stars such as Gary Cooper, William Holden, Lauren Bacall, Alan Ladd, Sophia Loren and John Wayne.

It may be that his decline was a direct result of the break-up of the studio system. The latter years of the decade had involved Warner Brothers in the investigation of the Committee of Un-American Activities into the extent of Communist involvement in Hollywood production; a delegation protesting against the methods of the Committee, headed by Humphrey Bogart, John Huston, Lauren Bacall and others had fragmented as pressure was brought to bear, but it had not been good publicity for the studios to have their stars involved. John Garfield was another "under suspicion"; whilst Curtiz's *Mission to Moscow* (1943), an ably written (by Howard Koch) pro-Stalinist propaganda piece, commissioned by President Roosevelt, according to Jack Warner in his biography *My First Hundred Years in Hollywood,* came under fire from the Committee members. It has since had few viewings in Britain, and remains one of

The American Ambassador's daughter (Eleanor Parker) meets a crack Russian ski-troop on manoeuvres. From left: Helmut Dantine, Eleanor Parker, Richard Travis, Ray Teal, in MISSION TO MOSCOW

the few major works of Curtiz to be re-assessed. The sale of a number of Warner pictures to television did little to improve the careers of the stars and directors on their payroll, and Curtiz, lacking the firm control of the studio system, dominated by Jack Warner and his successive production heads such as Hal B. Wallis, worked steadily but without his old impetus.

He made two films with Lauren Bacall in 1950; the first being one of his last studies of ambition, *Young Man with a Horn* (GB: *Young Man of Music*), co-starring her with Kirk Douglas. Bacall had originally interested Wallis in signing Douglas for his first film role, and he had risen rapidly to stardom. *Young Man with a Horn* was the second script which Carl Foreman had written for Douglas, casting him as a greedy swell-headed fool, who bullocks his way to the top of his field, but destroys himself through his infatuation with a *femme fatale.* The script, co-authored by Edmund H. North from a novel by Dorothy Baker, meatily characterised the Douglas figure, but did little justice to Bacall or Doris Day, who played Douglas's long-suffering, faithful singer companion. Bacall was over-written as a jealous neurotic with an inferiority complex, who marries and nearly ruins the young trumpeter. Occasionally, the film sparks to life above the conventional run of the plot, as for instance in the scene where Day warns Douglas to avoid the hard, fast-talking trainee psychiatrist(!) Bacall, only to find that they have just married; or with the image of Bacall playing Chopin idly on the piano with a cigarette dangling vulgarly out of the corner of her mouth, later to be described as having the same characteristics as her apartment: ". . . big, rich but empty, save for erotic lampshades and a parrot." She fared much better in *Bright Leaf,* playing a "tart-with-a-heart" who loves tobacco tycoon Gary Cooper, but it was a good performance in a mediocre film.

After a schmaltzy series of musical biographies of Gus Kahn (*I'll See You in My Dreams,* 1952), and Will Rogers (*The Story of Will Rogers,* 1952); and a re-make of *The Jazz Singer* (1953), Curtiz began to work at other studios including Twentieth Century-Fox and Paramount. He also embarked on a project with his wife, Bess Meredyth, and Frances Marion to launch an independent film company, which would release their product through Warner Brothers, but it never ventured beyond the planning stage due to lack of finance. His first film at Fox was *The Egyptian,* an early film made in CinemaScope; according to cameraman Leon Shamroy it was: ". . . also all Hollywood; it might have been better if Marlene Dietrich had been playing the old hooker—the old whore. And Marlon Brando should have been the man; but he hated Mike Curtiz, he disliked Bella Darvi and he wasn't too fond of the script." (*Hollywood Cameramen* by Charles Higham. Secker and Warburg.)

White Christmas (1954), the first film in VistaVision, was a successful Bing Crosby/Danny Kaye musical, and a re-make of *Four Daughters* entitled *Young at Heart* (1955), with Frank Sinatra playing the John Garfield role was also a box-office success, but neither match up to *The Best Things in Life Are Free* (1956), a biography of the successful song-writing team of De Sylva, Henderson and Brown. A superb score included "Happiness Is Just a Memory," "Broken-Hearted," "Button Up Your Overcoat," "Lucky Day," "Lucky in Love," "It All Depends on You," "Good News," "Don't Hold Everything," "Black Bottom" (which was a superb burlesque on the early gangster films), "One More Time," "Birth of the Blues" (the high-light of all the numbers), "Somebody Else," "Together," "Sunny Side Up" and the theme song. The development of the plot was predictable, but it was entertainingly played and exceptionally well mounted.

Henderson (Dan Dailey) is mistaken for an agency pianist, and hired by song writers De Sylva (Gordon MacRae) and Brown (Ernest Borgnine). They become a team ("You get 33⅓% of nothing"). After some hesitation on Henderson's part (to Brown: "Do you mind a suggestion?" Brown: "Usually . . . YES!" He sells "This Is the Missus," and success escalates rapidly—three shows running on Broadway simultaneously. Following the success of "George White's Scandals," De Sylva feels the urge to produce, and the chance comes from a well-known gangster, played by Murvyn Vye, who is a childhood friend of Brown. When Brown refuses to involve himself in a girlie show, the gangster is rather upset ("What are you? Some kind of religious maniac?"), but the deal goes ahead. It includes Vye's talentless girl, and results in a brawl during rehearsals when De Sylva fires her. The team opens the show under police pro-

On the death of his father, Akhnaton (Michael Wilding) takes the throne of Egypt as the new Pharaoh, in Curtiz's THE EGYPTIAN

tection, but it proves uncalled for because Vye is "rubbed out" at the barber shop.

Jolson rings up for a song, so they compose what they feel to be a quick stinker while awaiting the notices for their most recent show, but both the show and "Sonny Boy" turn up trumps. Henderson talks De Sylva out of taking a careless fling at marriage, so the energetic De Sylva turns his attention to Hollywood, running his partners ragged with his ambition until they are signed up by Winfield Sheehan. Not satisfied, De Sylva announces his desire to produce movies as well; this results in the break-up of the team, with Brown and Henderson trying a two man show which flops, but all ends well as a repentent De Sylva joins them again . . .

Curtiz and Ann Blyth were reunited in a bathetic soap-opera, purporting to be the life story of torchsinger Helen Morgan (GB: *Both Ends of the Candle*), but could do little with an atrocious script which had none of the smooth professionalism or subtlety of *Mildred Pierce*. Both Blyth and Paul Newman gave patchy performances, which was a very unusual occurrence in any work done by Curtiz. He made up for it in his next film, *The Proud Rebel* (1958), a gentle Western family drama starring Alan Ladd and Olivia De Havilland. The latter was rather surprised to be asked by Curtiz to play in the film, since she had always been a secondary item on the agenda of his earlier works, and she was pleased to find him somewhat mellowed by the passage of time. As Allen Eyles noted for a recent revival of the film: "Westerns are generally action pictures and rarely have difficulty in pleasing audiences on that score. *The Proud Rebel* largely dispenses with this built-in asset, and instead relies on a quiet charm. Films about small children and dogs are usually to be shied away from (except as afternoon viewing in the company of one's children)—and when one considers that the boy in *The Proud Rebel* is a deaf mute, there is room for apprehension.

"But *The Proud Rebel* seems to me a film of great beauty and understanding. Principal credit must belong to the veteran director Michael Curtiz—never a sentimental director—who handles the script and actors with a tight rein. Alan Ladd, too, is a relatively inexpressive actor, and as such does not overplay the situation of the father, while his real-life son, David, is outstandingly good as the deaf mute son, and Olivia De Havilland—long regarded in Hollywood as the most attractive "plain-featured" woman when such parts need casting—sensitively portrays the solitary woman who gives Ladd's proud "Reb" and his son a helping hand.

"The photography of Ted McCord is strikingly good, and the score by Jerome Moross is another asset of a film that is a calm triumph of old-fashioned, honest sentiment without lapsing into sentimentality as a fault." (National Film Theatre programme note.)

★ ★ ★

Raymond Massey (on steps with rifle) and his friends make a last stand in Curtiz's SANTA FE TRAIL

Michael Curtiz died in Hollywood on April 11, 1962, a few months after finishing work on a rousing John Wayne Western, *The Comancheros* (1961), which bears his stamp of proficiency with regard to the performances. But the plentiful action sequences are generally attributed to the second unit director, Cliff Lyons, in an ironic climax to the career of one of Hollywood's best action specialists. Curtiz's own attempts at self-promotion were clumsy, and did him harm more often than not. An ungallant man, he is spoken of better by some of his actors than by the technicians with whom he collaborated. Thus Paul Henreid described his working methods: "He had an instinctual visual flair . . . quite different from the way actors visualise. Every now and again he would stop the camera and say 'There's something wrong here, I don't know what it is.' By and by he'd realise what it was, and we'd begin the scene again." ("Films in Review", November 1970.) This impression is totally at odds with James Wong Howe's: "*Yankee Doodle Dandy,* the George M. Cohan musical, had very few photographic opportunities; I had to create them. Mike Curtiz knew almost nothing about lighting; he couldn't even tell the cameraman how he wanted the lights to look. He was very dominating, and many of his ideas would not work." "*Hollywood Cameramen* by Charles Higham. Secker and Warburg.)

Even if this is completely true, and Curtiz did have to depend on his cameraman to create the correct look for his images (as Charlie Chaplin's favourite cameraman, Rollie Totheroth, depended on his assistants), there is still no denying that his overall craftsmanship, and the skill with which he judged and guided the pace of his films, has come to represent the cream of film-making at Warner Brothers in the Thirties and Forties. Outside the industry and the minority group of film buffs, he is not one to be identified with his films as are Alfred Hitchcock, John Ford or Ingmar Bergman, but the Warner style itself certainly does have a more immediate association for the general film-going public. Thus the cynicism and cinema of Michael

A strikingly expressionistic use of shadows as Arthur Carewe waits to pounce on an unsuspecting Glenda Farrell in Curtiz's THE MYSTERY OF THE WAX MUSEUM

Curtiz live on, and audiences still flock to see *Casablanca,* while tourists still search for Rick's Café in Casablanca, and real-life facsimiles of "The Blue Parrot" and "Mildred's" feed hungry students on American campuses, perpetuating the cult of Michael Curtiz's cinema.

A highly-charged emotional scene between Bette Davis and Richard Cromwell in Curtiz's CABIN IN THE COTTON

MICHAEL CURTIZ Filmography

Hungary and Denmark
MA ES HOLNAP (1912). First feature made in Hungary; possibly directed by Curtiz.
RABLELEK (1913).
ATLANTIS (1913). Danish film directed by August Blom with Curtiz as an actor.
? (1913). Danish film of unknown title, made with Curtiz directing, and released in 1914 after his return to Hungary.
AZ EJSZAKA (1914). Curtiz acted and directed.
A KOLCSONKERT CSECSEMOK (1914).
BANK BAN (1914). Curtiz's first commercial success as a director.
A TOLONC (1914).
AKIT KETTEN SZERETNEK (1915). Curtiz acted and directed.
AZ EZUST KECSKE (1916).
A MEDIKUS (1916). Curtiz acted and directed.
DOCKTOR UR (1916).
A FARKAS (1916).
A FEKETE SZIVARVANY (1916).
MAKKHETES (1916).
A KARTHAUZI (1916).
A MAGYAR FOLD EREJE (1916).
AZ ARENDAS ZSIDO (1917).
EGY KRAJCAR TORTENETE (1917).
AZ EZREDES (1917).
A FOLD EMBERE (1917).
A HALALCSENGO (1917).
A KURUZSLO (1917).
A SZENTJOBI ERDO TITKA (1917).
A SENKA FIA (1917).
TAVASZ A TELBEN (1917).
ZOARD MESTER (1917).
TATARJARAS (1917).
KILENCVENKILENC (1918).
JUDAS (1918).
LULU (1918).
AZ ORDOG (1918).
A NAPRAFORGOS HOLGY (1918).
ALRAUNE (1918).
A VIG OZVEGY (1918).
VARAZSKERINGO (1918).
LU, A KOKOTT (1918).
LILIOM (1919). Unfinished when Curtiz fled the Béla Kun *régime*. Some sources list the following films as being made by Curtiz after he left Hungary but there is no evidence to support these claims:
Sweden
WELLINGTON REJTELY (1919).
ODETTE ET L'HISTOIRE DES FEMMES ILLUSTRES (1919). Supposedly featuring a fourteen year old Garbo as Marie Antoinette, but this is probably a false attribution!
Germany
DIE SPINNEN: DER GOLDENE SEE (1919). Rumoured to have been a version of Part I of Fritz Lang's serial, made with an all Hungarian cast.
The next accepted credits cover the films which Curtiz made for *Sascha-Film.*
Austria
DIE DAME MIT DEM SCHWARZEN HANDSCHUH (1919).
DIE GOTTESGEISSEL (1919).
DER STERN VON DAMASKUS (1920).
DIE DAME MIT DEN SONNENBLUM (1920).
HERZOGIN SATANELLA (1920).

BOCCACCIO (1920).

Italy

MISS TUTTI FRUTTI (1920).

Austria

CHERCHEZ LA FEMME (1921).

(FRAU) DOROTHY'S BEKENNTNIS (1921).

WEGE DES SCHRECKENS/LABYRINTH DES GRAUENS (1921).

SODOM UND GOMORRAH: PART 1 (1922).

SODOM UND GOMORRAH: PART 2 (1923).

SAMSON UND DALILA (1923). Directed by Alexander Korda with Curtiz possibly functioning as a supervising director.

DER LAWINE/AVALANCHE (1923).

DER JUNGE MEDARDUS (1923).

NAMENLOS (1923).

EIN SPIEL UMS LEBEN (1924).

HARUN AL RASCHID (1924).

DIE SLAVENKOENIGIN (1924). Released in the U.S.A. as MOON OF ISRAEL.

France

CELIMENE, POUPEE DE MONTMARTRE (1925). Austrian title: DAS SPIELZEUG VON PARIS. Shown in the U.S.A. as RED HEELS.

DER GOLDENE SCHMETTERLING (1926). A Danish/Austrian co-production released in the U.S.A. as THE ROAD TO HAPPINESS.

Germany

FIAKER NR. 13 (1926). An Austrian/German co-production.

U.S.A.

THE THIRD DEGREE (1926). A circus story about a mother eloping with a scoundrel, who is hired, years later to break up *her* daughter's marriage. *Sc:* Graham Baker (from Charles Klein play "The Music Master"). *Ph:* Hal Mohr. *Ed:* Clarence Kolster. *Assist. dir:* Henry Blanke. *With* Jason Robards Sr. (*Howard Jeffries Jnr.*), Dolores Costello (*Annie Daly*), Kate Price (*Mrs. Chubb*), Louise Dresser (*Alicia Daly*), Rockliffe Fellowes (*Underwood*), Tom Santschi, Harry Todd, David Torrence, Mary Louise Miller, Michael Vaviten, Fred Kelsey. *Prod:* for Warner Brothers/First National. 8r.

A MILLION BID (1927). The heroine is married, against her will, to a husband who apparently dies in a storm, only to reappear with amnesia. But on discovering her love for a surgeon, the husband vanishes again. *Sc:* Robert Dillon (short story by George Cameron). *Ph:* Hal Mohr. *Assist. dir:* Henry Blanke. *With* Dolores Costello (*Dorothy Gordon*), Warner Oland (*Geoff Marsh*), Malcolm McGregor (*Dr. Robert Brent*), Betty Blythe (*Mrs. Gordon*), William Demarest (*George Lamont*), Douglas Gerrard, Grace Gordon. *Prod:* Warner Brothers/First National. 7r.

GOOD TIME CHARLEY (1927). A tragic drama of a song and dance man. *Sc:* Ilona Fulop (adapted by Anthony Coldeway and Owen Francis from a story "The Rainbow Chaser," by Darryl F. Zanuck). *Ph:* Barney McGill. *With* Warner Oland (*Good Time Charley*), Helene Costello (*Rosita Keene*), Clyde Cook (*Billy Collins*), Montagu Love (*John Hartwell*), Hugh Allan (*John Hartwell Jnr.*), Mary Carr, Julanne Johnston. Assoc. *Prod:* Darryl F. Zanuck for Warner Brothers/First National. 7r.

THE DESIRED WOMAN (1927). An officer's wife creates a furore among the men at a lonely Sahara fortress. *Sc:* Anthony Coldeway (short story by Mark Canfield). *Ph:* Conrad Wells. *Assist. dir:* Henry Blanke. *With* Irene Rich (*Diana Maxwell*), William Russell (*Capt. Maxwell*), William Collier Jnr. (*Lieut. Trent*), John Miljan (*Lieut. Kellogg*), Richard Tucker (*Sir Sydney Vincent*), Douglas Gerrard, John Ackroyd. Assoc. *Prod:* Darryl F. Zanuck for Warner Brothers/First National. 7r.

TENDERLOIN (1928). A drama about a cabaret dancer rehabilitating a hardened criminal. Curtiz's first part talkie. *Sc:* E. T. Lowe Jnr. (story by Melville Crosman). *Ph:* Hal Mohr. *Titles:* Joseph Jackson. *Ed:* Ralph Dawson. *With* Conrad Nagel (*Chuck White*), Dolores Costello (*Rose Shannon*), Mitchell Lewis (*The Professor*), Dan Wolheim (*Lefty*), Pat Hartigan (*The Mug*), George Stone, Fred Kelsey, G. Raymond Nye, Evelyn Pierce, Dorothy Vernon, John Miljan. Assoc. *Prod:* Darryl F. Zanuck for Warner Brothers/First National. 8r.

NOAH'S ARK (1929). Part talkie Biblical epic with a parallel First World War story. A number of extracts later used in a 1953 short, *Magic Movie Moments,* while a *silent* version was re-issued in America in 1957. *Sc:* Anthony Coldeway (from story by Darryl F. Zanuck). *Ph:* Hal Mohr and Barney McGill. *Dialogue:* B. Leon Anthony. *Editor/Titles:* Harold McCord. *With* Dolores Costello (*Mary/Miriam*), George O'Brien (*Travis/Japheth*), Noah Beery Sr. (*Nickoloff/King Nephiliu*), Louise Fazenda (*Hilda/Tavern Maid*), Guinn Williams (*Al/Ham*), Paul McAllister, William V. Mong, Anders Randolf, Nigel De Brulier, Armand Kaliz, Malcolm Waite, Myrna Loy, Noble Johnson, Otto Hoffman, Joe Bonomo. *Assoc. Prod:* Darryl F. Zanuck for Warner Brothers/First National. 75 m.

THE GLAD RAG DOLL (1929). A rich boy falls for a show girl who appears to be a gold-digger. *Sc:* Graham Baker (story by Harvey Gates). *Ph:* Byron Haskin. *With* Dolores Costello (*Annabel Lee*), Ralph Graves (*John Fairchild*), Audrey Ferris (*Bertha*), Albert Grant (*Nathan Fairchild*), Maude Turner Gordon (*Aunt Fairchild*), Claude Gillingwater, Arthur T. Rankin, Thomas Ricketts, Dale Fuller, Andre Beranger, Douglas Gerrard, Lee Moran, Tom Kennedy, Stanley Taylor, Louise Beavers. *Prod:* Warner Brothers/First National. 8r.

MADONNA OF AVENUE A (1929). A night club hostess has an associate framed for murder, unaware that he is her son-in-law, and commits suicide when she finds out. *Sc:* Ray Doyle (story by Mark Canfield). *Ph:* Byron Haskin. *Ed:* Ray Doyle. *With* Dolores Costello (*Maria*), Grant Withers (*Slim*), Douglas Gerrard (*Arch Duke*), Louise Dresser (*Georgia Morton*), Otto Hoffman (*Monk*), William Russell, Lee Moran. *Prod:* Warner Brothers/First National. 8r.

HEARTS IN EXILE (1929). Drama about love and exile in Siberia, filmed with two alternative endings. *Sc:* Harvey Gates (story by John Oxenham). *Ph:* Bill Rees. *Title:* B. Leon Anthony. *Ed:* Thomas Pratt. *Mus:* Howard Jackson. *With* Dolores Costello (*Vera Ivanova*), Grant Withers (*Paul Pavloff*), James Kirkwood (*Serge Palma*), David Torrence (*Governor*), Olive Tell, Tom Dugan, George Fawcett, William Irving, Rose Dione, Carrie Daumery. *Prod:*

Warner Brothers/First National. 8r.

THE GAMBLERS (1929). A young man saves his father's name by taking the blame when company directors play the market unwisely with shares. *Sc:* J. Grubb Alexander (story by Charles Klein). *Ph:* William Reese. *Ed:* Thomas Pratt. *With* H. B. Warner (*James Darwin*), Lois Wilson (*Catherine Darwin*), Jason Robards Sr. (*Carvel Emerson*), George Fawcett (*Emerson Snr.*), Johnny Arthur (*George Cowper*), Frank Campeau, Pauline Garan, Charles Sellon. *Prod:* Warner Brothers/First National. 7r.

MAMMY (1930). Backstage murder vehicle for Jolson with a musical score by Irving Berlin, and some Technicolor sequences. *Sc:* L. G. Rigby (from Irving Berlin musical "Mr. Bones"; adapted by Joseph Jackson). *Ph:* Barney McGill. *Mus:* Irving Berlin. *With* Al Jolson (*Al Fuller*), Lowell Sherman (*Westy*), Lois Moran (*Nora Meadows*), Hobart Bosworth (*Meadows*), Ray Cooke, Louise Dresser, Tully Marshall, Mitchell Lewis, Stanley Fields, Jack Curtis. *Prod:* Warner Brothers/First National. 84m.

UNDER A TEXAS MOON (1930). Romantic Western saga involving the adventures of two Mexicans in Texas. *Sc:* Joseph Jackson, Raymond Griffith (from short story "Two Gun Man," by Stewart W. White). *Ph:* William Reese. *Mus:* Ray Perkins. *With* Frank Fay (*Don Carlos*), Raquel Torres (*Raquella*), Myrna Loy (*Lita Romero*), Armida (*Dolores*), Noah Beery Sr. (*Jed Parker*), Georgie Stone, George Cooper, Fred Kohler, Jack Curtis, Betty Boyd, Charles Sellon, Sam Appel, Edythe Kramer, Tully Marshall, Mona Maris, Francisco Moran, Tom Dix, Jerry Barrett, Inez Gomez, Bruce Covington. *Prod:* Warner Brothers/First National. Technicolor. 82m.

THE MATRIMONIAL BED (GB: A MATRIMONIAL PROBLEM) (1930). Domestic comedy-drama set in Paris, involving amnesia and bigamy. *Sc:* Seymour Hicks, Harvey Thew (story by Yves Mirande, Andre Mouezy-Eon). *Ph:* Dev Jennings. *With* Lilyan Tashman (*Sylvaine*), Frank Fay (*Adolphe Noblet*), Florence Eldredge (*Juliette Corton*), James Gleason (*Gustave Corton*), Beryl Mercer (*Corinne*) Vivian Oakland, Arthur Edmund Carewe, Marion Byron, James Bradbury Sr. *Prod:* Warner Brothers/First National. 98m.

BRIGHT LIGHTS (1930). Drama about show girls, smugglers and true love. *Sc:* Humphrey Pearson (from his own story). *Ph:* Lee Garmes. *Mus:* Leo Forbestein. *With* Dorothy Mackaill (*Louanne*), Frank Fay (*Wally Dean*), Noah Beery Sr. (*Miguel Parada*), Inez Courtney (*Peggy North*), Eddie Nugent (*Windy Jones*), Daphne Pollard, Edmund Breese, Philip Strange, James Murray, Tom Dugan, Jean Bary, Edwin Lynch, Frank McHugh, Virginia Sale. *Prod:* Robert North for Warner Brothers/First National. 73m.

A SOLDIER'S PLAYTHING (GB: A SOLDIER'S PAY) (1930). Comedy-drama about First World War soldiers and their reasons for enlisting. *Sc:* Percy Vekroff (story by Vina Delmar). *Ph:* J. O. Taylor. *Dialogue:* Arthur Caesar. *Ed:* Jack Killifer. *With* Lotti Loder (*Gretshen*), Harry Langdon (*Tim*), Ben Lyon (*Georgie Wilson*), Jean Hersholt (*Grandfather Rittner*), Noah Beery Sr. (*Capt. Plover*), Fred

Kohler, Otto Mattieson, Lee Moran, Marie Astaire, Frank Campeau. *Prod:* Warner Brothers/First National. 71m.

RIVER'S END (1930). Fugitive takes place of Mountie sent to capture him, but runs into trouble when he falls in love with the dead man's girl. *Sc:* Charles Kenyon (story by James Oliver Curwood). *Ph:* Robert Kurrle. *Ed:* Ralph Holt. *With* Charles Bickford (*Keith/Conniston*), Evelyn Knapp (*Miriam*) J. Farrell MacDonald (*O'Toole*), Walter McGrail (*Martin*), Zasu Pitts (*Louise*), David Torrence, Junior Coughlan, Tom Santschi. *Prod:* Warner Brothers/First National. 74m. Re-made in 1940, directed by Ray Enright.

DAEMON DES MEERES (1931). A German version of *Moby Dick* shot at the same time as the version Lloyd Bacon filmed with John Barrymore. *Sc:* Oliver H. P. Garrett, Ulrich Steindorff (from Herman Melville's *Moby Dick*). *Ph:* Robert Kurrle. *With* William Dieterle (*Ahab*), Anton Pointer, Karl Eltinger, Liszly Arna, Carla Bartheel, Lothar Mayrong. *Prod:* Warner Brothers/First National. 75m. Later version filmed in 1956 with John Huston directing.

GOD'S GIFT TO WOMEN (GB. TOO MANY WOMEN) (1931). A lady-killer has to prove the honesty of his intentions when he really falls in love. *Sc:* Joseph Jackson, Raymond Griffith (from play "The Devil Was Sick," by Jane Hinton). *Ph:* Robert Kurrle. *Ed:* James Gribbon. *With* Joan Blondell, Frank Fay, Laura La Plante, Arthur Edmund Carewe, Charles Winninger, Ala Mowbray, Charles Judels, Tyrell Davis, Louise Brooks, Billy House, Yola D'Avril. *Prod:* Warner Brothers/First National. 71m.

THE MAD GENIUS (1931). An unsuccessful sequel to *Svengali* which Barrymore filmed the same year. *Sc:* J. G. Alexander, Harvey Thew (from play "The Idol," by Martin Brown). *Ph:* Barney McGill. *Art dir:* Anton Grot. *Ed:* Ralph Dawson. *With* John Barrymore (*Tsarakov*), Marian Marsh (*Nana*), Donald Cook (*Fedor*), Carmel Myers (*Preskoya*), Charles Butterworth (*Karminsky*), Luis Alberni, Andre Luget, Boris Karloff, Frankie Darro, Mae Madison. *Prod:* Warner Brothers/First National. 75m.

THE WOMAN FROM MONTE CARLO (1932). Drama about a faithless wife who betrays her aging naval officer husband. *Sc:* Harvey Thew (story by Claude Farrere, Lucien Napoty). *Ph:* Ernest Haller. *Ed:* Harold McLernon. *With* Lil Dagover (*Lottie*), Walter Huston (*Capt. Corlaix*), Warren William (*D'Ortelles*), John Wray (*Brambourg*), Robert Warwick (*Morbraz*), Ben Hendricks, George E. Stone, Matt McHugh, Maude Eburne, Dewey Robinson, Robert Rose, Reginald Barlow, Clarence Muse, Frederick Burton, Oscar Apfel, John Rutherford, Francis McDonald, Warner Richmond, Frank Leigh, Paul Porcasi, Jack Kennedy, Elinor Wesselhoeft. *Prod:* Warner Brothers/First National. 68m.

ALIAS THE DOCTOR (1932). A surgeon almost ruins his life by taking the rap for his foster brother's malpractice. *Dir:* Michael Curtiz, Lloyd Bacon. *Sc:* Houston Branch, Charles Kenyon (play by Charles Foeldes). *Ph:* Barney McGill. *Ed:* William Holmes. *With* Richard Barthelmess (*Karl Muller*), Marian Marsh (*Lotti*), Lucille La Verne (*Mother Brenner*), Norman Foster (*Stephen*), Adrienne Dore (*Anna*), Oscar Apfel,

John St. Polis, Wallis Clark, George Rosener, Reginald Barlow, Arnold Lucy, Harold Waldridge, Robert Farfan, Boris Karloff. *Prod:* First National. 69m.

THE STRANGE LOVE OF MOLLY LOUVAIN (1932). A flighty girl is loved by three men. *Sc:* Erwin Gelsey, Brown Holmes (from play "Tinsel Girl," by Maurice Watkins). *Ph:* Robert Kurrle. *Ed:* James Borby. *With* Ann Dvorak (*Molly*), Lee Tracy (*Scotty*), Richard Cromwell (*Jimmy*), Guy Kibbee (*Pop*), Leslie Fenton (*Nick*), Frank McHugh, Charles Middleton, Evalyn Knapp, Hank Mann, C. Henry Gordon, Mary Doran, Harry Beresford, Harold Waldridge, William Buress, Willard Robertson, Claire McDowell, Maurice Black, Ben Alexander, Richard Cramer, Donald Dillaway. *Prod:* Warner Brothers/First National. 70m.

DOCTOR X (1932). Horror film about a psychopathic strangler. *Sc:* Earl Baldwin, Robert Tasker (play by Howard W. Comstock, Allen C. Miller). *Ph:* Ray Rennahan and Richard Tower. *Art dir:* Anton Grot. *Ed:* George Amy. *With* Lionel Atwill (*Dr. Xavier*), Lee Tracy (*Lee*), Fay Wray (*Joan Xavier*), Preston Foster (*Dr. Welles*), John Wray, George Rosener, Leila Bennett, Arthur Edmund Carewe, Harry Beresford, Tom Dugan, Robert Warwick, Mae Busch, Willard Robertson, Thomas Jackson, Harry Holman. *Prod:* Warner Brothers/First National. 80m.

CABIN IN THE COTTON (1932). A rich plantation owner's spoilt daughter teases and loses her true love. *Co-dir:* William Keighley. *Sc:* Paul Green (novel by Harry Harrison Kroll). *Ph:* Barney McGill. *Ed:* George Amy. *With* Bette Davis (*Madge*), Richard Barthelmess (*Marvin*), Dorothy Jordan (*Betty*), Henry B. Walthall (*Old Eph*), Berton Churchill (*Lane Norwood*), Walter Percival, William LeMaire, Tully Marshall, Edmund Breese, Clarence Muse, John Marston, Russell Simpson, Erville Anderson, Dorothy Peterson, Snow Flake, Harry Cording, Trevor Bardette, Virginia Hammond, Charles King, Florine McKinney, David Landau, Dennis O'Keefe, J. Carrol Naish. *Prod:* Jack L. Warner for Warner Brothers/First National. 79m.

20,000 YEARS IN SING SING (1933). Penal drama featuring Tracy as a cocky criminal who walks the last mile for a murder (justifiably) committed by his moll. *Sc:* Wilson Mizner, Brown Holmes (adapted by Courtney Terrall, Robert Lord from Warden Lewis E. Lawes's book). *Ph:* Barney McGill. *Art dir:* Anton Grot. *Ed:* George Amy. *Mus:* Bernhard Kaun. *With* Spencer Tracy (*Tom Connors*), Bette Davis (*Fay*), Lyle Talbot (*Bud*), Sheila Terry (*Billie*), Louis Calhern (*Joe Finn*), Arthur Byron (*Warden*

Cocky Spencer Tracy pelts his guards with boots in 20,000 YEARS IN SING SING

Long), Edward McNamara, Warren Hymer, Spencer Charters, Sam Godfrey, Harold Huber, Grant Mitchell, Nella Walker, William LeMaire, Arthur Hoyt, George Pat Collins. *Prod:* Robert Lord for Warner Brothers/First National. 77m.

THE MYSTERY OF THE WAX MUSEUM (1933). Classic horror film about a mad sculptor who uses live models for his wax museum figures. *Sc:* Don Mullaly, Carl Erickson (story by Charles Beldes). *Ph:* Ray Rennahan. *Art dir:* Anton Grot. *Ed:* George Amy. *With* Lionel Atwill (*Ivan Igor*), Fay Wray (*Charlotte*), Glenda Farrell (*Florence*), Allen Vincent (*Ralph Burton*), Holmes Herbert (*Dr. Rasmussen*), Frank McHugh, Monica Bannister, Arthur Edmund Carewe, Gavin Gordon, Edwin Maxwell, DeWitt Jennings, Pat O'Malley, Harry Woods, Claude King, Matthew Betz. *Prod:* Hal B. Wallis for Warner Brothers/First National. Technicolor. 73m. Re-made as HOUSE OF WAX (1953, *d.* Andre De Toth).

THE KEYHOLE (1933). A suspicious husband engages a private eye to tail his wife. *Sc:* Robert Presnell (from short story "Adventuress," by Alice Duer Miller). *Dialogue:* Arthur Greville Collins. *Ph:* Barney McGill. *With* Kay Francis (*Anne Brooks*), George Brent (*Neil Davis*), Glenda Farrell (*Dot*), Allen Jenkins (*Hank Wales*), Monroe Owsley (*Brooks*), Helen Ware, Henry Kolker. *Prod:* Warner Brothers/First National. 66m.

PRIVATE DETECTIVE 62 (1933). A Government agent falls for a lady gambler whom he is meant to be investigating. *Sc:* Rian James (short story by Raoul Whitfield). *Ph:* Tony Gaudio. *Art dir:* Jack Okey. *With* William Powell (*Donald Free*), Margaret Lindsay (*Janet*), Ruth Donnelly (*Amy*), Gordon Westcott (*Bandor*), James Bell (*Whitey*), Arthur Byron, Nathalie Moorehead, Theresa Harris, Sheila Terry, Renee Whitney, Ann Hovey, Irving Bacon, Arthur Hohl, Hobart Cavanaugh. *Prod:* Warner Brothers/First National. 67m.

GOODBYE AGAIN (1933). An author's secretary prevents him from falling for an old flame yet again. *Sc:* Ben Markson (story by George Haight, Allan Scott). *Ph:* George Barnes. *Ed:* Thomas Pratt. *With* Warren William (*Kenneth Bixby*), Joan Blondell (*Anne*), Genevieve Tobin (*Julie Wilson*), Helen Chandler (*Elizabeth*), Wallace Ford, Hobart Cavanaugh, Hugh Herbert, Jay Ward, Ray Cooke, Ruth Donnelly, Ferdinand Gottschalk. *Prod:* Warner Brothers/First National. 65m. Re-made as HONEYMOON FOR THREE (1941, *d* Lloyd Bacon).

THE KENNEL MURDER CASE (1933). A Philo Vance murder yarn starring the urbane William Powell. *Sc:* Robert N. Lee, Peter Milne (story by S. S. Van Dine). *Ph:* William Reese. *Art dir:* Jack Okey. *Ed:* Harold McLarnin. *With* William Powell (*Philo Vance*), Mary Astor (*Hilda Lake*), Eugene Pallette (*Heath*), Ralph Morgan (*Raymond Wrede*), Helen Vinson (*Doris Delafield*), Etienne Girardot (*Doremud*), Paul Cavanaugh, Jack La Rue, Robert Barrat, Arthur Hohl, Henry O'Neill, Robert McWade, Frank Conroy, Spencer Charters, Charles Wilson, James Lee. *Prod:* Robert Presnell for Warner Brothers/First National. 65m.

FEMALE (1933). A career woman, used to her own way, falls for a strong-minded architect. *Co-dir:* William Dieterle. *Sc:*

Gene Markey, Kathryn Scola (novel by Donald Henderson Clark). *Ph:* Sid Hickox. *Art dir:* Jack Okey. *Ed:* Jack Killifer. *With* Ruth Chatterton (*Nancy*), George Brent (*Jim Thorne*), Philip Faversham (*Claybourne*), Ruth Donnelly (*Miss Frothingham*), Johnny Mack Brown (*Cooper*), Ferdinand Gottschalk, Philip Reed, Lois Wilson, Huey White, Eric Wilton, Rafaelo Ottiano, Walter Walker, Charles Wilson, Kenneth Thompson, Edward Cooper, Douglas Dumbrille, Samuel S. Hinds, Usay O'Davern, Sterling Holloway, Spencer Charters, Robert Greig, Robert Warwick, Laura Hope Crews, Gavin Gordon. *Prod:* Henry Blanke for Warner Brothers/First National. 60m.

MANDALAY (1934). Melodrama about a fairly unsavoury heroine disposing of an unwanted lover. *Sc:* Austin Parker, Charles Kenyon (from short story by Paul Hervey Fox). *Ph:* Tony Gaudio. *Art dir:* Anton Grot. *Ed:* Thomas Pratt. *With* Kay Francis (*Tanya*), Ricardo Cortez (*Tony Evans*), Warner Oland (*Nick*), Lyle Talbot (*Dr. Greg Barton*), Ruth Donnelly (*Mrs. Peters*), Shirley Temple (*Betty Shaw*), Reginald Owen, Rafaela Ottiano, David Torrence, Halliwell Hobbes, Etienne Girardot, Lucien Littlefield, Herman Bing, Bodil Rosing, Hobart Cavanaugh, Harry C. Bradley, James B. Leong, Lillian Harmer, Torben Meyer. *Assoc. Prod:* Robert Presnell for Warner Brothers/First National. 65m.

BRITISH AGENT (1934). Mostly fictional story of British diplomat's efforts to prevent Soviet/German peace negotiations during First World War. *Sc:* Laird Doyle (based on Bruce Lockhart's memoirs). *Ph:* Ernest Haller. *Art dir:* Anton Grot. *Ed:* Tom Richards. *Music:* Leo Forbestein. *With* Leslie Howard (*Stephen Locke*), Kay Francis (*Elena*), Irving Pichel (*Stalin*), J. Carrol Naish (*Trotsky*), William Gargan (*Medill*), Philip Reed (*Le Farge*). Ivan Simpson, Walter Byron, Cesar Romero, Halliwell Hobbes, Arthur Aylesworth, Alphonse Ethier, Tenen Holt, Doris Lloyd, Marina Schubert, George Pearce, Gregory Gaye, Paul Porcasi, Addison Richards, Walter Armitage. *Sup. Prod:* Henry Blanke. *Assoc. Prod:* Robert Presnell for Warner Brothers/First National. 81m.

JIMMY THE GENT (1934). A madcap farce with Cagney exposing a missing heir racket. *Sc:* Bertram Milhauser (story "The Heir Chaser," by Laird Doyle, Ray Nazzaro). *Ph:* Ira Morgan. *Art dir:* Edsras Hartley. *Ed:* Tom Richards. *With* James Cagney (*Jimmy Corrigan*), Bette Davis (*Joan*), Alice White (*Mabel*), Allen Jenkins (*Louie*), Arthur Hohl, Alan Dinehart, Mayo Methot, Philip Reed, Hobart Cavanaugh, Rolf Harolde, Nora Lane, Joe Sawyer, Philip Faversham, Howard Hickman, Jane Darwell, Joseph Crehan, Robert Warwick, Harold Entwhistle, Eddie Featherstone, Renee Whitney, Myrna Kennedy, Dennis O'Keefe. *Prod:* Jack L. Warner for Warner Brothers/First National. 66m.

THE KEY (1934). A "Black-and Tan" philanderer becomes involved with a married woman during the Irish troubles. Re-issued in 1960 as HIGH PERIL. *Sc:* Laird Doyle (from a play by R. Gore Browne, J. L. Hardy). *Ph:* Ernest Haller. *Art dir:* Robert Haas. *Ed:* William Clemens and Thomas Richards. *With* Edna Best (*Nora*), William Powell (*Capt. Jennant*), Colin Clive (*Andrew Kerr*), Maxine Doyle (*Pauline*), Donald Crisp

Bette Davis prevents a typically aggressive James Cagney from punching Alan Dinehart while Allen Jenkins watches menacingly in JIMMY THE GENT

(*Conlan*), Hobart Cavanaugh, Halliwell Hobbes, Phil Regan, Arthur Treacher, Arthur Aylesworth, Dawn O'Day (later Anne Shirley), Gertrude Short, Henry O'Neill, J. M. Kerrigan. *Prod:* Robert Presnell for Warner Brothers. 72m.

BLACK FURY (1935). Social drama casting Muni as a simple miner used by a gang of racketeering strike breakers to destroy a union. *Sc:* Abem Finkel, Carl Erickson (from story "Jan Volkanik," by Judge M. A. Mussmano and play "Bohunk," by Harry R. Irving). *Ph:* Byron Haskin. *Art dir:* John J. Hughes. *Ed:* Tom Richards. *With* Paul Muni (*Joe Radek*), William Gargan (*Slim Johnson*), Tully Marshall (*Tommy Poole*), Karen Morley (*Anna Novak*), Mae Marsh (*Mary Novak*), Barton MacLane, John Qualen, J. Carroll Naish, Vince Barnett, Wade Boteler, Henry O'Neill, Effie Ellsler, Willard Robertson, Egon Brecher, George Pat Collins, Ward Bond, Joseph Crehan, Akim Tamiroff, Purnell Pratt, Eddie Schubert, Sara Haden, Selmar Jackson, Pat Moriarty, Edith Fellows, Bobby Nelson, June Ebberling, Dorothy Gray, Jack Bleifer, George Offerman Jnr., Floyd

Shackelford, Mickey Rentschler, Wally Albright, Pedro Regan. *Prod:* Robert Lord for Warner Brothers. 92m.

THE CASE OF THE CURIOUS BRIDE (1935). An episode from another popular crime series, featuring Warren William as Perry Mason. *Sc:* Brown Holmes, Tom Reed (novel by Erle Stanley Gardner). *Ph:* David Abel. *Art dir:* Carl Jules Weyl, Anton Grot. *Ed:* Terry Morse. *Mus:* Bernard Kaun. *With* Warren William (*Perry Mason*), Margaret Lindsay (*Rhoda*), Donald Woods (*Carl*), Claire Dodd (*Della*), Allen Jenkins (*Spudsy*), Philip Reed (*Dr. Claude Millsap*), Barton MacLane, Winifred Shaw, Olin Howland, Henry Kolker, Errol Flynn, Charles Richman, Thomas Jackson, Robert Gleckler, Mayo Methot, James Donlan, George Humbert, Warren Hymer, Paul Hurst. *Prod:* Harry Joe Brown for Warner Brothers. 68m.

FRONT PAGE WOMAN (1935). The making of a good female newspaper reporter. *Sc:* Laird Doyle, Roy Chanslor, Lillie Hayward (from a story "Women Are Born Newspapermen," by Richard Macauley). *Ph:* Tony Gaudio. *Art dir:* John Hughes. *Ed:* Terry Morse. *Mus:* Heinz Roemheld. *With* Bette Davis (*Ellen*), George Brent (*Curt*), June Martel (*Olive*), Joseph Crehan (*Spike Kiley*), Roscoe Karns (*Toots*), Dorothy Dare, Winifred Shaw, J. Carroll Naish, Joseph King, Walter Walker, J. Farrell MacDonald, De Witt Jennings, Grace Hale, Huntley Gordon, Adrian Rosley, George Renavent, Selmar Jackson, Gordon Westcott, Addison Richards, Mike Monk. *Prod:* Samuel Bischoff for Warner Brothers. 80m.

LITTLE BIG SHOT (1935). A vehicle for Warner Brothers' answer to Shirley Temple, Sybil Jason, who is kidnapped by Broadway gangsters in this minor crime drama. *Sc:* Jerry Wald, Julius J. Epstein, Robert Andrews (story by Harrison Jacobs). *Ph:* Tony Gaudio. *Art dir:* Hugh Retticher. *Ed:* Jack Killifer. *Mus:* Leo Forbestein. *With* Sybil Jason (*Gloria Gibbs*), Glenda Farrell (*Jean*), Robert Armstrong (*Steve Craig*), Edward Everett Horton (*Mortimer Thompson*), Edgar Kennedy, Jack La Rue, Mary Foy, Arthur Vinton, Addison Richards, Joseph Sawyer, Tammany Young, Emma Dunn, Ward Bond, Murray Alper, Guy Usher, Marc Lawrence. *Prod:* Sam Bischoff for Warner Brothers. 78m.

CAPTAIN BLOOD (1935). Sabatini's famous story of the gentleman doctor Peter Blood, forced into piracy by his opposition to James II. *Sc:* Casey Robinson (novel by Rafael Sabatini). *Ph:* Hal Mohr. *Art dir:* Anton Grot. *Ed:* George Amy. *Mus:* Erich Wolfgang Korngold. *With* Errol Flynn (*Peter Blood*), Olivia De Havilland (*Arabella Bishop*), Lionel Atwill (*Colonel Bishop*), Basil Rathbone (*Levasseur*), Ross Alexander (*Jeremy Pitt*), Henry Stephenson (*Lord Willoughby*), Guy Kibbee, Robert Barrat, Mary Forbes, Hobart Cavanaugh, Donald Meek, Jessie Ralph, Forrester Harvey, Frank McGlynn Sr., Holmes Herbert, Pedro de Cordoba, David Torrence, J. Carroll Naish, George Hassell, Harry Cording, Leonard Mudie, Ivan Simpson, E. E. Clive, Stuart Casey, Dennis D. Adburn, Colin Kenny, Maude Leslie, Gardner James, Vernon Steele. *Prod:* Harry Joe Brown for Warner Brothers/

First National. 117m. Previously filmed in 1924 (*d* David Smith).

THE WALKING DEAD (1936). An innocent man, framed and convicted for a murder, is raised from the dead to wreak vengeance on his criminal enemies. *Sc:* Ewart Adamson, Peter Milne, Robert Adams, Lillie Hayward. *Ph:* Hal Mohr. *Ed:* Thomas Pratt. *With* Boris Karloff (*John Ellman*), Ricardo Cortez (*Nolan*), Marguerite Churchill (*Nancy*), Edmund Gwenn (*Dr. Beaumont*), Warren Hull (*Jimmy*), Barton MacLane, Henry O'Neill, Addison Hehr, Ruth Robinson, Mike Morita, Eddie Acuff, Kenneth Harlan, Adrian Risley, Joseph King, Joe Sawyer, Paul Harvey, Robert Strange, Addison Richards. *Prod:* Warner Brothers. 66m.

STOLEN HOLIDAY (1936). A Parisian model marries a fortune-hunting Russian swindler in order to shield him from the law, and tries to reform him. *Sc:* Casey Robinson (story by Warren Duff and Virginia Kellogg). *Ph:* Sid Hickox. *Art dir:* Anton Grot. *Ed:* Terry Morse. *Mus:* Leo Forbestein. *With* Kay Francis, (*Nicole Picot*), Claude Rains (*Stefan Orloff*), Ian Hunter (*Anthony Wayne*), Alison Skipworth (*Suzanne*), Alexander D'Arcy (*Anatole*), Walter Kingsford, Betty Lawford, Charles Halton, Egon Brecher, Frank Reicher, Frank Conroy, Robert Strange, Kathleen Howard, Wedgewood Howell. *Prod:* Hal B. Wallis. *Assoc. Prod:* Harry Joe Brown for Warner Brothers. 84m.

THE CHARGE OF THE LIGHT BRIGADE (1936): Rousing adventure yarn set in India concerning the lives of two brothers who fall out over a woman, and their subsequent careers in the Lancers. *Sc:* Michel Jakoby, Rowland Leigh (poem by Alfred Tennyson). *Ph:* Sol Polito, Fred Jackman: *Art dir:* John Hughes. *Ed:* George Amy. *Mus:* Max Steiner. *Charge sequence mounted by:* B. Reeves Eason. *With* Errol Flynn (*Major Geoffrey Vickers*), Olivia De Havilland (*Elsa Campbell*), Patric Knowles (*Capt. Perry Vickers*), Henry Stephenson (*Sir Charles Macefield*), Nigel Bruce (*Sir Benjamin Warrenton*), David Niven (*Capt. Randall*), C. Henry Gordon, Donald Crisp, E. E. Clive, G. P. Hartley Jnr., Robert Barrat, J. Carroll Naish, Spring Byington, Walter Holbrook, Charles Sedgewick, Scotty Beckett, Princess Baigum, George Regas, Colin Kenny, Gordon Hart, Helen Sanborn, Frank Jenks. *Prod:* Hal B. Wallis. *Assoc. Prod:* Sam Bischoff for Warner Brothers. 116m. Re-made in 1968, with Tony Richardson directing.

KID GALAHAD (1937). A hick becomes a boxing champion but finds the going heavy under the pressure of his ruthless manager and the interest of the big-time gangsters who want to control him. *Sc:* Seton I. Miller (from novel by Francis Wallace). *Ph:* Tony Gaudio. *Art dir:* Carl Jules Weyl. *Ed:* George Amy. *Mus:* Heinz Roemheld and Max Steiner. *With* Wayne Morris (*Ward Guisenberry*), Edward G. Robinson (*Nick Donati*), Bette Davis (*Fluff*), Humphrey Bogart (*Turkey Morgan*), Jane Bryan (*Marie*), Harry Carey (*Silver Jackson*), Soledad Jiminez, William Haade, Veda Ann Borg, Ben Welden, Joseph Crehan, Harland Tucker, Horace MacMahon, Frank Faylen, Joyce Compton, Bob Evans, Hank

Hankinson, Bob Nestell, Jack Kranz, George Blake, Joe Cunningham. *Prod:* Hal B. Wallis for Warner Brothers/First National. 100m. Shown on American TV as THE BATTLING BELLHOP. Loosely re-made in 1962 as KID GALAHAD (*d* Phil Karlson).

MOUNTAIN JUSTICE (1937). A mountain girl struggles to make her family recognise her rights and her medical knowledge. *Sc:* Norman Reilly Raine, Luci Ward (story by Reilly, Ward). *Ph:* Ernest Haller. *Art dir:* Max Parker. *Ed:* George Amy. *With* Josephine Hutchinson (*Ruth Harkins*), Guy Kibbee (*Doc Barnard*), George Brent (*Paul Cameron*), Robert McWade (*Horace Bamber*), Robert Barrat (*Jeff Harkins*), Mona Barrie (*Evelyn Wayne*), Edwin Pawley (*Tod Miller*), Margaret Hamilton, Fuzzy Knight, Elizabeth Risdon, Marcia Mae Jones, Granville Bates, Russell Simpson, Sibyl Harrison, Guy Wilkerson. *Prod:* Warner Brothers, 83m.

THE PERFECT SPECIMEN (1937). Comedy about a handsome, athletic young millionaire who escapes from the sheltered existence imposed upon him by his grandmother. *Sc:* Norman Reilly Raine, Lawrence Riley, Brewster Morse, Fritz Frankenstein (story by Samuel Hopkins Adams). *Ph:* Charles Rosher. *Art dir:* Robert Haas. *Ed:* Terry Morse. *Mus:* Heinz Roemheld. *With* Errol Flynn (*Gerald Wicks*), Joan Blondell (*Mona Carter*), Hugh Herbert (*Killigrew Shawe*), Dick Foran (*Jink Carter*), Beverly Roberts (*Alicia*), Edward Everett Horton, May Robson, Allen Jenkins, Dennie Moore, Hugh O'Connell, James Burke, Granville Bates, Harry Davenport, Tim Henning, Spencer Charters. *Prod:* Hal B. Wallis. *Assoc. Prod:* Harry Joe Brown for Warner Brothers/First National. 98m.

GOLD IS WHERE YOU FIND IT (1938). Western dealing with feuds between the miners and the ranchers in California after the Civil War. *Sc:* Warren Duff, Robert Buckner (story by Clements Ripley). *Ph:* Sol Polito. *Spec. eff. ph:* Byron Haskin. *Art Dir:* Ted Smith. *Ed:* Clarence Kolster. *Mus:* Max Steiner. *With* Errol Flynn (*Jared Whitney*), Olivia De Havilland (*Serena Ferris*), Claude Rains (*Colonel Ferris*), Margaret Lindsay (*Rosanne*), John Litel (*Ralph Ferris*), Marcia Ralston, Barton MacLane, Tim Holt, Sidney Toler, Henry O'Neill, Willie Best, Robert McWade, George Hayes, Russell Simpson, Harry Davenport, Clarence Kolb, Moroni Olsen, Granville Bates, Robert Homans, Eddie Chandler. *Prod:* Hal B. Wallis for Warner Bros. 94m.

THE ADVENTURES OF ROBIN HOOD (1938). The classic swashbuckling tale of the gentleman outlaw of Sherwood Forest received the full expertise of talent and ability available at Warners, and still holds its own as a genuinely exciting and entertaining film. *Co-dir:* Michael Curtiz, William Keighley. *2nd Unit Dir:* B. Reeves Eason. *Sc:* Norman Reilly Raine, Seton I. Miller (from their story). *Ph:* Tony Gaudio, Sol Polito, W. Howard Greene. *Art Dir:* Carl Jules Weyl. *Ed:* Ralph Dawson. *Mus:* Erich Wolfgang Korngold. *With* Errol Flynn (*Robin Hood*), Olivia De Havilland (*Maid Marian*), Basil Rathbone (*Sir Guy of Gisborne*), Claude Rains (*Prince John*), Patric Knowles (*Will Scarlet*), Alan Hale (*Little John*), Eugene Pallette (*Friar*

Tuck), Ian Hunter, Melville Cooper, Una O'Connor, Herbert Mundin, Montague Love, Leonard Willey, Robert Noble, Kenneth Hunter, Robert Warwick, Colin Kenny, Lester Matthews, Harry Cording, Howard Hill, Ivan Simpson, Leonard Mudie, Charles McNaughton, John Sutton. *Prod:* Hal B. Wallis for Warner Bros. Technicolor. 105m. Thirteen other versions have been filmed between 1909 and 1971; the most notable being *Robin Hood* (1922, Allan Dwan), *The Bandit of Sherwood Forest* (1946, George Sherman, Henry Levin), *Rogues of Sherwood Forest* (1950, Gordon Douglas) which used stock footage from the Curtiz version, and *The Story of Robin Hood* (1952, Ken Annakin), filmed for Disney. The majority bear little relation to the legends, while some use the name or feature sons or daughters of Robin Hood.

FOUR DAUGHTERS (1938). Phenomenally successful soap-opera which led to Warners making three sequels, two of which were directed by Curtiz, while Gordon Douglas later re-made *Four Daughters* as *Young at Heart* (1954). *Sc:* Julius J. Epstein, Lenore Coffee (from novel *Sister Act* by Fannie Hurst). *Ph:* Ernest Haller. *Art Dir:* John Hughes. *Ed:* Ralph Dawson. *Mus:* Max Steiner. *With* Claude Rains (*Adam Lemp*), Jeffrey Lynn (*Felix Deitz*), John Garfield (*Mickey Borden*), Frank McHugh (*Ben Crowley*), May Robson (*Aunt Etta*), Rosemary Lane, Lola Lane, Priscilla Lane, Gail Page (*the Four Daughters*), Dick Foran, Vera Lewis, Tom Dugan, Eddie Acuff. *Prod:* Hal B. Wallis for Warner Bros. 90m.

FOUR'S A CROWD (1938). Comedy about a wealthy heiress and her many beaus. *Sc:* Casey Robinson, Sig Herzig (novel *All Rights Reserved* by Wallace Sullivan). *Ph:* Ernest Haller. *Art dir:* Max Parker. *Ed:* Clarence Kolster. *Music:* Heinz Roemheld, Ray Heindorf. *With* Errol Flynn (*Bob Lansford*), Olivia De Havilland (*Lorri Dillingwell*), Rosalind Russell (*Jean Christy*), Patric Knowles (*Patterson Buckley*), Walter Connolly (*John P. Dillingwell*), Hugh Herbert, Melville Cooper, Franklin Pangborn, Herman Bing, Margaret Hamilton, Joseph Crehan, Joe Cunningham, Dennie Moore, Gloria Blondell, Carole Landis, Rene Rivero. *Assoc. Prod:* David Lewis for Warner Bros. 91m.

ANGELS WITH DIRTY FACES (1938). Two slum kids go their different ways; one becomes a priest while the other takes to crime. They come into conflict when the criminal returns to his home environment where he is seen as a hero. *Sc:* John Wexley, Warren Duff (story by Rowland Brown). *Ph:* Sol Polito. *Art dir:* Robert Haas. *Ed:* Owen Marks. *Mus:* Max Steiner. *With* James Cagney (*Rocky Sullivan*), Pat O'Brien (*Father Jerry Connolly*), Humphrey Bogart (*James Frazier*), Ann Sheridan (*Laury Ferguson*), George Bancroft (*Mac Keefer*), Bobby Halop, Gabriel Dell, Leo Gorcey, Bobby Jordan, Huntz Hall, Bernard Punsley, Joe Downing, Frankie Burke, Adrian Morris, William Tracy, Marilyn Knowlden, St. Brendan's Church Choir. *Assoc. Prod:* Sam Bischoff for Warner Bros. 99m.

DODGE CITY (1939). The first of a series of large-scale Westerns with Flynn and De Havilland, this deals with troubles in Kansas as the railroad heads westwards. *Sc:* Robert Buckner (from his story). *Ph:* Sol Polito. *Art dir:* Ted Smith. *Ed:* George Amy. *Mus:* Max Steiner. *With* Errol Flynn (*Wade Hatton*), Olivia De Havilland (*Abbie*), Ann Sheridan (*Ruby*), Bruce Cabot (*Jeff Surrett*), Frank McHugh (*Joe Clemens*), Alan Hale, John Litel, Henry Travers, Henry O'Neill, Victory Jory, Bobs Watson, Guinn "Big Boy" Williams, Gloria Holden, Charles Halton, Douglas Fowley, Georgia Caine, Cora Witherspoon, Ward Bond, Russell Simpson, Monte Blue, William Lundigan. *Prod:* Robert Lord for Warner Bros. Technicolor. 105m.

SONS OF LIBERTY (1939). Short starring Claude Rains as Haym Solomon raising funds for George Washington's army. *Sc:* Crane Wilbur. *With* Claude Rains. *Prod:* Warner Brothers. 20m.

DAUGHTERS COURAGEOUS (1939). The second in the series about the New England family and their four daughters, deals with the return of the father after twenty years as his wife is about to remarry, and the romance between the youngest girl and a delinquent bum. *Sc:* Julius J. Epstein and Philip G. Epstein (from a play by Dorothy Bennett and Irving White based on characters created by Fannie Hurst). *Ph:* James Wong Howe. *Ed:* Ralph Dawson. *Mus:* Max Steiner. *With* Claude Rains (*Jim Masters*), John Garfield (*Gabriel Lopez*), Jeffrey Lynn (*Johnny Henning*), Fay Bainter (*Nan Masters*), Donald Crisp (*Sam Sloane*), Frank McHugh, Gail Page, Lola Lane, Priscilla Lane, Rosemary Lane, Dick Foran, George Humbert, Berton Churchill. *Prod:* Hal B. Wallis for Warner Bros. *Assoc. Prod:* Henry Blanke. 107m.

Warners' top romantic team, Errol Flynn and Olivia De Havilland, in a happy moment from DODGE CITY

THE PRIVATE LIVES OF ELIZABETH AND ESSEX (1939). A lavishly mounted vehicle for Bette Davis, starring as Elizabeth I of England. *Sc:* Norman Reilly Raine, Aeneas MacKenzie (from play "Elizabeth the Queen," by Maxwell Anderson). *Ph:* Sol Polito and W. Howard Greene. *Art dir:* Anton Grot. *Ed:* Owen Marks. *Mus:* Erich Wolfgang Korngold. *With* Bette Davis (*Elizabeth I*), Errol Flynn (*Earl of Essex*), Olivia De Havilland (*Lady Penelope Gray*), Donald Crisp (*Francis Bacon*), Alan Hale (*Earl of Tyrone*), Vincent Price (*Sir Walter Raleigh*), Henry Daniell, Leo G. Carroll, Henry Stephenson, Maris Wrixon, Nanette Fabares (Fabray), Rosella Towne, Ralph Forbes, Robert Warwick, Forrester Harvey, John Sutton, Guy Bellis, Doris Lloyd, Stanford I. Jolley.

Prod: Hal B. Wallis for Warner Bros. Technicolor. 105m. U.S. TV title is ELIZABETH THE QUEEN.

FOUR WIVES (1939). The third in the series sees the four daughters all married. *Sc:* Julius J. Epstein and Philip G. Epstein (based on novel *Sister Act* by Fannie Hurst). *Ph:* Sol Polito. *Art dir:* John Hughes. *Ed:* Ralph Dawson. *Mus:* Max Steiner. *With* Claude Rains (*Adam Lemp*), Priscilla Lane (*Ann Lemp Borden*), Rosemary Lane (*Kay Lemp*), Lola Lane (*Thea Lemp Crowley*), Jeffrey Lynn (*Felix Deitz*), Eddie Albert, May Robson, Frank McHugh, Dick Foran, Henry O'Neill, Vera Lewis, John Qualen. *Prod:* Hal B. Wallis for Warner Bros. *Assoc. Prod:* Henry Blanke. 110m.

VIRGINIA CITY (1940). Civil War conflict between Flynn and Scott with the latter being aided by Miriam Hopkins, while all are preyed upon by bandit Humphrey Bogart. *Sc:* Robert Buckner. *Ph:* Sol Polito. *Spec. eff. Ph:* H. F. Koenekamp. *Art dir:* Ted Smith. *Ed:* George Amy. *Mus:* Max Steiner. *With* Errol Flynn (*Kerry Bradford*), Miriam Hopkins (*Julia Haynes*), Randolph Scott (*Vance Irby*), Humphrey Bogart (*John Murrell*), Frank McHugh (*Mr. Upjohn*), Guinn Williams, Douglas Dumbrille, John Litel, Moroni Olsen, Dickie Jones, Russell Simpson, Frank Wilcox, Victor Kilian, Charles Middleton, Paul Fix, Russell Hicks, Billy Bevan. *Prod:* Hal B. Wallis for Warner Bros. *Assoc. Prod:* Robert Fellows. 121m.

THE SEA HAWK (1940). Swashbuckling drama about English privateers foiling a Spanish naval invasion after harassing the Spaniards in the colonies. *Sc:* Howard Koch, Seton I. Miller. *Ph:* Sol Polito. *Spec. eff. Ph:* Byron Haskin, H. F. Koenekamp. *Art Dir:* Anton Grot. *Ed:* George Amy. *Mus:* Erich Wolfgang Korngold. *With* Errol Flynn (*Geoffrey Thorpe*), Brenda Marshall (*Dona Maria*), Claude Rains (*Don Jose Alvarez de Cordoba*), Donald Crisp (*Sir John Burleson*), Flora Robson (*Queen Elizabeth I*), Gilbert Roland, Alan Hale, Henry Daniell, Una O'Connor, James Stephenson, William Lundigan, Julien Mitchell, Montagu Love, David Bruce, J. M. Kerrigan, Fritz Leiber, Clifford Brooke, Francis MacDonald, Clyde Cook, Ellis Irving, Pedro de Cordoba, Ian Keith, Jack La Rue, Halliwell Hobbes, Alec Craig, Victor Varconi, Robert Warwick, Harry Cording, Jay Novello. *Prod:* Jack L. Warner, Hal B. Wallis for Warner Bros. *Assoc. Prod:* Henry Blanke. 127m.

SANTA FE TRAIL (1940). Largely fictionalized Western involving George Armstrong Custer in tracking down and bringing to justice John Brown. *Sc:* Robert Buckner. *Ph:* Sol Polito. *Art dir:* John Hughes. *Ed:* George Amy. *Mus:* Max Steiner. *With* Errol Flynn (*Jeb Stuart*), Olivia De Havilland (*Kit Carson Holliday*), Ronald Reagan (*George Armstrong Custer*), Van Heflin (*Rader*), Raymond Massey (*John Brown*), Alan Hale, Gene Reynolds, Guinn Williams, Henry O'Neill, Joe Sawyer, Alan Baxter, John Litel, Moroni Olsen, Charles D. Brown, David Bruce, Hobart Cavanaugh, Frank Wilcox, Ward Bond, Russell Simpson, Charles Middleton, Erville Alderson, Spencer Charters, Suzanne Carabon, William Marshall, George Haywood, Susan Peters, Douglas Fowley. *Prod:* Jack L. Warner for Warner Bros. *Assoc. Prod:* Robert Fellows. 110m.

THE SEA WOLF (1941). Exciting version of Jack London's story of a psychopathic sea captain. *Sc:* Robert Rossen (story by Jack London). *Ph:* Sol Polito. *Ed:* George Amy. *Mus:* Erich Wolfgang Korngold. *With* Edward G. Robinson (*Wolf Larsen*), Ida Lupino (*Ruth Webster*), John Garfield (*George Leach*), Gene Lockhart (*Dr. Louie*), Barry Fitzgerald (*Cooky*), Alexander Knox, Stanley Ridges, David Bruce, Francis McDonald, Howard Da Silva, Frank Lackteen, Wilfrid Lucas. *Prod:* Jack L. Warner, Hal B. Wallis for Warner Bros. *Assoc. Prod:* Henry Blanke. 100m. Made in 1926 as *The Sea Beast* (d. Millard Webb) and in 1958 as *Wolf Larsen.*

DIVE BOMBER (1941). Drama about the medical problems related to flying high speed planes. *Sc:* Frank Wead and Robert Buckner (from story by Wead). *Ph:* Bert Glennon and Winton C. Hoch. *Aerial Ph:* Elmer Dyer and Charles Marshall. *Art dir:* Robert Haas. *Ed:* George Amy. *Mus:* Max Steiner. *With* Errol Flynn (*Doug Lee*), Fred MacMurray (*Joe Blake*), Ralph Bellamy (*Dr. Lance Rogers*), Alexis Smith (*Linda Fisher*), Robert Armstrong (*Art Lyons*), Herbert Anderson, Regis Toomey, Allen Jenkins, Craig Stevens, Moroni Olsen, Dennie Moore, Louis Jean Heydt, Cliff Nazzaro, Gig Young (Byron Barr), Addison Richards. *Prod:* Hal B. Wallis for Warner Bros. *Assoc. Prod:* Robert Lord. Technicolor. 133m.

CAPTAINS OF THE CLOUDS (1942). Melodramatic tribute to the Royal Air Force, similar in plot to Henry King's *A Yank in the R.A.F.* (1941) with a recalcitrant American learning discipline and comradeship. *Sc:* Arthur T. Norman, Richard Macauley, Norman Reilly Raine. *Ph:* Winton C. Hoch and Sol Polito. *Aerial Ph:* Elmer Dyer and Charles Marshall. *Ed:* George Amy. *Mus:* Max Steiner. *With* James Cagney (*Brian MacLean*), Dennis Morgan (*Johnny Dutton*), Brenda Marshall (*Emily Foster*), Alan Hale (*Tiny Murphy*), George Tobias (*Blimp Lebec*), Clem Bevans, Russell Arms, Reginald Gardiner, Reginald Denny, Air Marshal W. A. Bishop, Paul Cavanaugh, J. Farrell MacDonald, Patrick O'Moore, Sqd.-Ldr. O. Cathcart-Jones. *Prod:* Hal B. Wallis for Warner Bros. *Assoc. Prod:* William Cagney. Technicolor. 113m.

YANKEE DOODLE DANDY (1942). Musical biography of intensely patriotic song-writer and showman George M. Cohan, portrayed by James Cagney in an Oscar winning performance. *Sc:* Robert Buckner, Edmund Joseph (from Buckner story). *Ph:* James Wong Howe. *Art dir:* Carl Jules Weyl. *Ed:* George Amy. *Montage:* Don Siegel. *Mus:* George M. Cohan. *With* James Cagney (*George M. Cohan*), Walter Huston (*Jerry Cohan*), Joan Leslie (*Mary*), Richard Whorf (*Sam Harris*), Jeanne Cagney (*Josie Cohan*), Irene Manning, George Tobias, Rosemary De Camp, Frances Langford, George Barbier, S. Z. Sakall, Eddie Foy Jnr., Walter Catlett, Douglas Croft, Minor Watson, Chester Clute, Odette Myrtil, Patsy Lee Parsons, Capt. Jack Young, Mary Wickes. *Prod:* Jack L. Warner and Hal B. Wallis for Warner Bros. *Assoc. Prod:* William Cagney. 126m.

CASABLANCA (1943). Classic patriotic drama with existentialist hero Bogart coming to terms with a lost love and opting for life again to help her hero husband escape from the Nazi *régime*. *Sc:* Julius J. Epstein, Philip G. Epstein, Howard Koch (from an unperformed play by Murray Burnett and Joan Alison). *Ph:* Arthur Edeson. *Art dir:* Carl Jules Weyl. *Ed:* Owen Marks. *Montage:* Don Siegel, James Leicester. *Mus:* Max Steiner. *With* Humphrey Bogart (*Rick*), Ingrid Bergman (*Ilsa Lund*), Paul Henreid (*Laszlo*), Claude Rains (*Captain Renault*), Conrad Veidt (*Col. Strasser*), Peter Lorre (*Bugati*), Dooley Wilson (*Sam*), Sydney Greenstreet (*Señor Ferrari*), S. Z. Sakall, Joy Page, John Qualen, Madeleine LeBeau, Curt Bois, Leonid Kinskey, Helmut Dantine, Marcel Dalio, Corinna Mura, Ludwig Stossel, Ilka Gruning, Frank Puglia, Dan Seymour, Evelyn Varden. *Prod:* Hal B. Wallis for Warner Bros-First National. 102m.

MISSION TO MOSCOW (1943). Adaptation of a book by Joseph Davies, a former U.S. Ambassador to Russia, which achieved a notorious reputation during the McCarthy witch-hunt in the Fifties, but which is a classic propaganda work in its own stylistic right. *Sc:* Howard Koch (from Joseph Davies's memoirs). *Ph:* Bert Glennon. *Art dir:* Carl Jules Weyl. *Ed:* Owen Marks. *Mus:* Max Steiner. *Montage:* Don Siegel and James Liecester. *Tech. Adv:* Jay Leyda. *With* Walter Huston (*Joseph E. Davies*), Ann Harding (*Mrs. Davies*), Oscar Homolka (*Maxim Litvinov*), George Tobias (*Freddie*), Gene Lockhart (*Molotov*), Henry Daniell, Frieda Inescourt, Eleanor Parker, Richard Travis, Helmut Dantine, Victor Francen, Barbara Everest, Dudley Field Malone, Roman Bohnen, Maria Palmer, Moroni Olsen, Minor Watson, Vladimir Sokoloff, Maurice Schwartz, Jerome Cowan, Konstantin Shayne, Mannart Kippen, Kathleen Lockhart, Jean Del Val, Kurt Katch, Felix Basch, Frank Puglia, John Abbott, Charles Trowbridge, Leigh Whipper, George Renavent, Clive Morgan, Alex Chirva, Olaf Hytten, Art Gilmore, Dan Clayton, George Sorel, Duncan Renaldo, Doris Lloyd, Frank Reicher, Daniel Ocko, David Hoffman, Ivan Triesault, Ivan Lebedeff, Peter Goo Chong, Emile Rameau, Peter Michael, Nino Bellini, Fred Schuman-Heinck, Rolf Lindau, George Davis, Emory Parnell, J. Pat O'Malley, Mark Strong, Albert D'Arno, Rudolph Steinbeck, Gino Corrado, Glenn Strange, Oliver Cross, Ray Walker, Capt. Jack Young, Ernest Hauserman, Frank Faylen, Joseph Crehan, Ross Ford, Warren Douglas, Barbara Brown, Isabel Withers, George Lossey, Wallis Clark, Hans Schumm, Dr. Ernest Golm, Lisa Golm, Henry Victor, Luis Arco, Alfred Zeisler, Richard Ryan, Erwin Kaler, Pierre Watkin, Edward Van Sloan, Esther Zeitlin, Nina Blagio, Tania Somova, Nicholai Celikhovsky, Michael Visaroff, Nicholas Kobliansky, Gabriel Lenoff, Alex Akimoff, Sam Savitsky, George Glebeff, Michael Guttman, Robert Baikoff, Mischa Westfall, Elizabeth Archer, Rosa Margot, Valya Terry, Sandor Szabo, Virginia Christine, Lumsden Hare, Robert C. Fischer, Charles La Torre, Alex Caze, Leonid Snegoff, Edgar Licho, Marie Melesch, Michael Mark, Martin Noble, Lee Tung Foo, Victor Wong, Luke Chan, Allen Jung, John Dilson, Jean De Briac, Ted E. Jacques, Billie Louie, Loulette Sablon, Marian Lessing, Joan Winfield, Tina Menard, Peggy Watts, Irene Pedrini, Louis Jean Heydt, John Hamilton, Frank Ferguson, Bill Kennedy, William Forrest, Alex Melesch, Marek Windheim, Gregory Golubeff, Jack Gardner, Sam Goldenberg, Egon Brecher, Zina Torchina, Vera Richkova, Jean Wong, Irina Semochenko, Joseph Kamaryt, Christine Gordon, Alexander Granach, Baroness Yvonne Hendricks, Tamara Shayne, Olga Uljanovskaja, Patricia Fung, Igorde Navratsky, James Flavin, William B. Davidson, Herbert Heyes, George Carlton, Francis Pierlot, Forbes Murray, Edward Keane, William Gould, Harry Cording, Zoia Karabanova, Betty Roadman, Hooper Atchley, Eugene Eberly, Arthur Loft, Alec Campbell, Mike Mazurki, Nicko Romoff, Noel Cravat, Tom Tully, Lionel Royce, Eugene Borden, Feodor Chaliapin, John Maxwell, Jacqueline Dalya, Herbert Ashley, Oliver Prickett, Monte Blue, Frank Penny, Ernie Adams, Eddie Kane, Ed Cobb, Howard Mitchell, Frank Wayne, Jack Kenny, Ben Erway, Mauritz Hugo, Gene Gary, Frank Jacquet, Fred Essler, John Wengraf, Robert Shayne, Michael Panaieff, Lily Norwood, Cyd Charisse. *Prod:* Robert Buckner for Warner Brothers. 123m. Joseph Davies is also credited as co-director in some sources, but probably acted only in an advisory capacity.

THIS IS THE ARMY (1943). Technicolor romp about staging musical shows for the Army, made as part of Warner Bros. contribution to the war effort. *Sc:* Casey Robinson and Capt. Claude Binyon (story by Irving Berlin). *Ph:* Bert Glennon and Sol Polito. *Art dir:* Lt. John Koenig, John Hughes. *Ed:* George Amy. *Mus:* Irving Berlin. *With* George Murphy (*Jerry Jones*), Joan Leslie (*Eileen Dibble*), George Tobias (*Maxie Twardofsky*), Alan Hale (*Sgt. McGhee*) Charles Butterworth (*Eddie Dibble*), Dolores Costello, Una Merkel, Stanley Ridges, Rosemary De Camp, Kate Smith, Ruth Donnelly, Dorothy Peterson, Frances Langford, Gertrude Niesen, Ilka Gruning, Lieut. Ronald Reagan, Sgt. Joe Louis, Sgt. Tom D'Andrea, Sgt. James Burrell, Sgt. Ross Elliott, Sgt. Julie Oshins, Sgt. Robert Shanley, Capt. Herbert Anderson, Sgt. Phil Truex, Capt. Ralph Magelssen, Cpl. James McColl, Cpl. Tileston Perry, Cpl. Larry Weeks, The Allon Trio, Pte. Joe Cook Jnr., Cpl. Sidney Robin, Cpl. William Roerich, Pfc. Henry Jones, Sgt. Dick Bernie, Interlocutor Sgt. Alan Manson, Guard Cpl. John Draper, Sgt. Richard Irving, Sgt. Fred Kelly, Pfc. Hank Henry, Sgt. J. P. Mandes, Sgt. Gene Berg, S/Sgt. Arthur Steiner, Sgt. Belmonte Cristiani, Cpl. Pinkie Mitchell. *Prod:* Jack L. Warner, Hal B. Wallis for Warner Bros. Technicolor. 121m.

PASSAGE TO MARSEILLE (1944). Star-studded but over-elaborately scripted adventure yarn about a group of convicts who try to escape from Devil's Island to join the Free French forces. *Sc:* Casey Robinson and James Norman Hall. *Ph:* James Wong Howe. *Art dir:* Carl Jules Weyl. *Ed:* Owen Marks. *Mus:* Max Steiner. *With* Humphrey Bogart (*Matrac*), Claude Rains (*Capt. Freycinet*), Michèle Morgan (*Paula*), Sydney Greenstreet (*Major Duval*), Philip Dorn (*Renault*), Peter Lorre (*Marius*), George Tobias, Helmut Dantine, John Loder, Victor Francen, Vladimir Sokoloff, Eduardo Ciannelli, Corinna Mura, Konstantin Shayne, Stephen Richards (Mark Stevens), Charles La Torre, Hans Conreid, Monte Blue, Billy Roy, Frederic Brunn, Louis Mercier. *Prod:* Hal B. Wallis for

Warner Bros. 110m.

JANIE (1944). Juvenile boy in the army meets and wins girl comedy, taken from a Broadway success. *Sc:* Charles Hoffman and Agnes Christine Johnston (play by Josephine Butler and Herschel W. Williams Jnr.). *Ph:* Carl Guthrie. *Art dir:* Robert Haas. *Ed:* Owen Marks. *Mus:* Heinz Roemheld. *With* Joyce Reynolds (*Janie*), Robert Hutton (*Pte. Dick Lawrence*), Edward Arnold (*Charles Conway*), Ann Harding (*Lucille Conway*), Robert Benchley (*John Van Brunt*), Ruth Tobey, Virginia Patton, Colleen Townsend, Georgia Lee Settle, William Frambes, Peter Stackpole, Russell Hicks, Michael Harrison, Alan Hale, Clara Foley, Barbara Brown, Hattie McDaniel, Ann Gillis, Dick Erdman. *Prod:* Alex Gottlieb for Warner Bros. 106m.

ROUGHLY SPEAKING (1945). Long, comedy-drama about an ambitious woman raising a large family and shaping her shiftless husband's business affairs. *Sc:* Louise Randall Pierson (from her story). *Ph:* Joseph Walker. *Art dir:* Robert Haas. *Ed:* David Weisbart. *Mus:* Max Steiner. *With* Rosalind Russell (*Louise Randall*), Jack Carson (*Harold Pierson*), Alan Hale (*Mr. Morton*), Donald Woods (*Rodney Crane*), Robert Hutton (*John*), Jean Sullivan, Andrea King, Ray Collins, Kathleen Lockhart, Cora Sue Collins, Ann E. Todd, Andy Clyde, Arthur Shields, Helen Thimig, Eily Malyon, Greta Granstedt, Ann Doran, Hobart Cavanaugh, John Alvin, Craig Stevens, Mary Servoss, Francis Pierlot, Manart Kippen, George Carleton, George Mender, Frank Puglia, John Qualen, Chester Clute, Irving Bacon, Barbara Brown, Sig Arno, Ann Lawrence, Mona Freeman, Mickey Kuhn, Johnny Treal, John Colkins, Richard Willaker, John Sheridan, Jo Ann Marlowe, Patsy Lee Parsons, Gregory Moradian, Robert Arthur, Johnny Sheffield. *Prod:* Henry Blanke for Warner Bros. 117m.

MILDRED PIERCE (1945). The overriding ambition of a mother destroys her marriage, alienates her from her vicious daughter and involves her in blackmail, corruption and murder. *Sc:* Ranald MacDougall and Catherine Turney (novel by James M. Cain). *Ph:* Ernest Haller. *Art dir:* Anton Grot. *Ed:* David Weisbart. *Mus:* Max Steiner. *With* Joan Crawford (*Mildred Pierce*), Jack Carson (*Wally*), Zachary Scott (*Monty Berrigan*), Ann Blyth (*Veda Pierce*), Bruce Bennett (*Pierce*), Eve Arden, Jo Ann Marlowe, Margaret Kippen, Lee Patrick, Moroni Olsen, Butterfly McQueen, George Tobias, John Sheffield, Barbara Brown, Charles Trowbridge, John Compton, Chester Clute. *Prod:* Jerry Wald for Warner Bros. 111m.

NIGHT AND DAY (1946). Fictionalised biography of Cole Porter. *Sc:* Charles Hoffman, Leo Townsend, William Bowers. *Adaptation:* Jack Moffitt. *Ph:* J. Peverell Marley, William V. Skall. *Art dir:* John Hughes. *Ed:* David Weisbart. *Spec. eff. Ph:* Robert Burks. *Mus:* Cole Porter, Max Steiner. *With* Cary Grant (*Cole Porter*), Alexis Smith (*Linda Lee*), Monty Woolley (*Himself*), Ginny Sims (*Carole Hill*), Jane Wyman (*Gracie Harris*), Victor Francen, Eve Arden, Mary Martin, Alan Hale, Dorothy Malone, Tom D'Andrea, Selena Royle, Donald Woods, Sig Ruman, Henry Stephenson, Paul Cavanaugh, Carlos Ramirez, Milada Mladova, George Zoritch, Adam and Jane Di Gatano, Estelle Sloan, Clarence Muse, John Pearson, John Alvin, George Riley, Howard Freeman, Billy Watson, Herman Bing. *Prod:* Arthur Schwartz for Warner Bros. 128m.

LIFE WITH FATHER (1947). A beautifully observed cameo of family life in New York during the 1880s. *Sc:* Donald Ogden Stewart. *Ph:* J. Peverell Marley, William V. Skall. *Art dir:* Robert Haas. *Ed:* George Amy. *Mus:* Max Steiner. *With* William Powell (*Father*), Irene Dunne (*Vinnie*), Elizabeth Taylor (*Mary*), Edmund Gwenn (*Rev. Dr. Lloyd*), Zasu Pitts (*Cora*), Jimmy Lydon, Emma Dunn, Moroni Olsen, Elizabeth Risdon, Derek Scott, John Calkins, Monte Blue, Martin Milner, Heather Wilde, Mary Field, Nancy Evans, Queenie Leonard, Clara Blandick, Frank Elliott, Douglas Kennedy. *Prod:* Robert Buckner for Warner Bros. 118m.

THE UNSUSPECTED (1947). A starring role for Claude Rains as a demented radio personality who specialises in recreating murder mysteries for his public, and in the absence of a suitable script, tries to get away with the perfect murder himself. *Sc:* Ranald MacDougall (story by Charlotte Armstrong). *Adaptation:* Ben Meredyth. *Ph:* Woody Bredell. *Art dir:* Anton Grot. *Ed:* Frederick Richards. *Mus:* Franz Waxman. *With* Claude Rains (*Victor Grandison*), Joan Caulfield (*Matilda Frazier*), Audrey Totter (*Althea Keane*), Constance Bennett (*Jane Moynihan*), Hurd Hatfield (*Oliver Keane*), Michael North, Fred Clark, Jack Lambert, Harry Lewis, Ray Walker, Walter Baldwin, Nana Bryant, George Eldredge, Douglas Kennedy, Rory Mallinson. *Prod:* Charles Hoffman for Warner Bros. 103m.

ROMANCE ON THE HIGH SEAS (GB: IT'S MAGIC) (1948). Slight romantic comedy set against a cruise background with Doris Day in her first screen role. *Sc:* Julius J. Epstein and Philip G. Epstein (story by S. Pondal Rios, Carlos A. Olivari). *Ph:* Woody Bredell. *Art dir:* Anton Grot. *Ed:* Rudi Fehr. *Mus:* Leo Forbestein (*dir*). *With* Doris Day (*Georgia Garrett*), Jack Carson (*Peter Virgil*), Janis Paige (*Elvira Kent*), Don De Fore (*Michael Kent*), Oscar Levant (*Oscar Farrar*), S. Z. Sakall, Eric Blore, Franklin Pangborn, Fortunio Bonanova, Leslie Brooks, William Bakewell, Johnny Berkes, Avon Loug, Kenneth Britton, Sir Lancelot, The Samba Kings, The Page Cavanaugh Trio. *Prod:* Alex Gottlieb for Warner Bros. 99m.

MY DREAM IS YOURS (1949). A follow-up to the success of *Romance on the High Seas,* using the same leads with Bugs Bunny in a routine show business musical. *Sc:* Harry Kurnitz and Dane Lurrier. *Ph:* Ernest Haller. *Art dir:* Robert Haas. *Ed:* Folmar Blangsted. *Mus:* Harry Warren. *With* Doris Day (*Martha Gibson*), Jack Carson (*Doug Blake*), Lee Bowman (*Gary Mitchell*), Adolphe Menjou (*Thomas Hutchings*), Eve Arden (*Vivian Martin*), S. Z. Sakall, Selena Royle, Edgar Kennedy, Sheldon Leonard, Frankie Carle, Duncan Richardson, John Berkes, Ada Leonard. *Prod:* Michael Curtiz for Warner Bros. Technicolor. 99m.

FLAMINGO ROAD (1949). Another strong Crawford vehicle with her falling for a heel and becoming involved in murder. *Sc:* Robert Wilder (from his and Sally Wilder's play). *Ph:* Ted Mc-

Cord. *Art dir:* Leo K. Kuter. *Ed:* Folmar Blangsted. *Mus:* Ray Heindorf. *With* Joan Crawford (*Lane Bellamy*), Zachary Scott (*Fielding Carlisle*), Sydney Greenstreet (*Titus Semple*), David Brian (*Dan Reynolds*), Gladys George (*Lute Mae Saunders*), Virginia Huston, Fred Clark, Gertrude Michael, Alice White, Sam McDaniel, Tito Vuolo. *Prod:* Jerry Wald for Warner Bros. 94m.

THE LADY TAKES A SAILOR (1949). Knockabout comedy concerning a girl who cannot help constantly telling the truth. *Sc:* Everett Freeman (story by Jerry Graskin). *Ph:* Ted McCord. *Art dir:* Edward Carrere. *Ed:* David Weisbart. *Mus:* Max Steiner. *With* Jane Wyman (*Jennifer*), Dennis Morgan (*Bill*), Eve Arden (*Susan*), Robert Douglas (*Tyson*), Allyn Joslyn (*Ralph Whitcomb*), Tom Tully, Lina Ronay, Fred Clark, William Frawley, Charles Meredith, Craig Stevens, Stanley Prager, Kenneth Britton. *Prod:* Harry Kurnitz for Warner Bros. 98m.

YOUNG MAN WITH A HORN (GB: YOUNG MAN OF MUSIC) (1950). Drama, partially factual, about a dedicated trumpet player who nearly destroys himself through his fanatical ambition. *Sc:* Carl Foreman and Edmund H. North (novel by Dorothy Baker). *Ph:* Ted McCord. *Art dir:* Edward Carrere. *Ed:* Alan Crosland Jnr. *Mus:* Ray Heindorf. *With* Kirk Douglas (*Rick Martin*), Lauren Bacall (*Amy North*), Doris Day (*Jo Jordan*), Hoagy Carmichael (*Smoke Willoughby*), Juano Hernandez (*Art Hazard*), Jerome Cowan, Mary Beth Hughes, Orley Lindgren, Dan Seymour, Harry James, Nestor Paiva, Walter Reed, Alex Gerry. *Prod:* Jerry Wald for Warner Bros. 112m.

BRIGHT LEAF (1950). Dramatic story of Gary Cooper's rise to wealth as a tobacco grower, and the two women in his life. *Sc:* Ranald MacDougall (story by Foster Fitzsimmons). *Ph:* Karl Freund. *Art dir:* Stanley Fleischer. *Ed:* Owen Marks. *Mus:* Victor Young. *With* Gary Cooper (*Brant Royle*), Laureen Bacall (*Sonia Kovac*), Patricia Neal (*Margaret Jane Singleton*), Jack Carson (*Chris Malley*), Donald Crisp (*Major James Singleton*), Jeff Corey, Gladys George, Elizabeth Patterson, Taylor Holmes, Thurston Hall, Jimmy Griffith, Marietta Canty, William Walker. *Prod:* Henry Blanke for Warner Bros. 110m.

THE BREAKING POINT (1950). The second of three very individual versions of a Hemingway story about a hapless charter-boat owner lured into smuggling against his better nature. *Sc:* Ranald MacDougall (from novel *To Have and Have Not* by Ernest Hemingway). *Ph:* Ted McCord. *Art dir:* Edward Carrere. *Ed:* Alan Crosland Jnr. *Mus:* Ray Heindorf. *With* John Garfield (*Harry Morgan*), Patricia Neal (*Leona Charles*), Phyllis Thaxter (*Lucy Morgan*), Juano Hernandez (*Wesley Park*), Wallace Ford (*Duncan*), Edmond Ryan, Ralph Dumke, Guy Thomajan, Peter Brocco, William Campbell, John Doucette, James Griffith, Victor Sen Yung, Donna Jo Boyce, Sherry Jackson. *Prod:* Jerry Wald for Warner Bros. 97m. Previously made in 1944 (*To Have and Have Not,* Howard Hawks), and later in 1958 (*The Gun Runners,* Don Siegel).

JIM THORPE—ALL AMERICAN (GB: MAN OF BRONZE) (1951). Sports tale about the American Indian who rose from obscure beginnings to become a national sporting hero. Thorpe also played extra and bit parts in films. *Sc:* Douglas Morrow and Everett Freeman. *Ph:* Ernest Haller. *Art dir:* Edward Carrere. *Ed:* Folmar Blangsted. *Mus:* Max Steiner. *With* Burt Lancaster (*Jim Thorpe*), Charles Bickford (*"Pop" Warner*), Steve Cochran (*Peter Allendine*), Phyllis Thaxter (*Margaret Miller*), Dick Wesson (*Ed Guyac*), Jack Big Head, Suni Warcloud, Al Mejia, Hubie Kerns, Billy Gray, Nestor Paiva, Jimmy Moss. *Prod:* Everett Freeman for Warner Bros. 105m.

FORCE OF ARMS (1951). A love affair between an Army officer and a young WAC during the Second World War. *Sc:* Orin Jannings (story by Richard Tregaskin). *Ph:* Ted McCord. *Art dir:* Edward Carrere. *Ed:* Owen Marks. *Mus:* Max Steiner. *With* William Holden (*Peterson*), Nancy Olson (*Eleanor*), Frank Lovejoy (*Major Blackford*), Gene Evans (*McFee*), Dick Wesson (*Klein*), Paul Picerni, Ross Ford, Katherine Warren, Ron Hagerthy, Argentina Brunetti, Mario Siletti, Amelia Cova, Don Gordon, Bob Roark, Slatts Taylor. *Prod:* Anthony Veiller for Warner Bros. 98m.

I'LL SEE YOU IN MY DREAMS (1952). Sentimental biography of songwriter Gus Kahn. *Sc:* Jack Rose and Melville Shavelson. *Ph:* Ted McCord. *Art dir:* Douglas Bacon. *Ed:* Owen Marks. *Mus:* Gus Kahn, *directed by* Ray Heindorf. *With* Danny Thomas (*Gus Kahn*), Doris Day (*Grace LeBoy Kahn*), Frank Lovejoy (*Walter Donaldson*), Patricia Wymore (*Gloria Knight*), James Gleason (*Fred Thompson*), Mary Wickes, Julie Oshins, Jim Backus, Minna Gombell, Harry Antrim, William Forrest, Dick Simmons, Elsie Neft, Bunny Lewbel, Robert Lyden, Mimi Gibson, Christy Olson. *Prod:* Louis F. Edelman for Warner Bros. Warnercolor. 109m.

THE STORY OF WILL ROGERS (1952). Slow-moving biography of the great American humourist with his son playing the leading role. *Sc:* Stanley Roberts and Frank Davis. *Ph:* Wilfrid M. Cline. *Art dir:* Edward Carrere. *Ed:* Folmar Blangsted. *Mus:* Victor Young. *With* Will Rogers Jnr. (*Will Rogers*), Jane Wyman (*Mrs. Will Rogers*), James Gleason (*Bert Lynn*), Carl Benton Reid (*Clem Rogers*), Eddie Cline (*Himself*), Eve Miller, Noah Beery Jnr., Richard Kean, Slim Pickens, Mary Wickes, Steve Brodie, Virgil S. Taylor, Pinky Tomlin, Margaret Field, Brian Daly, Jay Silverheels, William Forrest, Earl Lee. *Prod:* Robert Arthur for Warner Bros. Warnercolor. 109m.

THE JAZZ SINGER (1953). Jewish boy follows a show business singing career instead of becoming a cantor. *Sc:* Frank Davis, Leonard Stern, Louis Meltzer (play by Samson Raphaelson). *Ph:* Carl Guthrie. *Art dir:* Leo K. Kuter. *Ed:* Alan Crosland Jnr. *Mus:* Ray Heindorf. *With* Danny Thomas (*Jerry Golding*), Peggy Lee (*Judy Lane*), Mildred Dunnock (*Mrs. Golding*), Eduard Franz (*Cantor Golding*), Tom Tully (*McGurney*), Alex Geray, Harold Gordon, Allyn Joslyn. *Prod:* Louis F. Edelman for Warner Bros. Technicolor. 105m. Silent version 1927 (*d* Alan Crosland).

TROUBLE ALONG THE WAY (1953). Sentimental story of a tough, two-fisted football coach. *Sc:* Melville Shavelson and Jack Rose. *Ph:* Archie Stout. *Art dir:* Leo K. Kuter. *Ed:* Owen Marks. *Mus:*

Max Steiner. *With* John Wayne (*Steve Williams*), Donna Reed (*Alice Singleton*), Charles Coburn (*Father Burke*), Tom Tully (*Father Malone*), Sherry Jackson (*Carol*), Marie Windsor, Tom Helmore, Dabs Greer, Leif Erickson, Douglas Spencer, Lester Matthews, Chuck Connors, Bill Radovich. *Prod:* Melville Shavelson for Warner Bros. 109m.

THE BOY FROM OKLAHOMA (1954). A quiet, peace-loving sheriff confronts the villains who run Bluerock in an effort to restore law and order. *Sc:* Winston Miller and Frank Davis (story by Michael Ferrier). *Ph:* Robert Burks. *Art dir:* Leo K. Kuter. *Ed:* James Moore. *Mus:* Max Steiner. *With* Will Rogers Jnr. (*Tom Brewster*), Nancy Olson (*Katie Brannigan*), Lon Chaney Jnr. (*Crazy Charlie*), Anthony Caruso (*Barney Turlock*), Wallace Ford (*Wally Higgins*), Louis Jean Heydt, Clem Bevans, Merv Griffin, Slim Pickens, Sheb Wooley, Tyler MacDuff, Skippy Torgenson, James Griffith, Charles Watts. *Prod:* David Weisbart for Warner Bros. Warnercolor. 88m.

THE EGYPTIAN (1954). Curtiz's first film away from Warners; a Biblical spectacular with a stellar cast, notable for its lavish sets and costume design. *Sc:* Philip Dunne and Casey Robinson (novel by Mika Waltari). *Ph:* Leon Shamroy. *Art dir:* Lyle R. Wheeler and George W. Davis. *Ed:* Barbara McLean. *Mus:* Alfred Newman and Bernard Herrmann. *With* Jean Simmons (*Merit*), Victor Mature (*Horenheb*), Gene Tierney (*Baketamon*), Michael Wilding (*Akhnatan*), Bella Darvi (*Nefer*), Edmund Purdom (*The Egyptian*), Peter Ustinov, Judith Evelyn, Henry Daniell, John Carradine, Carl Benton Reid, Tommy Rettig, Ian MacDonald, Donna Martell, Mike Mazurki, Anitra Stevens, Mimi Gibson, Carmen de Lavallade, Harry Thompson, George Melford, Lawrence Ryle, Tiger Joe Marsh, Karl Davis, Peter Raynolds, Michael Granger, Don Blackman, Joan Winfield. *Prod:* Darryl F. Zanuck for 20th Century-Fox. Color De Luxe. CinemaScope. 139m.

WHITE CHRISTMAS (1954). First film made in VistaVision. Kaye and Crosby are two Army buddies who make a hit in show business, and then help several old friends out. Thin plot merely an excuse for fifteen good numbers. *Sc:* Norman Krasna, Norman Panama, Melvin Frank. *Ph:* Loyal Griggs. *Art dir:* Hal Pereira and Roland Anderson. *Ed:* Frank Bracht. *Mus:* Irving Berlin. *With* Bing Crosby (*Bob Wallace*), Danny Kaye (*Phil Davis*), Rosemary Clooney (*Betty*), Vera-Ellen (*Judy*), Dean Jagger (*General Waverly*), Mary Wickes, John Brascia, Anne Whitfield, Richard Shannon, Grady Sutton, Sig Ruman, Robert Crosson, Richard Keane, Herb Vigran, Johnny Grant, Gavin Gordon, Marcel de la Brosse, James Parnell, Percy Helton, Elizabeth Holmes, Barrie Chase, Stanford I. Jolley, Mike Donovan, Glen Cargyle, Lorraine Crawford, Joan Bayley, Lester Clark, Ernest Flatt, Bea Allen. *Prod:* Robert Emmett Dolan for Paramount. Technicolor. VistaVision. 120m.

WE'RE NO ANGELS (1955). Stagey comedy about three Devil's Island escapees taking over a French store-keeper's shop, and introducing some fair but unconventional changes! *Sc:* Ranald Mac-

Dougall (play "La Cuisine des Anges," by Albert Husson). *Ph:* Loyal Griggs. *Art dir:* Hal Pereira and Roland Anderson. *Ed:* Arthur Schmidt. *Mus:* Frederick Hollander. *With* Humphrey Bogart (*Joseph*), Peter Ustinov (*Jules*), Joan Bennett (*Amelie Ducotel*), Aldo Ray (*Albert*), Basil Rathbone (*Andre Trochard*), Leo G. Carroll, Gloria Talbott, John Baer, Lea Penman, John Smith. *Prod:* Pat Duggan for Paramount. Colour. VistaVision. 106m.

THE SCARLET HOUR (1956). Highly charged drama about an eternal triangle, also produced by Curtiz. *Sc:* Rip Van Ronkel, Frank Tashlin, John Meredyth Lucas. *Ph:* Lionel Lindon. *Art dir:* Hal Pereira and Tambi Larsen. *Ed:* Everett Douglas. *Mus:* Leith Stevens. *With* Tom Tryon (*"Marsh" Marshall*), Carol Omhart (*Pauline Nevins*), James Gregory (*Ralph Nevins*), Jody Lawrence (*Kathy*), David Lewis (*Sam*), Elaine Stritch, E. G. Marshall, Edward Binns, Maureen Hurley, Nat "King" Cole. *Prod:* Michael Curtiz for Paramount. VistaVision. 94m.

THE VAGABOND KING (1956). Shoddy version of much-filmed story of François Villon, the King of the Beggars in Paris, during the reign of Louis XI, who aids Louis in outsmarting the treachery of the Duke of Burgundy. *Sc:* Ken Englund, Noel Langley (from operetta–music by Rudolf Friml; book/lyrics by William H. Post, Brian Hooker; from play "If I Were King," by Justin Huntly McCarthy). *Ph:* Robert Burks. *Art dir:* Hal Pereira and Henry Bumstead. *Ed:* Arthur Schmidt. *Mus:* Rudolf Friml (additional songs by Friml and Johnny Burke). *With* Oreste (*François Villon*), Kathryn Grayson (*Catherine De Vaucelles*), Rita Moreno (*Huguette*), Cedric Harwicke (*Tristan*), Walter Hampden (*King Louis XI*), Leslie Nielsen, William Prince, Jack Lord, Billy Vine, Florence Sundström, Harry McNaughton, G. Thomas Duggan, Ralph Sumpter, Gregory Morton, Lucie Lancaster. *Prod:* Pat Duggan for Paramount. Technicolor. VistaVision. 89m. Previously filmed as *The Beloved Rogue* (1926, Alan Crosland); *The Vagabond King* (1930, Ludwig Berger) and as *If I Were King* (1938, Frank Lloyd); the latter and the silent version being nonmusical.

THE BEST THINGS IN LIFE ARE FREE (1956). Tuneful biography of song writers of the Twenties: Da Sylva, Brown and Henderson, which charts their rise and the near collapse of the team through Da Sylva's ambition. *Sc:* William Bowers and Pheobe Ephron (story by John O'Hara). *Ph:* Leon Shamroy. *Art dir:* Lyle R. Wheeler and Maurice Ransford. *Ed:* Dorothy Spencer. *Mus:* Lionel Newman. *With* Gordon MacRae (*Da Sylva*), Ernest Borgnine (*Brown*), Dan Dailey (*Henderson*), Sheree North (*Kitty*), Tommy Noonan (*Carl*), Murvyn Vye, Phyllis Avery, Larry Keating, Tony Galento, Norman Brooks, Jacques d'Amboise, Roxanne Arlen, Byron Palmer, Eugene Borden, Linda Brace, Patty Lou Hudson, Julie Van Zandt, Larry Kerr, Charles Victor, Harold Miller, Emily Belser, Paul Glass, Bill Foster. *Prod:* Henry Ephron for 20th Century-Fox. Eastmancolor. CinemaScope. 104m.

THE HELEN MORGAN STORY (GB: BOTH ENDS OF THE CANDLE) (1957). Poorly written biography of famed torch singer of the Twenties and Thirties; the second and last occasion Curtiz worked with Ann Blyth. *Sc:* Stephen

Longstreet, Oscar Saul, Dean Riesner, Nelson Gidding. *Ph:* Ted McCord. *Art dir:* Tom Beckman. *Ed:* Frank Bracht. *Mus:* Larry Prinz. *With* Ann Blyth (*Helen Morgan*), Paul Newman (*Larry*), Richard Carlson (*Wade*), Gene Evans (*Whitney Krause*), Alan King (*Ben*), Cara Williams, Walter Woolf King, Virginia Vincent, Warren Douglas, Dorothy King, Ed Platt, Sammy White, Walter Winchell, Jimmy McHugh, Rudy Vallee, Peggy De Castro, Babette De Castro, Cheri De Castro. *Prod:* Martin Rackin for Warner Bros. CinemaScope. 118m.

THE PROUD REBEL (1958). Understated story of a Civil War veteran and his mute son, who take a job on a farm while the father searches for a doctor to cure his son, and falls foul of the local villains in the process. *Sc:* Joe Petracca, Lillie Hayward. *Ph:* Ted McCord. *Art dir:* McClure Capps. *Ed:* Aaron Stell. *Mus:* Jerome Moross. *With* Alan Ladd (*John Chandler*), Olivia De Havilland (*Linnett Moore*), Dean Jagger (*Harry Burleigh*), David Ladd (*David Chandler*), Cecil Kellaway (*Dr. Enos Davis*), Thomas P. Haran, Henry Hull, Eli Mintz, James Westerfield, John Carradine, Dean Stanton, Thomas Pittman, King. *Prod:* Samuel Goldwyn Jr. for Buena Vista (Disney). Colour. 103m.

KING CREOLE (1958). Curtiz handled Elvis Presley well in this tale of a bus boy who narrowly escapes juvenile delinquency by finding success as a night club singer. *Sc:* Herbert Baker and Michael V. Gazzo (novel *A Stone for Danny Fisher* by Harold Robbins). *Ph:* Russell Harlan. *Art dir:* J. MacMillan Johnson. *Ed:* Warren Low. *Mus:* Walter Scharf. *With* Elvis Presley (*Danny Fisher*), Carolyn Jones (*Ronnie*), Dolores Hart (*Nellie*), Dean Jagger (*Mr. Fisher*), Walter Matthau (*Maxie Fields*), Lillian Montevecchi, Vic Morrow, Jan Shepherd, Paul Stewart, Brian Hutton, Jack Grinnage. *Prod:* Hal B. Wallis for Paramount. VistaVision. 116m.

THE HANGMAN (1959). Tough Western about a grim lawman determined to get his man even if he has to take on a whole town to do it. *Sc:* Dudley Nichols. *Ph:* Loyal Griggs. *Art dir:* Hal Pereira and Henry Bumstead. *Ed:* Terry Morse. *Mus:* Harry Sukman. *With* Robert Taylor (*MacKenzie Bovard*), Tina Louise (*Selah Jennison*), Fess Parker (*Buck Weston*), Jack Lord (*Johnny Bishop*), Mickey Shaugnessy (*Al Cruse*), Gene Evans, Shirley Harmer. *Prod:* Frank Freeman Jnr. for Paramount. 86m.

THE MAN IN THE NET (1959). A murder case drama involving Alan Ladd as an artist trying to clear himself from the position of prime suspect. *Sc:* Reginald Rose (story by Patrick Quentin). *Ph:* John Seitz. *Art dir:* Hildyard Brown. *Ed:* Richard Heermance. *Mus:* Hans J. Salter. *With* Alan Ladd (*John Hamilton*), Carolyn Jones (*Linda*), Diane Brewster (*Vickie Carey*), John Lupton (*Brad Carey*), Charles McGraw (*Steve Ritter*), Betty Lou Holland, Tom Helmore, John Alexander, Kathryn Givney, Edward Binns, Alvin Children, Barbara Baird, Susan Gordon, Charles Herbert, Mike McGreery, Stephen Perry. *Prod:* Walter Mirisch for Mirisch-Jaguar Productions. 97m.

THE ADVENTURES OF HUCKLEBERRY FINN (1960). Photography and atmosphere were the main credits of this version of the famous Mark Twain story.

Sc: James Lee (novel by Mark Twain). *Ph:* Ted McCord. *Art dir:* George W. Davis and McClure Capps. *Ed:* Frederic Steinkamp. *Mus:* Jerome Moross. *With* Tony Randall (*The King*), Eddie Hodges (*Huck Finn*), Archie Moore (*Jim*), Patty McCormack (*Joanna*), Neville Brand (*Pap*), Mickey Shaugnessy, Judy Canova, Andy Devine, Sherry Jackson, Buster Keaton, Finlay Currie, John Carradine, Josephine Hutchinson, Parley Baer, Royal Dano, Dolores Hawkins, Sterling Holloway, Dean Stanton. *Prod:* Sam Goldwyn Jnr. for M-G-M. Metrocolor. CinemaScope. 107m. Previous version in 1938, directed by Norman Taurog.

A BREATH OF SCANDAL (I: OLYMPIA) (1960). A young American's romance with a princess whose life he has saved is hampered by court protocol. *Sc:* Walter Bernstein (from play "Olympia," by Ferenc Molnar). *Ph:* Mario Montuori. *Art dir:* Gene Allan. *Ed:* Howard Smith. *Mus:* B. Cicognini. *With* Sophia Loren (*Olympia*), John Gavin (*Charlie*), Maurice Chevalier (*Philip*), Isabel Jeans (*Eugenie*), Angela Lansbury (*Lina*), Tullio Carminati, Roberto Risso, Carlo Hintermann, Milly Vitale, Adrienne Gessner, Frederick Ledebur. *Prod:* Carlo Ponti and Marcello Girosi for Titanus/Ponti-Girosi/Paramount. Technicolor. 98m.

FRANCIS OF ASSISI (1961). Lavish but cumbersome tale of St. Francis and his struggles to found his order in the Thirteenth Century. *Sc:* Eugene Vale, James Forsyth, Jack Thomas (from book *Joyful Beggar* by Louis de Wohl). *Ph:* Piero Portalupi. *Art dir:* Edward Carrere. *Ed:* Louis R. Loeffler. *Mus:* Mario Nascimbene. *With* Bradford Dillman (*St. Francis*), Dolores Hart (*Clare*), Stuart Whitman (*Paolo*), Eduard Franz (*Pietro*), Pedro Armendariz (*Sultan*), Cecil Kellaway, Athene Seyler, Finlay Currie, Mervyn Johns, Russell Napier, Harold Goldblatt, John Welsh, Edith Sharpe, Jack Lambert, Malcolm Keen, Oliver Johnston, Evi Manardi, Manuel Ballard, Jule Mauro, Uti Hof, Paul Muller, John Karlssen, Jack Savage, David Maunsell, Cyrus Elias, Curt Lowen, Renzo Cesana, Walter Marlow. *Prod:* Plato A. Skouras for Perseus. De Luxe Color. CinemaScope. 111m.

THE COMANCHEROS (1962). Well-mounted Western combining humour and action in its tale of a lawman infiltrating a gang which is selling whiskey and guns to the Indians. *Sc:* James Edward Grant and Clair Huffaker (Novel by Paul I. Wellman). *Ph:* William H. Clothier. *Art dir:* Jack Martin Smith and Alfred Ybarra. *Ed:* Louis R. Loeffler. *Mus:* Elmer Bernstein. *Action scenes directed by* Cliff Lyons. *With* John Wayne (*Capt. Jake Cutter*), Stuart Whitman (*Paul Regret*), Ina Balin (*Pilar*), Nehemiah Persoff (*Graile*), Lee Marvin (*Crow*), Michael Ansara, Bruce Cabot, Pat Wayne, Joan O'Brien, Jack Elam, Edgar Buchanan, Henry Daniell, Richard Devon, Steve Baylor, John Dierkes, Roger Mobley, Bob Steele, Luisa Triava, Iphegenie Castiglioni, Aiessa Wayne, George J. Lewis. *Prod:* George Sherman for 20th Century-Fox. DeLuxe Color. CinemaScope. 107 m. Unofficially re-made as *Rio Conchos* (1964, Gordon Douglas).

Raoul Walsh: The Rugged Individualist.

Raoul Walsh was critically re-discovered in the Sixties by French *cinéastes* after receiving little or no recognition from both film historians and serious critics. This fact emphasises the flaws in having narrow criteria and the need for constant and extensive re-evaluation of cinema history while the rapidly diminishing material is still available.

For while Walsh has received scant attention from serious sources, the so-called lower echelons of the critical hierarchy, namely the newspaper and magazine critics, have been consistent in pointing out the merits of a fair proportion of his work over five decades. How many other directors of equal but forgotten competence have the proof of their ability disintegrating in canisters of old film or yellowing newspaper files?

Walsh's claim to fame in the French view lies in the totality of his films. The action in his cinema represents the sum of all the qualities and abilities with which his characters are endowed; this action is accomplished by means of a simple, direct technique, lacking any pretensions, but one which represents the consummate skill and knowledge of a master craftsman. This suggests a native instinct and animal energy as being constituent elements of his film-making personality, but not the total limits of his ability as other critics have suggested. Walsh became a case in point for a disagreement over the validity and usage of the *auteur* theory between Pauline Kael and Andrew Sarris some years ago.

The first criterion or circle of Sarris's theory states that a director's worth depends on his technical competence. Sarris cited an example of a scene in Walsh's *Every Night at Eight* in which George Raft talks in his sleep, revealing his inner fears to his girl, who has accidentally entered the room, thus overhearing him. The same device was used in Walsh's *High Sierra,* featuring Humphrey Bogart and

Raoul Walsh shares a meal with natives of a far inland village on Tahiti while filming PASSIONS OF THE SEA

Ida Lupino. To Sarris, this was "a virile director using a feminine narrative device to dramatise the emotional vulnerability of his heroes." Kael countered that Sarris had earlier called Walsh's style pleasingly unpretentious, but that this statement contradicted the former by suggesting that Walsh was being profound. If Sarris was using the term as a general comment on Walsh's style, Kael is correct in her interpretation.

High Sierra (1941) is an unbalanced film because the main body of the film consists of a fast-paced, sardonic gangster work dominated by the convincing characterisations of Bogart and Lupino, woven into an unconvincingly sentimental sub-plot which creates sympathy for Bogart's anti-social public enemy, Roy "Mad Dog" Earle, by having him fall in love with a simple country girl, Velma (Joan Leslie), who is badly crippled. Earle partially redeems himself by forcing a "gang doctor" to operate on her and restore her to health but she then jilts Earle—as a censorial punishment for his past sins? Unable to find a place in society, he returns to his faithful moll and careers to his final death in the Sierras. The death scene, which becomes a public spectacle as newspaper and radio reporters lure onlookers to the spot, is only one of a number of social comments in the film. These comments, balanced against a routine studio vehicle such as *Every Night at Eight*, do have certain pretensions—but not in any derogatory sense.

However, if Sarris was applying the term specifically as a comment on *Every Night at Eight*, Walsh is perfectly entitled, as Kael acknowledges, to borrow from himself and to repeat techniques or devices. A brief glance at his work will indicate that he has done so fairly often; the point being that the result has invariably been a refinement or improvement, seldom a regression. What is more to the point is the question as to whether the borrowing or repetition of a device amounts to technical competence? As I have said before, the repetition in Walsh's work has usually been an improvement; also one has to take into consideration the fact that he was a studio director making at least three films a year on average. Therefore it is quite feasible—artistic considerations apart—that he may have had certain decisions regarding the form of his work imposed upon him, or that he may have decided to use certain tried *formulae* to save or improve a poor vehicle. As well as his credited work, he was one of Warner Brothers' most prolific "picture-doctors," and some of these uncredited stints which have been identified in recent years are listed in the filmography. Taking "technical competence" to mean a sound working knowledge of the equipment and all other factors involved in completing a motion picture, there can be no doubt whatsoever about Walsh's credentials.

He was born on March 11, 1887 in New York City in a residential section of what is now East Manhattan. He came of mixed parentage; his Irish father was a builder with an acknowledged interest in horse-racing, and his mother was Spanish. His younger brother George (*b.* 1892) was destined to become a leading star in silent films, many of which Raoul directed. Raoul Walsh was an adventurous child; he ran away to Fall River in Massachusetts during his teens, and briefly attended several academic institutions, including the College of St. Francis Xavier and Seton Hall University. He then travelled to Europe as a hand on a cattle boat, before settling in Texas as a cowpuncher where a horse fell on his leg, laying him up for a while. He spent his recuperation at a local theatre, learning a new trade, and eventually went on tour with the company, returning to New York in 1909 as an experienced actor. At this time the Pathe Brothers were looking for cowboy actors, and his ranching experience and horsemanship earned him a job as a movie heavy. (General information about Walsh's silent career obtained from Walter Conley's article in "The Silent Picture," No. 9—Winter 1970/71.)

The first significant influence on his later development was Paul Armstrong, a successful playwright and friend of the Walsh family, who taught Walsh how to assemble material. I have touched on the question of authorship earlier when referring to repetition of devices in his films, and this is something that tends to be overlooked in his work—the fact that he wrote the bulk of his films between 1914 and 1921, and subsequently used writers such as James T. O'Donohue (on his silent work), John Twist, Jerry Wald, Niven Busch, Borden

Chase, Richard Macaulay, Ivan Goff and Ben Roberts consistently as well as allowing authors to develop their own material for the screen. This suggests that he obviously values the importance of the writer, and the idea of a film as the work of a team is reinforced by his repeated use of certain cameramen and other technicians. Knowing the abilities and limitations of his team enabled him to function prolifically within the studio system while maintaining a reasonable standard in the finished product.

Most probably, he realised the value of working as part of a team while under contract to D. W. Griffith, who had seen some of his acting performances in Pathe Westerns, and signed him as an actor and assistant director. Walsh's rough and ready upbringing particularly suited him for the latter capacity since many of Griffith's extras were unruly cowboys who spent most of their non-working hours living it up in saloons. He had been signed by Griffith in 1912 while the director was at Biograph, but the following year Griffith and his *protégé* moved to Mutual where Walsh was given the opportunity to involve himself in the type of project that in later years was to become his trademark—filming the exploits of Pancho Villa, the Mexican bandit. Walsh filmed Villa during battles, addressing his followers, in camp and on the move across Mexico. Villa was only too pleased by this and was constantly upstaging the camera, but later the project was taken out of Walsh's hands when Mutual decided to give the material some shape. They filmed weak linking and replacement footage (released as *The Battle of Torreon* (1914) in a double bill with *The Life of General Villa*) with Walsh playing the young Villa in the latter film on which the direction was attributed to Christy Cabanne—although much of the footage shot by Walsh was inserted into Cabanne's work.

It was as an actor that Walsh's break came when he was assigned the role of John Wilkes Booth in Griffith's *The Birth of a Nation.* His success enabled him to obtain better terms with Reliance-Majestic who gave him the chance of directing one and two reel action films. He turned out films prolifically, establishing a reputation for speed, economy and efficiency, and proved that he had assimilated Griffith's influence so well that he was prepared to improve on it—i.e. Griffith's films usually employed "blacked-up" white actors to portray blacks or Indians, whereas Walsh preferred realism in casting his ethnic roles.

Winfield Sheehan signed him up as a director for the newly formed Fox Film Company in early 1915, and assigned him a six reel social drama entitled *The Regeneration.* A review in the Motion Picture World noted: "The production is most accurate in presenting the depressing squalor of tenement life on the East Side. It is strong and true in its characterisations, and as a spectacle there is a wonderfully realistic depiction of a fire aboard a crowded excursion boat. Director Walsh was fortunate in his selection of types that are in no way an exaggeration of those to be found on the streets of the East Side. There is a grim sort of humour in many of the scenes; there is an abundance of excitement in others, and throughout the picture carries a genuine heart interest."

This humour was to reappear frequently in his work, losing its grim base and substituting for it a bawdy virility as Walsh worked prolifically, searching for the right subjects. His output at Fox covered heavy drama (*Carmen,* starring Theda Bara), social reform pictures (*The Honor System,* which dealt with prison conditions and was largely filmed on location at the Arizona State Prison), Westerns (*Blue Blood and Red,* which made a star of his brother in the Fairbanks athletic mould; *The Conqueror* which was a biography of Sam Houston featuring William Farnum, Fox's top male star, in the leading role), and an eccentric comedy *This Is the Life,* based on a "Merton of the Movies" type portrayal of an avid movie fan who has some lively dreams (while under a gas anesthetic at the dentist) involving himself and a pretty girl whom he has just seen leaving the dentist's office. These dreams are worked out as part of the action until the hero is supposed to be having his throat cut; at that instant he wakes up to find that his decayed tooth has been removed.

Soon after completing *This Is the Life,* Walsh returned to the east coast to make *The Pride of New York* (1917), and rumours began to circulate that he was leaving Fox when his contract expired. He signed a contract with Goldwyn Pictures in late November, but there was a snag. He had not realised that Fox had written a renewal option clause into their original contract with him, and since he was one of their hottest properties they had no intention of letting him film elsewhere. The matter was settled, and he continued to work for Fox until 1920, although the quality of his projects declined after *The Pride of New York* (which was the only Walsh film to have a Great War setting). A love story between a construction worker and a rich, unspoiled girl with settings ranging from New York to the battlefields of France, it significantly combined much wit with its realistic action scenes.

Walsh's last "class" project was *Evangeline*, based on Longfellow's poem, shown in New York twice daily on a reserved seat basis. According to Walsh, it had a special significance: "*Evangeline* got the most wonderful write-ups of any picture I ever made. There were editorials written about it. But it didn't make a quarter. So I decided then to play to Main Street and to hell with art."

Walsh's first film away from Fox when his contract expired was based on a play by his original mentor, Paul Armstrong, entitled *The Deep Purple* (1920) but it met with little praise. His popularity began to decline as his next four pictures, including one for Goldwyn, flopped; but the tide changed after he had completed *The Thief of Bagdad* (1924), an elaborate spectacle written by its swashbuckling star Doug Fairbanks Sr., who also received the best notices for the film. Fairbanks's faith in Walsh's abilities, coupled with the box-office

Drama as the Princess's maid, Anna May Wong, tries to poison her sleeping mistress, Julanne Johnson, in THE THIEF OF BAGDAD, the film that restored Walsh's flagging reputation in 1924

success of the film, earned the director a five film deal at Paramount. These five films, including a Biblical epic based on the tale of the Prodigal Son, which included a spectacular sequence (tinted) of a burning city, did little to further Walsh's reputation, and so he returned finally to Fox.

The return was marked with a certain irony; he had latterly been unhappy there and his work had suffered as a result, but on gaining his independence he had achieved little bar the Fairbanks picture. Yet as soon as he returned to Fox, he was given the film that represents the synthesis of his style and ability in the silent cinema, *What Price Glory?* (1926).

A touching moment from Walsh's WHAT PRICE GLORY? as Dolores Del Rio kneels in prayer among the battlefield graves

It was based on a popular stage success, but there was no sign of any staginess in the scenario, which revolved around the rivalry between two tough, brawling Marines over a young French girl. The attempts to resolve the rivalry were presented by means of a virile, robust, gutsy humour, with the two actors (Victor McLaglen and Edmund Lowe) fitting perfectly into Walsh's conception. As a counterpoint, the war scenes were grimly realistic and dramatic (i.e. the death scene of the Mother's Boy); the idea was so successful that Walsh and his actors made a number of sequels, while the original was remade by John Ford in 1952 for Fox. A comparison between the two versions underlines the difference between the directors. Ford retains the basic plot and gives James Cagney his head as Captain Flagg, but Dan Dailey's Sergeant Quirt is much less pugnacious and more resourceful than Lowe's; Walsh's heroes were like two bulls in a china shop but then Walsh was concerned with their adventures while Ford uses their escapades and reactions to develop his point about the behaviour patterns of men in war, with the girl representing a civilising influence on their anarchic, aggressive natures. Ford is also more concerned with the visual terms of reference in his film, outlining men against the sky in poetic images or representing the tragedy of war through the shots of deserted villages.

Walsh continued making box-office successes with the offbeat *The Monkey Talks* being followed rapidly by *The Loves of Carmen,* in which humour and burlesque replaced the straight drama of his version fifteen years earlier. Walsh also demonstrated with his acting in *Sadie Thompson* that he was capable of a quieter, more natural style. The film, and its conception, stemmed from the enthusiasm of its star (Gloria Swanson) for the project: ". . . Swanson boldly announced she would make a movie of "Rain," the play in which Jeanne Eagels had made such a hit. After Miss Swanson bought the film rights to Somerset Maugham's short story, "Miss Thompson," upon which "Rain" had been based, the Hays Office refused to sanction the characterisation of Reverend Davidson, a man of God who secretly and hypocritically lusts for a harlot. To satisfy the Hays Office Davidson became a self-appointed morals reformer of no religious denomination named Oliver Hamilton. Lionel Barrymore was signed for the role, and Raoul Walsh to direct.

" 'I practically had to blackmail Raoul into playing O'Hara,' says Miss Swanson, 'He just didn't want to act anymore.' *Sadie Thompson* emerged as a gutsy and moving film and had Miss Swanson's best performance to date. She was nominated for an Academy Award—the first year they were given—but lost to Janet Gaynor who had been nominated for *three* performances. . . . Miss Swanson said recently: 'I had better luck with *Sadie* than any other movie star because I had the advantage of making a good silent of it. If you have to censor Sadie's language, how can you really portray her' ?" ("Films in Review," April 1965.)

Me, Gangster (1928) used the gimmick of sub-titles supposedly written in the young hoodlum hero's hand, and presented a realistic view of criminals and prison life again. The year 1929 proved to be an eventful one for Walsh. While working on location in Zion County, Utah, he set a precedent in film history by using sound

A key point in Walsh's THE YELLOW TICKET, as Laurence Olivier unwittingly betrays Elissa Landi to the villain (Lionel Barrymore)

equipment on location for the first time; he was also playing the lead in the film, *In Old Arizona,* as the Cisco Kid, but one night as he was driving home along a rough road, his headlights mesmerised a jack-rabbit which leapt through his window screen. Walsh was pulled out of the wreckage, and rushed to a hospital in Salt Lake where it was found necessary to remove his right eye, hence the black patch he has worn ever since. The film was taken over by director Irving Cummings and Warner Baxter replaced Walsh as the Cisco Kid, winning an Oscar for his performance. Undaunted, Walsh returned to direction with the first Flagg/Quirt sequel, *The Cock-Eyed World,* shown in both silent and sound versions just weeks before the stock market crash of 1929.

He followed this with an even more ambitious project, a Western epic shot in two versions—one in normal 35mm ratio, the other in a 70mm "grandeur" process—using fourteen cameramen, and a little-known bit player, John Wayne, as his star. The film was not well received, and Wayne returned to the ranks of secondary performers until John Ford made him a box-office star with *Stagecoach.* Walsh's career remained equally static throughout the Thirities because he had trouble finding the right studio to develop his talent. Fox had been a major company in the late silent days, but due to financial and other crises with the coming of sound, it was over-shadowed by Warner Brothers, Metro and Paramount. Its overall output remained steady, and the studio roster included many good players and technicians, but the films lacked a uniform style, unlike those of its rivals.

Walsh remained at Fox until 1935, during which period he made two more Flagg and Quirt yarns, several vehicles for Joan Bennett and Charles Farrell, and the unusual *Yellow Ticket.* The latter was an anti-Russian adventure story told in strong terms, dominated by some good camerawork by James Wong Howe—especially mobile during the panic that ensues in the streets as war is declared between

Germany and Russia. Other footage in a Russian prison appears to have been "borrowed" from an earlier work, but the rest of the film is typically Walshian, showing an avid, earthy interest in the problems of a Jewish girl, forced by circumstance to become a prostitute, and hounded by a lewd chief of the secret police.

"Out of Michael Morton's old play *The Yellow Ticket* . . . Raoul Walsh has produced a rugged, unrestrained but often effective pictorial drama, in which Lionel Barrymore and Elissa Landi give clever interpretations of their respective roles. Mr. Barrymore acts the sinister Baron Andrey, the head of the Czarist secret police, and Elissa Landi appears as Marya Varenka, a Jewish girl, who secures a yellow ticket—a pass given to abandoned women—in order to be able to go to St. Petersburg, where she has reason to believe her father is lying ill.

"There are several excellent ideas in this production, particularly that in which a stage sketch recalls to the Baron where he saw Marya, who is known by another name on her yellow ticket. After learning that her father has been killed, Marya encounters Julian Rolph, a young British journalist who is in Russia to write articles for his own country's newspapers and those in America. Marya enlightens this writer, with the result that the tenor of his contributions changes and this is noticed by the secret police. The Baron, after hearing that Marya has been persecuted by his men, gives the girl his own card, which he tells her will save her from further trouble. This scoundrel, however, intends it to serve another purpose —to bring the attractive girl to his place. When she goes to see him the Baron endeavours to embrace her and Marya finally shoots him and escapes." (National Film Theatre programme note.)

★ ★ ★

Walsh also worked on several minor films at Metro before joining Paramount, where he was given romantic comedies and musicals featuring some of the studio's younger players such as Henry Fonda,

Cary Grant and Alice Faye as well as established comics like George Burns, Gracie Allen and Jack Benny. One of the best of them, *Klondike Annie* (1935), cast Mae West and Victor McLaglen as a romantic team whose courting had a robust authenticity combined with a crudely disguised vulgarity, and provided Miss West with some sparkling throwaways such as, "Between two evils, I always pick the one I never tried before"; "Women are as old as they feel—and men are old when they lose their feelings"; "Give a man a free hand and he'll try to put it all over you"; and, "Too many girls follow the line of least resistance—but a good line is hard to resist." Walsh also made two films in England, using American leads and British supporting players in both productions, but the turning point of his career came in 1939, when he took over the direction of *The Roaring Twenties* from Anatole Litvak at Warner Brothers.

It has never been established precisely why he took it over, because Litvak had just finished *Confessions of a Nazi Spy,* a highly successful propaganda piece starring Edward G. Robinson which was a box-office smash. The finished film shows possible evidence of "doctoring" in terms of the large chunks of montage and special effects inserted into the narrative but it remains an important film today, for it covers the whole span of events from the end of the First World War to the repeal of the Eighteenth Amendment in more detail than any of the other Thirties crime films.

Eddie Bartlett (James Cagney), George Hally (Humphrey Bogart) and Lloyd Hart (Jeffrey Lynn), three soldier pals, go their own ways after the Armistice with George becoming chief hood for a mobster, Nick Brown (Paul Kelly), while Eddie becomes a taxi-driver and Lloyd a lawyer. Eddie has many let-downs including the loss of his girl Jean (Priscilla Lane) to Lloyd, and drifts into making bath-tub gin when Prohibition comes in. He is arrested and fined when delivering a "parcel" to a well-known lady, Panama Smith (Gladys George). She pays his fine, and he is soon established

A young John Wayne in his first starring role in Walsh's spectacular but unsuccessful THE BIG TRAIL

as a big wheel in the booze business, using his taxi service as a legitimate front. His business interests conflict with those of Brown who sends George to deal with Eddie. Instead the two pals become partners, basing the agreement on the fact that since neither really trusts the other a pretty good basis for a partnership exists. They take Lloyd in on the deal as Eddie's lawyer, and he falls in love with Jean, whom Eddie has promoted from a chorus line to sing in one of his clubs.

A key sequence of the film which reflects Walsh's capacity for handling action lies in their biggest coup as they raid a government warehouse, equipped with newly issued light sub-machine guns, stealing a million dollars worth of liquor from under the noses of the night watchmen. George reveals his true psychotic colours, killing two of them, one of whom was his former sergeant in the trenches and against whom George has long nursed a grudge. The partnership runs aground during the 1929 Wall Street stock market crash, and Eddie is ruined. He sells his interest to George and returns to driving a taxi, while Lloyd turns honest and becomes a crusading attorney. George expands his activities, but when these threaten Lloyd and Jean, Eddie goes to his house and kills him. But he is in turn gunned down by George's men on the steps of a church, dying in Panama's arms as the film closes with the famous exchange—Cop: "What was his business?" Panama: "He used to be a big shot."

Cagney is in good form as the pugnacious little Eddie, but the acting honours go to Bogart, alternately rasping threats or lisping hard-boiled wise-cracks (Frank McHugh announces his intention to dance, and Bogie snarls: "That'll be a break for some dame!") in the first of four strong performances for Walsh. The low-key photography is studio-bound, creating mood, but not necessarily credibility, unlike that of *They Drive by Night*.

Released as *Road to Frisco* in Britain, this film is a powerfully atmospheric, authentic view of life on the road for long-distance lorry drivers, picturing them as a rough fraternity existing in a philosophical acceptance of the tedium and violence in their lives. Joe Fabrini (George Raft) and his brother Paul (Bogart) haul freight for a corrupt boss, conning petrol along the way, and going to great lengths to avoid making payments on their truck. Joe is quiet but determined, while Paul is more volatile, and hates the life. Joe crashes and loses his load through a trick by the boss. The brothers pick up a waitress, Cassie (Ann Sheridan) on their journey;

a truck ahead of them on the road crashes when the driver falls asleep and he is burnt to death. Paul is upset on discovering that it was an old friend; later he meets Ed Carlsen (Alan Hale), an ex-driver who now owns his own fleet of trucks, and his wayward wife Lana (Ida Lupino). Carlsen gives the brothers a tip on a lemon consignment, and they make enough on the deal to pay the outstanding amount owing on their truck. But Paul falls asleep at the wheel and crashes, losing an arm and totally wrecking the truck, so that they are forced to go to work for Carlsen.

Lana makes a play for Joe, but he brushes her off. She is, however, a very determined lady; capitalising on her husband's weakness for drink, she murders him by locking him in the garage with the car motor running. A verdict of accidental death is recorded, and the naïve Joe becomes her partner. When he reveals his feelings for Cassie to Lana, she is so shocked that she reveals all to Joe, and frames him when he refuses to leave Cassie. Circumstantial evidence builds up a strong case against Joe but the perjury proves too much for Lana, who goes insane in the witness box.

Skilful acting and direction, plus taut, effective dialogue set aside some of the more blatant absurdities of the Bezzerides novel which acted as a basis for the plot. The greatest pity about the Warner Brothers system was that in milking their contractees as frequently as was their custom, they depleted a player's talent or range. Thus Ida Lupino was always seen as a second string Bette Davis, bringing a steely, brittle intensity to her unsympathetic roles—and nobody explored her capacity for going insane on the screen more frequently than Ida—or brought a more delicate, tragic air to her sympathetic roles. Thus in *They Drive by Night,* Ann Sheridan fades out after making a big impact in the early stages with some promising banter: "Here's the L.A. phone-book—make sure you bring back all the pages too!" "Barney had twelve hands, and I didn't like any of them"; "Love at first sight? It sure saves a lot of time." Equally Bogart fades

The cold, taut world of Warner gangsterdom is summed up in this image of Barton Maclane menacing Humphrey Bogart in Walsh's HIGH SIERRA

after his accident and some endearing patter: the collection agent tries to make off with the truck, which leads Bogart to snarl, "You'd look kinda funny with a monkey wrench growing outta your head." The man retorts that if Bogart touches him, he'll call a cop, to which Bogart replies, "If I touch you, you'll call an ambulance. We don't have to be nasty, but it's more fun." Raft is at his best, ambitious, moral ("I'm not playing around with the boss's wife. Goodnight MRS. Carlsen"), but reckless (buying the lemons with Bogart's share of the money, justifying himself with, "A guy's gotta be around to be asked"); while Lupino dominates the second half of the film, making amends for the switch from the manufactured but gripping realism to the obvious *clichés* of the court-room drama with a display of sheer acting *style*.

She and Bogart were teamed again in Walsh's *High Sierra*, a flawed but impressive gangster work. This performance summed up for Bogart all the qualities of range and style that had been slowly maturing in his previous ten years' acting experience. His weather-beaten face spoke of a world of experience; this was no longer the flash, loud punk who would last a few menacing reels before being rubbed out by the hero; here was a character of integrity, true to his own spirit—the Bogart existentialist hero was already developing as he summed up his past in one last great "heavy" role. Roy Earle is true to his own spirit because he won't abandon a stray dog he picks up, or the moll (Lupino) who attaches herself so faithfully to him. His integrity is contrasted with the treachery and cowardice of his companions. His doom is paralleled in the characterisations of the dispassionate "Doc" (Henry Hull) and the tough Marie.

"Mad Dog" Roy Earle is sprung by the Syndicate to mastermind a big robbery; he cases the joint and keeps in touch with a lame girl Velma (Joan Leslie) whom he has met on his journey to Palm Springs (in fact, Arrowhead Springs was used for location shooting since the August temperature at Palm Springs—125°—was considered too hot for reasonable working conditions). He dislikes his companions, chosen to pull the job with him, and quarrels over a girl with them. A visit to his Syndicate mentor, Big Mac (Barton MacLane) affords him an opportunity to air his feelings and to recall the old days, but Mac is ill and plays on Roy's conscience ("All the A1 guys are gone, or in Alcatraz," laments Mac, "All that's left are soda-jerks and jitterbugs"), persuading him to carry the job through. Earle's disillusion is complete after a gang doctor has successfully operated on Velma's foot; she spurns Roy (in a reasonably nice way) telling him that she has a sweetheart back in Ohio.

The sentimentality does not become the character since his motivation is rather dubious in the first place, and thus does him little credit. He returns to the hideout, with Velma's rebuff driving him into the arms of Marie. The robbery is neatly carried out, but then everything goes wrong. Red (Arthur Kennedy) and Babe (Alan Curtis), his two companions, are killed in a car crash, trying to evade the police, and the money burns with them. The inside man, Mendoza (Cornel Wilde), breaks down and fingers Earle, who becomes too hot for the Syndicate to aid, so he goes on the run across the heat of the white, blinding desert flats with Marie, forcing her to leave him when the going gets too rough. She hears a radio flash telling of his hopeless position, trapped on a hillside by a posse, and rushes to the scene with his dog. The dog breaks loose, and runs to Earle, who breaks cover to save the dog from police bullets—only to be mown down himself.

Walsh had the advantage of making *High Sierra* at the end of an era, and thus the film could benefit from a nostalgic appeal. Until the introduction of the censorship code by Will Hays, gangsters had been to a certain extent glorified on the screen; the press had given extensive coverage to their exploits, but in the mid-Thirties the emphasis changed. Most of the top names like Capone or Dillinger were either imprisoned or dead, and films were now glorifying the law enforcement agencies as were the press. *High Sierra* was indeed "the last swallow of the gangster's summer" for wartime gangsters in Hollywood films began to find the patriotic urge—in the interests of national morale.

★ ★ ★

Walsh has never been a great talker, preferring to make movies instead of talking about them. He has worked hard towards the goal of concealing his art, never indulging in gimmicks to draw attention to his style. He simply channels all the resources of a studio and his own experience to the benefit of a film as a cohesive form. *High*

Sierra is an example of extreme compact structure and camera placement. All the action is framed in a 4 x 5 ratio, never obviously by trick framing, but always directing attention to the main core of his scene. The professionalism entailed in the long series of shots detailing a car chase up the mountain, particularly the skilful pans, is a marvel of construction and co-ordination of stunt work. Today it would have been filmed with the use of a helicopter but it is debatable whether the result would surpass the original.

Sentimentality and nostalgia again played a large and valid role in *The Strawberry Blonde,* which Walsh also filmed as a musical some years later. It tells the story of a simple fellow with an ambition to be a dentist. He works hard to gain a correspondence school diploma; while he is studying he falls for the local belle but she runs off with a local boy who makes good so the dentist marries a prim and proper nurse with advanced views. After many happily wed years, he still has a secret yearning for his first love but he finds he has married the right girl since the belle has turned into a querulous nagging woman, who hen-pecks her husband despite his money. All this is told in flashback as the unfortunate husband calls on the dentist one Sunday for some emergency treatment.

Small town Americana at the turn of the century has long been a favourite topic with film directors. This film had been made before with Gary Cooper essaying the leading role, which Cagney portrayed for Walsh. Dilys Powell gave the film a moderate reception at the time of its original release on the grounds that it sacrificed the quiet simplicity and understated irony of the earlier version, and speeded it up to an unnatural pace. Yet she accepted it as agreeable by virtue of the acting. Seen today, without having the Cooper version available to balance one's judgements, the acting (with the exception of a rather flat Rita Hayworth) is certainly agreeable; Cagney is more rumbustious than Cooper would have been but this energy is an integral part of his screen personality, and as such,

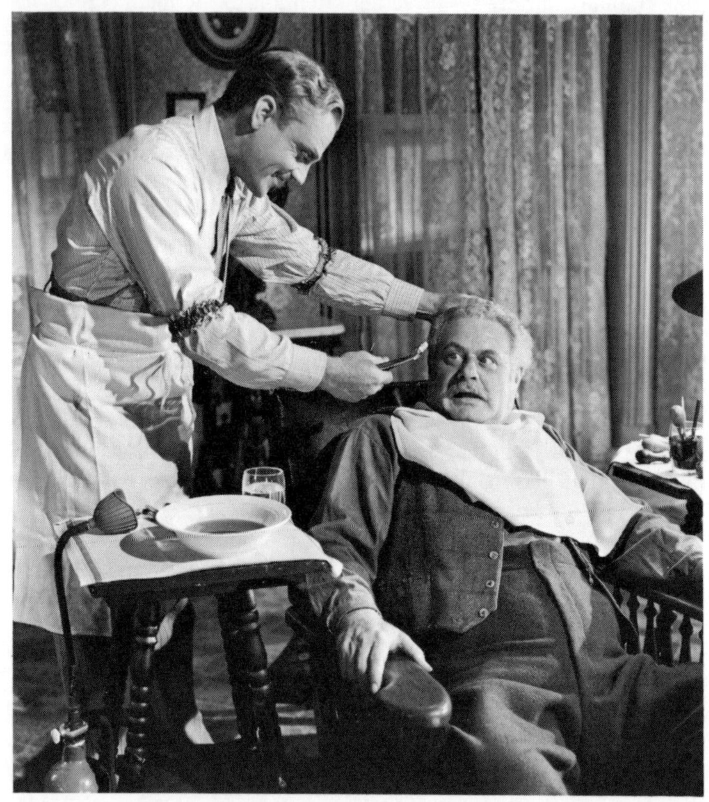

Ace dental student James Cagney proudly displays the result of his first extraction to his nervous guinea pig and father Alan Hale in Walsh's THE STRAWBERRY BLONDE works well in this role; Olivia De Havilland may well be too pretty to be taken for beauty's stooge, but this could be said of most of the "plain" roles that she undertook, and it certainly does not detract from her skill—i.e. the revelation scene in which is it shown to her that she does not practise what she preaches; and Jack Carson was always at home playing a louse.

Walsh's last film in 1941 typified the expertise of the Warner technicians in assembling action footage of consummate and unsurpassed quality. *They Died with Their Boots On* also marked the first of seven films the director made with Errol Flynn; his portrayal of George Armstrong Custer was a tailor made part for Flynn, full of gallantry and wholesome romantic adventure, paying vague attention to fact and presenting Custer in the then-fashionable sympathetic light.

"After a chequered career at West Point, George Armstrong Custer takes a conspicuous, if somewhat unorthodox, part in the Civil War. At the end of the War he takes command of the 7th Cavalry Regiment in the Dakota territories. His regime is successful and he concludes a treaty with the Sioux Indians agreeing that no white man shall encroach on their territories in the Black Hills. On account of this he falls foul of the owners of a trading company who are proposing to develop their interests in Indian territory. By a trick Custer is relieved of his command so that the trading company can go unhampered in their negotiations, but he manages to get back to his regiment for their last stand against the Indians, now infuriated by the broken treaty. Custer and the whole regiment are wiped out but die "with their boots on," fighting gloriously. A film so full of action and expertly directed and produced that even though unusually long it is remarkably realistic." ("Monthly Film Bulletin," March 1942.)

★ ★ ★

Walsh's work with Flynn was not always on large scale "A" films, as can be seen from *Northern Pursuit,* with Flynn heading a cast of minor and second-string players in a drama which is essentially aimed at the wartime adventure/propaganda market. It bore some resemblance to Michael Powell's *49th Parallel,* released in America as *The Invaders,* in that it represented a situation of Nazis landing in Canada on a mission of sabotage. Whereas Powell concentrated on characterisation and used the terrain as an integral part of his story, Walsh concentrates on the mounting of the action scenes such as an avalanche caused by the German agents shooting their Indian guides, which spectacularly engulfs the Nazi killers leaving only one survivor.

He is found by two patrolling Mounties, one of whom is played by Flynn. The remainder of the film revolves around the efforts of Flynn, who is supposed to be of Germanic origin, to penetrate the Nazi Fifth Column in Canada by pretending to be a traitor to the Mounties, and teaming up with this lone survivor until he discovers the man's mission.

Walsh was working with a script that related to the lowest common denominator in characterisation. For instance, the Nazi officer reprimands one of his associates for thinking too much when the man suggests that Flynn may be planted. Later Flynn capitalises on the Nazi's obvious contempt for an Indian guide to stir racial feelings up to such a pitch that the man makes a desperate, unsuccessful attempt to escape, being shot down in a ski chase. Flynn's Mountie partner is forever breaking into patriotic speech, and shows such a totally bigoted attitude towards the Nazi captive in the early section of the film that it comes as no surprise when the German later guns him down as he is surrendering, unarmed, to Flynn.

The predictability and the over-blown heroics such as Flynn's escaping from a mine, knocking out a German flyer and taking his place on a bomber heading for the St. Lawrence seaway, killing the rest of the crew and baling out to safety in spite of his wounds, fully justify the tag that was attached to a number of his war films about winning the war singlehanded. The performances are routine, the musical score as banal as that of a serial, but the film is enhanced by excellent atmospheric photography, especially the highlighting of plotting faces and suspicious eyes, and the reasonable staging of the action sequences such as the ski chase in which camera placement again substitutes for material that today would be shot with the use of sophisticated paraphernalia such as hand-held cameras and helicopters. Technique is also the key factor in the success of *Objective Burma,* the best of the Flynn/Walsh war films.

Errol Flynn and his patrol storm into action against the Japanese during OBJECTIVE BURMA

The opening sequences, and indeed most of the film which is very sparse on dialogue, depend on the images and incidental sounds to develop the narrative, and are reminiscent of a silent film. The slender story is thus developed through narrative imagery in almost documentary form, detailing the adventures of a company of paratroopers flown in to knock out a radio station. What dialogue there is is terse and earthy in the Walshian tradition. The mission is successful but the paras are ambushed while awaiting pickup, pursued to an alternative field and have to fight their way out. The ruthless commando warfare against the unseen Japanese is graphically depicted, especially in the eerie night scenes with bird calls

Troubled mother Judith Anderson and daughter Teresa Wright watch as Robert Mitchum moodily surveys the unconscious body of his half-brother John Rodney, whom he has just laid out in Walsh's PURSUED

and animal noises dominating the soundtrack. Walsh's direction constantly emphasises technique, for example the tracking shot down the river behind a broken branch which floats up to the hidden Japanese soldiers, betraying the American position. The action is short and bloody, with occasional overplaying, such as Flynn and Hull's eye-popping command, "Kill them all . . . every last one of them!" as they discover the bodies of some tortured colleagues. But on the whole there is little that is as offensive as one might have thought, considering the virulent press and public outcry against the film and its subsequent banning in Britain until 1952, when it was re-issued with an apologetic introduction denying any anti-British bias.

★ ★ ★

The odium attached to *Objective Burma* seemed to have an effect on Walsh's career since his next few films were totally innocuous vehicles until in 1947 *Pursued* placed him in the forefront once more. He had decried film as an art form in 1919 after *Evangeline* had failed at the box-office, and had seldom tried to introduce anything of intellectual complexity or density into his work. But *Pursued* cannot be interpreted as anything but a psychological Western, with its involved structure encompassing flashbacks and Freudian overtones.

The film opens with the hero, Jeb Rand (Robert Mitchum) waiting in the shadows for a lynch mob. In flashbacks he recalls the mysterious stranger who has always dogged his life. An orphan, he was raised by Medora Callum (Judith Anderson) with her two children, Adam (John Rodney) and Thorley (Teresa Wright). A recurring childhood recollection left him unsure of Medora and not trusting Adam. His adopted father, Grant Callum (Dean Jagger) persuades him that either he or Adam must enlist in the Spanish-American War. Thorley tosses a coin, and Jeb loses, declaring his love for her as he goes. He returns a wounded hero, and again on the spin of a coin, loses his share of the ranch to Adam after a quarrel. He wins a fortune in the saloon, but while returning home is ambushed by Adam, whom he has to kill. Tried and acquitted, he is still seen as guilty by the Callum family, yet months later Thorley agrees to marry him (telling Medora that in this way she may kill him). Her shot misses on their wedding night, and she grows to love him.

But Grant and his men force Jeb to flee to the old Rand ranch, where he is joined by Thorley. Grant arrives with a lynch mob; Jeb surrenders in order to save Thorley but as the rope is tied around his neck, Medora arrives and Thorley reveals the reason for Adam's hatred of Jeb, which dates back to a love affair between Medora and Jeb's real father. Medora shoots the avenging Grant, thus releasing the young lovers.

The film was strikingly photographed by James Wong Howe, and began a fruitful collaboration between Walsh and producer Milton Sperling, although its true status and importance only came to be recognised in later years. Many contemporary critics felt that it was using the Western format improperly, but with the production of Henry King's *The Gunfighter*, Delmer Daves's *Broken Arrow*, and Fred Zinnemann's *High Noon* in the early Fifties, a change of heart was conceded. The immediate effect for Walsh at Warner Brothers was that he was allowed to involve himself in projects which bore a more personal stamp, such as *Silver River* and *White Heat*.

The former cast Flynn in an unsympathetic role. Opening with a Civil War montage, it establishes Flynn as a Northern officer, Mike McComb, who is forced to flee with a payroll when Southern troops give chase (to his side-kick: "We could play a little poker"). He burns the cash, only to find himself under arrest; drummed out, he decides to live by his own rules. Expelled from a gambling hall, he dons his old uniform to order a troop of soldiers in to tear the place apart, stopping his side-kick from joining the fray with the comment, "YOU don't want to get hurt do you?" He becomes a gambler on the proceeds, and when his rival claims back the stolen goods, McComb holds a gun on him until the boat crosses the State line! A patriotic lady, Georgia Moore (Ann Sheridan) joins the boat collecting money for the troops, commandeering the only wagons aboard to unload her property. McComb wins them gambling, and leaves her high and dry.

Walsh employs a strong visual emphasis during the wagon journey to Silver City, using several medium/long shots, outlining and isolating the wagons against the terrain—with many of the compositions in the Fordian tradition.

Georgia refuses to help McComb's rival arrange a reception committee at Silver City; so McComb "gallantly" takes her on his wagon train when they meet again as a stage-coach overtakes the wagons and breaks down; this time he leaves his rival, Sweeney (Barton MacLane) stranded. The scene is accompanied by an emphatic epic score by Steiner, and Flynn and Sheridan are filmed in towering close shots of heroic proportions. Walsh introduces some earthy humour as a rainstorm bursts with McComb refusing to allow Georgia to shelter in his wagon, "Mrs. Moore, please! You could at least knock on the wheels before entering my wagon." She retaliates by riding off on his horse when the storm has subsided. A more decisive visual shorthand is used when Sweeney arrives, offering McComb peace and a partnership—two punches and a chair crashed on his skull lay him flat!

McComb meets an alcoholic lawyer, who comes to act as his conscience, and Georgia's husband, Stanley (Bruce Bennett), who offers him a share in a mine in return for aid (Mitchell: "Caesar was ambitious; he lived for it, and he died for it"). Georgia is wary of her husband's new business partner, with good reason, for when the mine goes badly McComb increases his share to fifty percent in return for financial aid. Sweeney stirs up feeling about McComb's not taking paper bonds money in his saloon, so McComb sets up a bank—taking a cut in every mine! When President Grant visits the town to encourage silver production, McComb sees his empire visions coming into being, and approaches Georgia openly ("I want . . .YOU"). She rebuffs him, but when his wagon boss is killed by hostile Indians McComb keeps quiet about it, sending Stanley to prospect in the Indian hills (Stanley sees it as his duty as a mining engineer). The lawyer, John Plato Beck, draws a parallel with David and Bathsheba; McComb knocks him to the saloon floor, but relents—too late to save Stanley. Beck's epitaph, as a man claiming the rewards of his treachery, incenses local feeling.

Georgia remains unsure of the relationship, but accepts McComb's word that she is the source of his motivation. Beck breaks up a party, organised to win over local businessmen; McComb is ostracised and a rival bank established. Beck enters politics; McComb determines to close all mines and Georgia at last becomes aware of the extent of local gossip, leaving after forcing a showdown. There is a run on the bank, and McComb pays out everything. He discovers that Georgia is working for Beck, but when he goes to see her, he is unable to prevent Sweeney killing Beck. McComb accepts his destiny, but nobody will follow him until Georgia shames them into doing so. He deploys his troops in military fashion, encircling Sweeney's men and restoring law and order to Silver City.

Walsh maintains the pace well, incorporating a visual consistency with the narrative development and capable acting performances; features which he perfected in *White Heat,* in which he elaborated his main theme of a man at odds with organised society within the clearly defined *genre* structure of the crime thriller. It is his most polished analysis of the criminal mind, laid out in simple psychological terms.

Cody Jarrett (James Cagney) engineers a train robbery, using an inside man, a car across the tracks and dynamite, escaping with the proceeds and leaving four dead men and a badly scalded gang member in his wake. He mistrusts his over-ambitious lieutenant, Ed Sommers (Steve Cochran) and his trollopy wife Verna (Virginia Mayo), relying on and loving only his mother—a latter day Ma Barker (Margaret Wycherley). Cody has trouble with recurrent brainstorms, and the police are hot on his tail, even if they lack the evidence to involve him. Cody murders a rival, hiding in a highway drive-in cinema, where he evolves a scheme for surrendering on a fake charge. The District Attorney orders undercover specialist Hank Fallon (Edmond O'Brien) to pose as a smalltime crook, Vic Pardo, in order to share a cell with Cody, and win his confidence. He briefs him on Cody's case history—insanity in the family and a psychopathic devotion to his mother.

Cody is very suspicious but eventually accepts Pardo. Cody controls his gang via instructions to his mother passed on every visiting day, unaware that Sommers and Verna are having an affair, and that Sommers is planning to have him killed in prison. Pardo saves his life, planting suspicion in Cody's mind; Ma promises to take care of Sommers ("When I can't take care of his type, I'll know I'm getting old"), but this only leads to Cody's having another brainstorm. When Pardo helps him again, Cody confides his plan to crash out, agreeing not to use guns at Pardo's instigation. But after another brainstorm he takes along a prisoner with a gun. As Cody escapes, the prison doctor hands the prison governor the results of medical tests, proving him to be totally insane. The escape is successful; as well as Pardo, Cody takes an old acquaintance and a "stool pigeon" whom he locks in a car boot before shooting him ("I'll give you some air"). Meanwhile Cody's mother has been killed by Sommers and Verna; the latter is about to leave on hearing of Cody's escape but Sommers threatens to put the blame on her ("Cody'll be mad when he hears she got it in the back"), but Verna reverses the story successfully when Cody catches up with them, and he guns Sommers down (pointing in silent triumph to the bullet holes in his back).

The gang have invested in a petrol tanker since Cody plans a robbery at a chemical factory—once suggested by his late mother.

Cody talks of conversing with a dead man when he discovers evidence to implicate Pardo in treachery; Pardo fools him long enough to plant a message for the police but then a convict hired especially for the factory job fingers him. Cody flips but the police refuse to do a deal to save Fallon's life. They surround the factory, isolate the gang, weaken them with tear gas and mow them down. Fallon is wounded while cornering Cody, who accidentally sets some gas alight, dying in the billowing flames of a gigantic explosion, insanely screaming, "Made it Ma! Top of the World!"

White Heat proved to be the apex of Walsh's career at Warner Brothers. Three films later, his contract expired and he worked at most of the major studios during the Fifties. For Universal on Westerns with Rock Hudson and Alan Ladd; for RKO on several pirate sagas plus a controversial adaptation of Norman Mailer's *The Naked and the Dead*; for Warners on vehicles for Cagney and Gable plus another lengthy Marine saga, *Battle Cry*; a mixed bag of drama and comedy for Fox, and another Gable vehicle for United Artists.

His last film to date, *A Distant Trumpet*, was made in 1964 at Warners, and proved to be an excellent Cavalry Western in terms of action though in other respects it showed the hand of age affecting the director's capabilities, notably in the lifeless plot and lack of historical setting. It remains a sad but rather touching epitaph to a great director whose career has spanned fifty-five years of involvement in film. But we may yet see a final work from Walsh, who has projects ready to go if he can overcome medical doubts about his health, which have been the cause of his inability to find backing for films.

ALAN LADD
SHELLEY WINTERS
O'Rourke of the
Royal Mounted (U)

Above: Mountie Alan Ladd metes out rough justice to crooked lawman Hugh O'Brian in O'ROURKE OF THE ROYAL MOUNTED (1954). Below: Jane Russell and Richard Egan in Walsh's THE REVOLT OF MAMIE STOVER

RAOUL WALSH Filmography

Actor: (1909–49):
Walsh began acting, mainly as a Western heavy, for Pathe in 1909; he moved to Biograph in 1912 as an actor and assistant director for D. W. Griffith, and left with Griffith to join Mutual in October 1913. These acting performances include:
THE LIFE OF GENERAL VILLA (1912, Christy Cabanne). Walsh acted as the young Villa, wrote the scenario and directed some of the film.
SANDS OF FATE (1914, Donald Crisp). As a romantic rival for the hand of Dorothy Gish.
THE AVAILING PRAYER (1914, Donald Crisp), As the romantic lead.
LEST WE FORGET (1914, ?).
THE GREAT LEAP (1914, ?).
THE DISHONORED MEDAL (1914, ?).
THE MYSTERY OF THE HINDU IMAGE (1914, Raoul Walsh).
SIERRA JIM'S REFORMATION (1914, ?).
FOR HIS MASTER (1914, ?).
THE DOUBLE KNOT (1914, Raoul Walsh). As the heavy.
THE FINAL VERDICT (1914, Raoul Walsh). As a heavy.
THE BIRTH OF A NATION (1915). In D. W. Griffith's epic film, Walsh played John Wilkes Booth, and acted as an assistant director.
THE SMUGGLER (1915, ?).
HIS RETURN (1915, Raoul Walsh).
THE GREASER (1915; Raoul Walsh). As a sympathetic villain.
A MAN FOR ALL THAT (1915, Raoul Walsh).
THE HONOR SYSTEM (1917, Raoul Walsh).
SADIE THOMPSON (1928, Raoul Walsh). As Sgt. Tim O'Hara.
IT'S A GREAT FEELING (1949, David Butler). As himself.

Director:
Walsh probably wrote the first thirteen films listed, although no scenario credits are available to support this supposition.
THE DOUBLE KNOT (1914). *With* Mary Alden, Raoul Walsh. Produced for Reliance. 2r.
THE MYSTERY OF THE HINDU IMAGE (1914). Produced for Majestic. 2r.
THE GUNMAN (1914). *With* Sam de Grasse, Eugene Pallette, Miriam Cooper, Ralph Lewis. Produced for Reliance. 2r.
THE FINAL VERDICT (1914). *With* Raoul Walsh, Franceila Billington, Joe Singleton, Eagle Eye. Produced for Majestic. 2r.
THE DEATH DICE (1915). *With* Irene Hunt. Produced for Reliance. 2r.
HIS RETURN (1915). *With* Elmer Clifton. Produced for Reliance. 2r.
THE GREASER (1915). *With* Elmer Clifton, Miriam Cooper, Raoul Walsh. Produced for Majestic. 2r.
THE FENCING MASTER (1915). *With* Thomas Jefferson, Frank Bennett, Teddy Sampson, George Walsh. Produced for Majestic. 2r.
A MAN FOR ALL THAT (1915). *With* Miriam Cooper, Tom Wilson, Elmer Clifton. Produced for Reliance. 2r.
ELEVEN-THIRTY (1915). *With* Loretta Blake, Eric von Ritzau, Al W. Filson, George Walsh. Produced for Majestic. 2r.
THE BURIED HAND (1915). *With* Miriam Cooper, William Hinckley, W. E.

Lowry, Cora Drew. Produced for Majestic. 2r.

THE CELESTIAL CODE (1915). *With* Irene Hunt, George Walsh, Harry James, Dark Cloud, Tote Du Crow, James Warnack. Produced for Reliance. 2r.

A BAD MAN AND OTHERS (1915). *With* George Walsh, Elmo Lincoln, Violet Wilkey, W. E. Lowry. Produced for Reliance. 2r.

THE REGENERATION (1915). A realistic depiction of the squalid tenement life on New York's East Side. *Sc:* Raoul Walsh, Carl Harbaugh (play by Owen Kildare, Walter Hackett). *With* Rockliffe Fellowes, Anna Q. Nilsson, Carl Harbaugh, William A. Sheer, James A. Marcus, Johnny McCann. Walsh is often credited as producer for Fox. 6r.

CARMEN (1915). Lively story of the loves of a Spanish gypsy girl. *Sc:* Raoul Walsh (novel by Prosper Mérimée). *With* Theda Bara (*Carmen*), Einar Linden (*Jose*), Elsie MacLoed (*Michaela*), Marie de Beneditto (*Jose's Mother*), James A. Marcus (*Inn-keeper*), Carl Harbaugh, Lilian Hathaway, Fay Tunis, Emil de Varney, Joseph P. Green. *Prod:* Raoul Walsh for Fox. 5r.

PILLARS OF SOCIETY (1916). *Supervising director and sc:* D. W. Griffith. *Dir:* Raoul Walsh. *Sc:* based on play by Henrik Ibsen. *With* Henry B. Walthall, Mary Alden, George Beranger, Josephine Cromwell, Olga Grey, Juanita Archer. *Prod:* Triangle. 5r.

THE SERPENT (1916). A Russian peasant girl, seduced by a duke, vows a serpentine revenge, and ends up as bride of the duke's son. *Sc:* Raoul Walsh and George Walsh (story "The Wolf's Claw" by Philip Bartholmae). *With* Theda Bara, Charles Craig, George Walsh, James A. Marcus, Lilian Hathaway, Charles Craig, Carl Harbaugh, Nan Carter, Barry Whitcomb. *Prod:* Raoul Walsh for Fox. 6r.

BLUE BLOOD AND RED (1916). An action-packed Western which used real people in rather outrageous portrayals that nearly resulted in law suits, but which also made George Walsh a new romantic star. *Sc:* Raoul Walsh (from his own story). *Ph:* George Benoit. *With* George Walsh, Doris Pawn, James A. Marcus, Vester Pegg, Martin Kinney. *Prod:* Raoul Walsh for Fox. 5r.

THE HONOR SYSTEM (1917). A drama advocating penal reform. *Sc:* Raoul Walsh (story by Henry C. Warnack). *Ph:* George Benoit. *Title Editor:* Hettie Gray Baker. *With* Milton Sills, George Walsh, Miriam Cooper, Gladys Brockwell, Cora Drew, James A. Marcus, Carrie Clark, Ward, Arthur Mackley, Charles Clary, Roy Rice, P. J. Cannon, Johnny Reese, William Ens (Eagle Eye), Thomas X. Brian, Countess Du Cello. *Prod:* Raoul Walsh for Fox. 10r.

THE CONQUEROR (1917). Biography of General Sam Houston. *Sc:* Henry C. Warnack, Raoul Walsh(?). *With* William Farnum (*Sam Houston*), Jewel Carmen, Charles Clary, James A. Marcus, Carrie Clark Ward, Robert Dunbar, Owen Jones, William Eagle Shirt, Chief Budhead, Little Bear, William Chisholm. *Prod:* Fox. 8r. Later films featuring Houston include *Man of Conquest* (1939, George Nichols Jr.); *Lone Star* (1952, Vincent Sherman); *The First Texan* (1956, Byron Haskin) and *The Alamo* (1960, John Wayne).

BETRAYED (1917). *With* Miriam Cooper. *Sc:* Raoul Walsh (story by Walsh and C. B. Clapp). *Prod:* Raoul Walsh for Fox. 5r.
THIS IS THE LIFE (1917). The fantasies of a movie-buff in a dentist's chair. *Sc:* Ralph Spence, Raoul Walsh (from their story). *With* George Walsh, Wanda Petit/Hawley, James A. Marcus, Ralph Lewis, John Eherts, Jack MacDonald, W. H. Tyne, Hector V. Sarno. *Prod:* Fox. 5r.
THE PRIDE OF NEW YORK (1917). First World War love story about a poor construction worker winning a nice rich girl from an upper-class rival. *Sc:* Raoul Walsh (from his story). *With* George Walsh, Regina Quinn, James A. Marcus, William Bailey. *Prod:* Fox. 5r.
THE SILENT LIE (1917). A lusty drama about life in the North-West. *Sc:* C. B. Clapp (story "Conahan" by Harry Evans). *With* Miriam Cooper, Ralph Lewis, Charles Clary, Monroe Salisbury, Henry C. Barrow, Howard C. Davis, William Eagle Shirt. *Prod:* Fox. 5r.
THE INNOCENT SINNER (1917). *Sc:* Raoul Walsh (story by Mary Synon). *With* Miriam Cooper, Charles Clary, Jack Standing, Jane Novak, Rosita Marstini, William E. Parsons, Johnny Reese, Jennie Lee. *Prod:* Fox. 6r.
THE WOMAN AND THE LAW (1918). Factually based murder drama. *Sc:* Raoul Walsh (based on the De Saulles case). *With* Miriam Cooper, Ramsay Wallace, Peggy Hopkins, George Humbert, Agnes Nielsen, Louis Daytch, John Laffe, Jack Connor, Lilian Satherwaite, Winifred Allen. *Prod:* Fox. 7r.
THE PRUSSIAN CUR (1918). A fashionable anti-German tirade incorporating newsreel clips with a melodramatic plot. *Sc:* Raoul Walsh (from his story). *With* Miriam Cooper, James A. Marcus, Patrick O'Malley, Lenora Stewart, Capt. Horst von der Goltz, Sidney Mason, Walter McEwan, William M. Black, Ralph Faulkner, Walter M. Lawrence, James Hathaway, William Harrison, P. C. Hartigan, J. E. Franklin. *Prod:* Fox. 8r.
ON THE JUMP (1918). *Sc:* Raoul Walsh (from his story). *Ph:* Roy Overbough. *With* George Walsh, Frances Burnham, Henry Clive, James A. Marcus, Ralph Faulkner. *Prod:* Fox. 6r.
EVERY MOTHER'S SON (1918). A family drama. *Sc:* Raoul Walsh (from his story). *With* Charlotte Walker, Percy Standing, Edwin Stanley, Ray Howard, Gareth Hughes, Corone Paynter, Bernard Thornton. *Prod:* Fox 5r.
I'LL SAY SO (1918). Comedy about a young man's attempts to enlist constantly ending in frustration. *Sc:* Ralph Spence. *Ed:* Ralph Spence. *With* George Walsh, Regina Quinn, William Bailey, James Black. *Prod:* William Fox for Fox Film Corp. 5r.
EVANGELINE (1919). A romantic tragedy based on Longfellow's poem. *Sc:* Raoul Walsh (from poem by H. W. Longfellow). *Ph:* J. D. Jennings. *With* Miriam Cooper (*Evangeline*), Albert Roscoe (*Gabriel*), Spottiswoode Aitken (*Benedict Bellefontaine*), James Marcus (*Basil*), Paul Weigel (*Father Felician*), William A. Wellman. *Prod:* Raoul Walsh for Fox. 5r.
THE STRONGEST (1919). A story of love overcoming selfishness, based on a tale by the Premier of France. *Sc:* Raoul Walsh (story by Georges Clémenceau). *With* Renee Adoree (*Claudia*), Carlo

Liten (*Henri, Marquis de Puymaufray*), Harrison Hunter (*Harle*), Florence Malone (*Claire Harle*), Madame Tressida (*Nanette*), Jean Gauthier de Trigny, Georgette Gauthier de Trigny, James A. Marcus, Hal Horne, C. H. de Lima. *Prod:* Fox. Shown with tinted sequences.

SHOULD A HUSBAND FORGIVE? (1920). A moral sex-comedy of the type made popular by Cecil B. DeMille. *Sc:* Raoul Walsh (from his story). *Ph:* J. D. Jennings. *With* Miriam Cooper (*Ruth Fulton*), Mrs. James C. Hackett (*Mary Carroll*), Eric Mayne (*John Carroll*), Vincent Coleman (*John Carroll Jr.*), Lyster Chambers (*Cad*), Percy Standing, Charles Craig, Martha Mansfield, James A. Marcus, Johnny Rees, Tom Brooke. *Prod:* Fox. 7r.

FROM NOW ON (1920). American boy falls in love with Italian girl. *Sc:* Raoul Walsh (story by Frank Packard). *Ph:* Joseph Ruttenberg. *With* George Walsh (*Dave Henderson*), Regina Quinn (*Teresa Capriano*), Mario Majeroni (*Capriano*), Paul Everton (*Booky Sharvan*), James A. Marcus (*Martin Tydeman*), Cesare Gravina, Robert Byrd, Tom Walsh. *Prod:* Fox. 7r. Shown with tinted sequences.

THE DEEP PURPLE (1920). A country girl is lured to the city by a criminal gang, but saved from a fate worse than death by the loving hero. *Sc:* Earle Brown (from play by Paul Armstrong, Wilson Mizner). *Ph:* Jacques Bizuel. *With* Miriam Cooper (*Doris Moore*), Helen Ware (*Kate Fallon*), Vincent Serrano (*Harry Leland*), Stuart Sage (*William Lake*), William B. Mack (*Gordon Laylock*), Bird Millman, W. J. Ferguson, Lincoln Plumer, Ethel Haller, Hal Horne, Lorraine Frost, Marjorie Brenner. *Prod:* Realart. 7r. Possibly a re-make of a 1915 film of the same title.

THE OATH (1921). A Gentile who marries a Jew without her father's consent becomes the chief suspect when her father is murdered. *Sc:* Ralph Spence (from novel "Idols" by W. J. Locke). *Ph:* Del Clawson. *With* Miriam Cooper (*Ninna Hart*), Conway Tearle (*Hugh Colman*), Robert Fischer (*Israel Hart*), Anna Q. Nilsson (*Irene Lansing*), Henry Clive (*Gerard Merriam*), Ricca Allen (*Anna Cassaba*). *Prod:* Raoul Walsh for Mayflower Photoplay Corp. 8r.

SERENADE (1921). Aristocratic Castilian rivals fight over the heroine in New Mexico. *Sc:* J. T. O'Donohue (play "Maria Del Carmen" by Jose Filny Codina). *Ph:* George Peters. *With* Miriam Cooper (*Maria Del Carmen*), George Walsh (*Pancho*), Rosita Marstini (*Mother*), James A. Marcus (*Pepuso*), James Swickard, Bertram Grassby, Noble Johnson, Adelbert Knott, William Eagle Eye/ William Ens, Ardita Milano, Peter Venezuela, John Eberts, Tom Kennedy. *Prod:* Raoul Walsh for Raoul Walsh Productions. 7r.

LOST AND FOUND ON A SOUTH SEA ISLAND (GB: LOST AND FOUND) (1922). A pirate drama shot on location in Tahiti. *Sc:* Paul Bern (story by Carey Wilson). *Ph:* Clyde De Vinna, Paul Kerschner. *Ed:* Kate Hilliker, H. H. Calvert. *With* House Peters (*Capt. Blackbird*), Pauline Stark (*Lorna*), Antonio Moreno (*Lloyd Warren*), Rosemary Theby (*Madge*), Mary Jane Irving (*Madge, as a baby*), George Siegmann, William V. Mong, Carl Harbaugh, David Wing. *Prod:* Goldwyn. 7r.

KINDRED OF THE DUST (1922). Rich man's son falls for a poor squatter's daughter. *Sc:* J. T. O'Donohue (story by Peter Kyne). *Ph:* Lyman Broening, Charles J. Van Enger. *Art dir:* William Cameron Menzies. *With* Miriam Cooper (*Nan of the Sawdust Pile*), Ralph Graves (*Don McKaye*), Lionel Belmore (*Laird of Tyee*), Eugenie Besserer (*Mrs. McKaye*), Maryland Morne (*Jane McKaye*), Bessie Peters, William J. Ferguson, Carolyn Rankin, Pat Rooney, Bruce Guerin, John Herdman. *Prod:* Raoul Walsh for R. A. Walsh Company Inc. 8r.

THE THIEF OF BAGDAD (1924). An Arabian Nights spectacle that gave Walsh his biggest break of the early Twenties. *Sc:* Lotta Woods (from an adaptation of "The Thousand and One Nights"—story written by Elton John (Douglas Fairbanks Sr.). *Ph:* Arthur Edeson. *Art Dir:* William Cameron Menzies. *Consultant Art Dir:* Irvin J. Martin. *Ed:* William Nolan. *Costumes:* Mitchell Leisen. *Technical Director:* Robert Fairbanks. *Mus:* Mortimer Wilson. *With* Douglas Fairbanks (*The Thief of Bagdad*), Julanne Johnson (*the Princess*), Anna May Wong (*her slave*), Brandon Hurst (*the Caliph*), Sojin (*the Mongol Prince*), Snitz Edwards, Charles Belcher, Winter Blossom, Etta Lee, Tote Du Crow, K. Nambu, Sadakichi Hartmann, Mathilde Comont, Noble Johnson, Charles Stevens, Sam Baker, Jesse Weldon, Scott Mattraw, Charles Sylvester. *Prod:* Theodore Reed for Douglas Fairbanks Pictures. 14r. British version 1940 (*d* Ludwig Berger, Michael Powell, Tim Whelan).

EAST OF SUEZ (1925). A Pola Negri vehicle casting her as an educated half-caste who falls in love with an English civil servent. *Sc:* Sada Cowan (play by Somerset Maugham). *Ph:* Victor Milner. *With* Pola Negri (*Daisy Forbes*), Edmund Lowe (*George Tevis*), Rockliffe Fellowes (*Harry Anderson*), Noah Beery (*Robert Tevis*), Sojin Kamiyama (*Lee Tai*), Mrs. Wong Wing, Florence Regnart, Charles Requa, E. H. Calvert. *Presented by* Adolph Zukor, Jesse Lasky for Famous Players Lasky Corp. (Paramount). 7r.

THE SPANIARD (GB: SPANISH LORE) (1925). A bullfighter abducts an English girl, and terrorises her before she eventually succumbs willingly to his passionate inclinations. *Sc:* J. T. O'Donohue (story by Juanita Savage). *Ph:* Victor Milner. *Art Dir:* Lawrence W. Hitt. *With* Jetta Goudal (*Dolores Annesley*), Ricardo Cortez (*Don Pedro de Barrego*), Noah Beery (*Gomez*), Emily Fitzroy (*Maria*), Bernard Seigel (*Manuel*), Florence Regnart, Mathilda Brundage, Renzo De Gardi. *Presented by* Adolph Zukor, Jesse Lasky for Famous Players Lasky Corp. (Paramount). 6,600 ft.

THE WANDERER (1925). Biblical tale based on the story of the Prodigal Son. *Sc:* J. T. O'Donohue (play by Maurice V. Samuels). *Ph:* Victor Milner. *Art Dir:* Lawrence W. Hitt. *With* Greta Nissen (*Tisha*), William Collier Jr. (*Jether*), Ernest Torrence (*Tola*), Wallace Beery (*Pharis*), Tyrone Power Sr. (*Jesse*), Kathryn Hill, Kathlyn Williams, George Rigas, Holmes Herbert, Snitz Edwards, Sojin. *Presented by* Adolph Zukor, Jesse Lasky for Paramount. 8,100 ft. Shown with tinted sequences.

THE LUCKY LADY (1926). Romantic adventures of a Princess in a small European principality, who falls in love with an American tourist. *Sc:* James T. O'Donohue (story by Robert Sherwood, Bertram Bloch). *Ph:* Victor Milner. *With* Greta Nissen (*Antoinette*), William Collier Jr. (*Jack Clarke*), Lionel Barrymore (*Count Ferranzo*), Marc McDermott (*Garletz*), Mme. Daumery (*Duchess*), Sojin. *Prod:* Raoul Walsh for Paramount. 6r.

THE LADY OF THE HAREM (1926). When the heroine is taken prisoner, the hero fights the Caliph by joining forces with the rebels, and regains his true love. *Sc:* James T. O'Donohue (play "Hassan" by James Elroy Flecker). *Ph:* Victor Milner. *With* Greta Nissen (*Pervaneh*), William Collier Jr. (*Rafi*), Ernest Torrence (*Hassan*), Louise Fazenda (*Yasmin*), Sojin (*Caliph*), Frank Leigh, Andre de Beranger, Noble Johnson, Daniel Makarenko, Christian Frank, Snitz Edwards, Chester Conklin, Leo White, Brandon Hurst. *Presented by* Adolph Zukor, Jesse L. Lasky for Paramount. 5,700 ft.

WHAT PRICE GLORY? (1926). A virile war comedy about the Marines which incorporated spectacular battle footage, and was so successful that Walsh and his stars made a number of sequels. *Sc:* Lawrence Stallings, Maxwell Anderson (from Anderson play). *Ph:* Barney McGill, John Marta, John Smith. *Mus:* Erno Rapee. *With* Victor McLaglen (*Sgt. Flagg*), Edmund Lowe (*Sgt. Quirk*), Dolores Del Rio (*Charmaine*), Phyllis Haver (*Shanghai Mabel*), Leslie Fenton (*Lieut. Moore*), Elena Jurado, Ted McNamara, Sammy Cohen, August Tollaire, Mathilde Comont, William V. Mong, Pat Rooney, Barry Norton, Jack Pennick, Mahlon Hamilton. *Prod:* William Fox for Fox. c116m. Shown with tinted sequences. Re-made by John Ford in 1952.

THE MONKEY TALKS (1927). Three stranded circus men persuade a dwarf to impersonate a monkey, making money by showing him as a talking monkey; but a lion-tamer replaces him with a real monkey with fatal results. *Sc:* L. G. Rigby (play by Rene Fauchois). *Ph:* L. William O'Connell. *With* Don Alvarado (*Fano*), Olive Borden (*Olivette*), Jacques Lerner (*Jacko Lerner*), Malcolm Waite (*Bergerin*), Raymond Hitchcock (*Lorenzo*), Ted McNamara, Jane Winton, August Tollaire. *Prod:* Raoul Walsh for Fox. 6r.

THE LOVES OF CARMEN (1927). A re-make of his 1915 version setting aside much of the intensity of the drama in favour of a characteristic bawdy humour. *Sc:* Gertrude Orr (novel by Prosper Mérimée). *Ph:* John Marta, Lucien Andriot. *Ed:* Kate Hilliker, H. H. Caldwell. *With* Dolores Del Rio (*Carmen*), Victor McLaglen (*Escamilio*), Don Alvarado (*Jose*), Nancy Nash (*Michaela*), Mathilde Comont (*Emilia*), Carmen Costello, Jack Baston, Fred Kohler, Rafael Valverda. *Prod:* William Fox for Fox. Later version (using same title) directed by Charles Vidor in 1947.

SADIE THOMPSON (1928). Censored version of Maugham's tale about a man of God who secretly and hypocritically lusts after a tart. *Sc:* Raoul Walsh (novel and play by Somerset Maugham). *Ph:* George Barnes, Oliver Marsh, Robert Kurrle. *Art Dir:* William Cameron Menies. *Ed:* C. Gardner Sullivan. *With* Gloria Swanson (*Sadie Thompson*), Lionel Barrymore (*Oliver Hamilton*), Blanche

Frederici (*Mrs. Hamilton*), Charles Lane (*Dr. McPhail*), Raoul Walsh (*Sgt. Tim O'Hara*), Florence Midgeley, James A. Marcus, Sophia Artega, Will Stanton. *Prod:* Gloria Swanson Productions Inc. 9r. Later filmed as RAIN (1932, *d* Lewis Milestone) and MISS SADIE THOMPSON (1953, *d* Curtis Bernhardt).

THE RED DANCE (GB: THE RED DANCER OF MOSCOW) (1928). Russian Revolutionary drama about a peasant girl who loves a Prince, and wins her happiness by saving his life. *Sc:* James Creelman (adapted by Pierre Collings, Philip Klein from a story by Eleanor Brown, H. L. Gates). *Ph:* Charles Clarke, John Marta. *Ed:* Louis Loeffler. *Mus:* S. L. Rothafel, Erno Rapee. *With* Dolores Del Rio (*Tasia*), Charles Farrell (*Grand Duke Eugene*), Ivan Linow (*Ivan Petroff*), Boris Charsky (*Agitator*), Dorothy Revier (*Princess Varvara*), Barry Norton, Andre Segurola, Demetrius Alexis. *Prod:* Raoul Walsh for Fox. 10r. Walsh's first film using sound effects.

ME, GANGSTER (1928). The rise and fall of a young hoodlum portrayed in a realistic vein. *Sc:* Charles Francis Coe, Raoul Walsh (from story by Coe). *Ph:* Arthur Edeson. *Ed:* Louis Loeffler. *With* June Collyer (*Mary Regan*), Don Terry (*Jimmy Williams*), Anders Randolf (*Russ Williams*), Stella Adams (*Lizzie Williams*), Walter James, Burr McIntosh, Al Hill, Gustav von Seyfferitz, Herbert Ashton, Bob Perry, Harry Castle, Carol Lombard, Joe Brown, Nigel de Brulier, Arthur Stone. *Prod:* William Fox for Fox. 7r.

HOT FOR PARIS (1929). A rough diamond sailor wins the French Grand National lottery, and the attentions of a vamp. *Sc:* Charles J. McGuirk (story by Raoul Walsh). *Ph:* Charles Van Enger. *Art. Dir:* David Hall. *Sets:* Ben Carre. *Ed:* Jack Dennis. *With* Victor McLaglen (*John Patrick Duke*), Fifi Dorsay (*Fifi Dupre*), El Brendel (*Axel Olson*), Polly Moran (*Polly*), Lennox Pawle, August Tollaire, George Fawcett, Charles Judels, Eddie Dillon, Rosita Marstini, Agostino Borgato, Yola D'Avril, Anita Maurray, Dave Valles. *Presented by* William Fox for Fox. 7r.

IN OLD ARIZONA (1929). Romantic triangle between the Cisco Kid, his pursuer and a money-grabbing girl who sacrifices her life for the Kid in the last reel. *Co-Dir:* Raoul Walsh, Irving Cummings. *Sc:* Tom Barry (from story "The Caballero's Way" by O. Henry). *Ph:* Arthur Edeson, A. Hansen. *Ed:* Louis Loeffler. *With* Warner Baxter–replacing Raoul Walsh– (*The Cisco Kid*), Dorothy Burgess (*Tonia Maria*), Edmund Lowe (*Sgt. Mickey Dunn*), J. Farrell McDonald (*Tad*), Alphonse Ethier (*Sheriff*), Ivan Linow, Soledad Jiminez, Fred Warren, Roy Stewart, Henry Armetta, James Bradbury Jr., James A. Marcus, Joe Brown, Frank Campeau, Tom Santschi, Pat Hartigan, John Dillon, Frank Nelson, Duke Martin. *Prod:* Fox. 7r.

THE COCK-EYED WORLD (1929). The first sequel to *What Price Glory? Sc:* Raoul Walsh (based on a story by Laurence Stallings, Maxwell Anderson). *Ph:* Arthur Edeson. *Ed:* Jack Dennis. *With* Victor McLaglen (*Sgt. Flagg*), Edmund Lowe (*Sgt. Quirt*), Lily Damita (*Elenita*), Leila Karnelly (*Olga*), El Brendel (*Olson*), Bobby Burns, Jean Laverty, Joe Brown, Stuart Erwin, Ivan Linow, Soledad Jiminez, Albert Dresden, Joe Rochay,

Jeanette Dagna, Jean Barry, Warren Hymer. *Presented by* William Fox for Fox. 12r. Released in both sound and silent versions.

THE BIG TRAIL (1930). Epic Western dealing with the opening up of the Oregon trail. *Sc:* Jack Peabody, Marie Boyle, Florence Postal (story by Hal G. Evarts). *Ph:* (ordinary version) Lucien Andriot, Don Anderson, Bill McDonald, Roger Sherman, Bobby Mack, Henry Pollack; (grandeur version): Arthur Edeson, Dave Ragin, Sol Halprin, Curt Fetters, Max Cohn, Harry Smith, L. Kunkel, Harry Dave. *Ed:* Jack Dennis. *Incidental Mus:* Arthur Kay. *With* John Wayne (*Breck Coleman*), Marguerite Churchill (*Ruth Cameron*), El Brendel (*Gussie*), Tully Marshall (*Zeke*), Tyrone Power Sr. (*Red Flake*), Russ Powell, David Rollins, Frederick Burton, Charles Stevens, Louise Carver, William V. Mong, Dodo Newton, Ward Bond, Marcia Harris, Marjorie Lee, Jack Peabody, Leslie Emerson, Frank Ramboth, Andy Shufford, Helen Parrish, De Witt Jennings, Gertrude Van Lent, Lucille Van Lent, Alphonse Ethier. *Prod:* Fox. Normal version 126m; 70mm. widescreen version 158m.

THE MAN WHO CAME BACK (1931). A melodrama starring the popular Farrell-Gaynor team. *Sc:* E. J. Burke (play by Jules Eckert Goodman, John Fleming Wilson). *Ph:* Arthur Edeson. *Ed:* Harold Schuster. *With* Janet Gaynor (*Angie*), Charles Farrell (*Stephen Randolph*), Kenneth McKenna (*Capt. Trevelyan*), William Holden (*Thomas Randolph*), Mary Forbes (*Mrs. Gaynes*), Ulrich Haupt, William Worthington, Peter Cawthorne, Leslie Fenton. *Prod:* Fox. 74m.

WOMEN OF ALL NATIONS (1931). Further adventures of Flagg and Quirt with Bogart in a small role. *Sc:* Barry Connors (from his story). *Ph:* Lucien Andriot. *Art Dir:* David Hall. *Ed:* Jack Dennis. *Mus:* Ray Bussett. *With* Victor McLaglen (*Sgt. Flagg*), Edmund Lowe (*Sgt. Quirt*), Greta Nissen (*Elsa*), El Brendel (*Olsen*), Fifi Dorsay (*Fifi*), Marjorie White, T. Roy Barnes, Bela Lugosi, Humphrey Bogart, Joyce Compton, Jesse De Vorska, Charles Judels. *Prod:* Fox. 72m.

YELLOW TICKET (GB: THE YELLOW PASSPORT) (1931). A Russian girl is forced to become a prostitute in pre-Revolutionary Russia, and her life is jeopardised by her love for a young British journalist for whom she has given information concerning the social ills of her country. *Sc:* Jules Furthman, Guy Bolton (play by Michael Morton). *Ph:* James Wong Howe. *Ed:* Jack Murray. *With* Elissa Landi (*Marya Kalish*), Lionel Barrymore (*Baron Andrey*), Laurence Olivier (*Julien Rolphe*), Walter Byron (*Prince Nikolai*), Sarah Padden (*Mother Kalish*), Arnold Koeff, Mischa Auer, Boris Karloff, Rita La Roy, Edwin Maxwell, Alex Mellish. *Prod:* Raoul Walsh for Fox. 88m.

WILD GIRL (GB: SALOMY JANE) (1932). Pioneering drama about a young girl on the run with a man who killed his sister's seducer. *Sc:* Doris Anderson, Edwin Justis Mayer (from Brett Harte story "Salomy Jane"). *Ph:* Norbert Brodine. *Ed:* Jack Murray. *With* Charles Farrell (*The Stranger*), Joan Bennett (*Salomy Jane*), Ralph Bellamy (*Jack Marbury*), Eugene Pallette (*Yuba Bill*), Irving Pichel (*Rufe Waters*), Minna Gombell, Sarah Padden, Willard Robertson, Ferdinand Munier, Louise Beavers, Morgan Wallace, James Durkin, Murdock MacQuarrie, Alphonse Ethier, Marilyn Harris, Delma Watson, Carmencita Johnson. *Prod:* Fox. 78m.

ME AND MY GAL (Also known as PIER 13) (1932). A young policeman romances a waitress whose sister falls for a hood. *Sc:* Arthur Kober (story by Barry Connors, Philip Klein). *Ph:* Norbert Brodine. *Art Dir:* Gordon Wiles. *Ed:* Jack Murray. *With* Spencer Tracy (*Dan*), Joan Bennett (*Helen*), Marion Burns (*Kate*), George Walsh (*Duke*), J. Farrell MacDonald (*Pop*), Noel Madison, Henry B. Walthall, Bert Hanlon, Adrian Morris, George Chandler. *Prod:* Fox. 78m.

SAILOR'S LUCK (1933). Romantic comedy about a homeless but spirited girl who meets a tough sailor. *Sc:* Marguerite Roberts, Charlotte Miller (from their story). *Ph:* Arthur Miller. *Ed:* Jack Murray. *With* James Dunn (*Jimmy Harrigan*), Sally Eilers (*Sally Brent*), Sammy Cohen (*Barnacle Benny*), Frank Morgan (*Bilge*), Victor Jory (*Baron Darrow*), Esther Muir, Will Stanton, Curley Wright, Jerry Mandy, Lucien Littlefield, Buster Phelps, Frank Atkinson. *Prod:* Fox. 78m.

THE BOWERY (1933). Rugged tale of the Gay Nineties featuring George Raft as the legendary Steve Brodie who is reputed to have jumped off Brooklyn Bridge. *Sc:* Howard Estabrook, James Gleason (novel by Michael Simmons, Bessie Rogow). *Ph:* Barney McGill. *Art Dir:* Richard Day. *Ed:* Allen McNeil. *Mus:* Alfred Newman. *With* George Raft (*Steve Brodie*), Wallace Beery (*Chuck Connors*), Jackie Cooper (*Swipes*), Fay

George Raft's attention wanders from Fay Wray in this scene from THE BOWERY

Wray (*Lucy Calhoun*), Pert Kelton (*Trixie*), George Walsh, Oscar Apfel, Ferdinand Munier, Herman Bing, Harold Huber, Fletcher Norton, Lillian Harmer, Tammany Young, Esther Muir, John Bleifer, John Kelly. *Prod:* William Goetz, Raymond Griffith for United Artists. 90m.

GOING HOLLYWOOD (1933). Girl loves crooner, and wins him from rival by making a brilliant Hollywood *début*. *Sc:* Donald Ogden Stewart (story by Frances Marion). *Ph:* George Folsey. *Ed:* Frank Sullivan. *With* Marion Davies (*Sylvia Bruce*), Bing Crosby (*Bill Williams*), Fifi Dorsay (*Lili*), Stuart Erwin (*Ernest P. Baker*), Ned Sparks (*Conroy*), Patsy Kelly, Bobby Watson, The Three Radio Rogues. *Prod:* Walter Walsh for Cosmopolitan–M-G-M. 80m.

UNDER PRESSURE (1935). The final Flagg/Quirt episode finds them heading a gang of "sand hogs" digging a tunnel under the East River between brawls. *Sc:* Borden Chase, Noel Pierce, Lester

Cole (story by Edward Doherty, Borden Chase). *Ph:* Hal Mohr. *Mus:* Louis De Francesco. *With* Edmund Lowe (*Shocker*), Victor McLaglen (*Jumbo*), Florence Rice (*Pat*), Marjorie Rambeau (*Amy*), Charles Bickford (*Nipper Moran*), Sig Rumann, Roger Imhoff, George Walsh, Warner Richmond, Jack Wallace, James Donlan. *Prod:* Fox. 69m.

BABY-FACE HARRINGTON (1935). A timid clerk with an inferiority complex and nagging wife becomes a hero by catching a crook. *Sc:* Nunnally Johnson, Edwin H. Knopf (play "Something to Brag About" by Edgar Selwyn, William Le Baron). *Ph:* Oliver T. Marsh. *Art Dir:* Cedric Gibbons, Howard Campbell, Edwin B. Willis. *Ed:* William S. Gray. *Mus:* Sam Wineland. *With* Charles Butterworth (*Willie Harrington*), Una Merkel (*Millicent Harrington*), Harvey Stephens (*Ronald Lawford*), Eugene Pallette (*Uncle Harry*), Nat Pendleton (*Rocky Bannister*), Ruth Selwyn, Donald Meek, Dorothy Libaire, Edward Nugent, Robert Livingston, Stanley Field, Raymond Brown, Wade Boteler, Bradley Page, Richard Carle, G. Pat Collins, Claude Gillingwater. *Prod:* Edgar Selwyn for M-G-M. 61m.

EVERY NIGHT AT EIGHT (1935). Musical romance detailing the rise to fame of an amateur band-leader and three girl singers. *Sc:* Gene Towne, Graham Baker (from story "Three on a Mike" by Stanley Garvey). *Ph:* James Van Trees. *Art Dir:* Alex Toluboff. *Ed:* W. Don Hayes. *Mus:* Sam Wineland. *With* George Raft (*Tops Cardona*), Alice Faye (*Dixie Foley*), Frances Langford (*Susan Moore*), Patsy Kelly (*Daphne O'Connor*), Walter Catlett (*Col. Bayes*), The Three Radio Rogues, Boothe Howard, Harry Barris, Eddie Conrad, Herman Bing, John H. Dillson, Louise Carver, Florence Gill. *Prod:* Walter Wanger for Wanger-Paramount. 80m.

KLONDIKE ANNIE (1936). Comedy-drama with Mae West on the run for murder, escaping to the Klondike by ship during the Gold Rush and becoming romantically involved with the skipper of the boat. *Sc:* Mae West, Marion Morgan, George B. Dowell, Frank Mitchell Dazey. *Ph:* George Clemens. *Art Dir:* Hans Dreier, Bernard Herzbrun, *Ed:* Stuart Heisler. *Mus:* Sam Coslow. *With* Mae West (*The Frisco Doll*), Victor McLaglen (*Capt. Bull Brackett*), Philip Reed (*Inspector Jack Forrest*), Helen Jerome Eddy (*Sister Annie Alden*), Harry Beresford (*Brother Bowser*), Harold Huber, Lucille Webster Gleason, Conway Tearle, Esther Howard, Soo Yong, Chester Gan, Gene Austin, Tetsu Komai, James Burke, Ted Oliver, George Walsh, John Rogers. *Prod:* William LeBaron for Paramount. 80m.

BIG BROWN EYES (1936). Detective and a manicurist solve a jewel robbery and expose an insurance racket. *Sc:* Raoul Walsh, Bert Hanlon (stories "Big Brown Eyes" and "Hahsit Babe" by James Edward Grant). *Ph:* George Clemens. *Art Dir:* Alexander Toluboff. *Ed:* Robert Simpson. *Mus:* Boris Moross. *With* Cary Grant (*Danny Barr*), Joan Bennett (*Eve Fallon*), Walter Pidgeon (*Richard Morey*), Lloyd Nolan (*Russ Cortig*), Alan Baxter (*Carey Butler*), Marjorie Gateson, Isabel Jewell, Douglas Fowley, Henry Kleinbach/Brandon, Joseph Sawyer, Harold Brown, Dorothy Casey, Edwin Maxwell, Sam Flint, Joe

Piccori, Charles Wilson, Charles Martin, Ed Jones, Francis McDonald, Eddie Conrad. *Prod:* Walter Wanger for Paramount. 77m.

SPENDTHRIFT (1936). Adventuress drains millionaire who divorces her, makes good again and marries his true love. *Sc:* Raoul Walsh, Bert Hanlon (story by Eric Hatch). *Ph:* Leon Shamroy. *Art Dir:* Alexander Toluboff. *Ed:* Robert Simpson. *Mus:* Boris Moross. *With* Henry Fonda (*Townsend Middleton*), Pat Paterson (*Boots O'Connell*), Mary Brian (*Sally Barnaby*), George Barbier (*Uncle Morton*), Edward Brophy (*Bill McGuire*), Jill Brewster, Halliwell Hobbes, Spencer Charters, Richard Carle, J. M. Kerrigan, Jerry Mandy, Greta Meyer, Micki Morita. *Prod:* Walter Wanger for Paramount. 70m.

O.H.M.S. (U.S.: YOU'RE IN THE ARMY NOW) (1937). A smalltime crook joins the British Army to evade the police, and dies a hero's death. *Sc:* Austin Melford, Bryan Wallace (story by Lester Samuels, Ralph Bettinson). *Ph:* Roy Kellino. *Art Dir:* Edward Carrick. *Ed:* Charles Saunders. *Mus:* Louis Levy. *With* Wallace Ford (*Jimmy Tracey*), John Mills (*Lance Corporal Bert Dawson*), Anna Lee (*Sally*), Grace Bradley (*Jean*), Frank Cellier (*Sgt-Major Briggs*), Peter Croft, Robertson Hare, Arthur Chesney, Lawrence Anderson, Frederick Leister, Leon von Porkorny, Athol Fleming, Arthur Seaton, Peter Evan Thomas, Ernest Jay, Richard Gray, Cyril Smith, Arnold Bell, Henry Hallat, Pat Vyvyvan, Donald Gadd, Leslie Roberts, Denis Cowles. *Prod:* Gaumont British. Filmed in England. 87m.

Barrack-room humour between Wallace Ford and a young John Mills (in vest) in Walsh's O.H.M.S.

JUMP FOR GLORY (U.S.: WHEN THIEF MEETS THIEF) (1937). A gentleman burglar becomes involved in blackmail and murder when he falls for one of his female victims. *Sc:* John Meehan (from novel "Jump for Glory" by Gordon McConnell). *Ph:* Cedric Williams, Victor Armenise. *Art Dir:* Edward Carrick. *Ed:* Conrad von Molo. *Mus:* Percival Mackey. *With* Douglas Fairbanks Jr. (*Ricky Morgan*), Valerie Hobson (*Gloria Howard*), Alan Hale (*Jim Dial, alias Col. Fane*), Jack Melford (*Thompson*), Anthony Ireland (*Sir Timothy Haddon*), Barbara Everest, Edward Rigby, Basil Radford, Esme Percy, Leo Genn, Ian Fleming, Frank Birch. *Prod:* Marcel Hellman for Criterion Film Prod. Filmed in England. 90m.

ARTISTS AND MODELS (1937). Romantic comedy dealing with the problems involved in selecting a Queen for a Charity Ball. *Sc:* Walter De Leon, Francis Martin (story by Sid Herzig, Gene

Thackeray adapted by Eve Greene, Harlan Ware). *Ph:* Victor Milner. *Art Dir:* Hans Dreier, Robert Usher. *Ed:* Ellsworth Hoagland. *Mus:* Ted Koehler, Victor Young, Harold Arlen, Frederick Hollander, Leo Robin. *With* Jack Benny (*Mac Brewster*), Ida Lupino (*Paula Sewell*), Richard Arlen (*Alan Tiwnsend*), Gail Patrick (*Cynthia Wentworth*), Ben Blue (*Jupiter Pluvius II*), Judy Canova, Cecil Cunningham, Hedda Hopper, Donald Meek, Kathryn Kay, Sandra Stone, The Yacht Club Boys, Martha Raye, Louis Armstrong, Andre Kostelanetz, Peter Arno, Russell Patterson and his Marionettes, McClelland Barclay, John La Gatta, Arthur William Brown, Rube Goldberg, Connie Boswell, Mary Shepher, Gloria Wheedon, Madelon Grey, Alan Birmingham, Dell Henderson, Harry Hayden, Antrim Short, Alexander Pollard, Virginia Brissac, John Marshall, Henry Johnson, Harry Johnson, Jack Story, Harvey Poirer, Pat Moran, Jack McAfee, Irene McAfee, Elsa Connor, Nick Lukats, Ethel Clayton, Gloria Williams, Jack Daley, David Newell, Carl Harbaugh, Little Billy, Dale Armstrong, Arthur Shank, Edward Earle, James G. Spacey, Alphonse Martel, Jane Weir, Howard Hickman, Reginald Simpson, Jerry Jerome, Bernie La Mont, Bert Le Baron. *Prod:* Adolph Zukor, Lewis E. Gensler for Paramount. 97m.

HITTING A NEW HIGH (1937). An impresario tries to train a new discovery as an opera singer, but she returns to working in cabaret. *Sc:* John Twist, Gertrude Purcell (story by Robert Harari, Maxwell Shane). *Ph:* J. Roy Hunt. *Art Dir:* Van Nest Polglase. *Ed:* Desmond Marquette. *Mus:* Andre Kostelanetz. *With* Lily Pons (*Suzette*), John Howard (*Jimmy*), Jack Oakie (*Corny*), Eric Blore (*Cosmo*), Eduardo Ciannelli (*Mazzini*), Jack Arnold, Vinton Haworth, Luis Alberni, Leonard Carey. *Prod:* Jesse L. Lasky for RKO. 85m.

COLLEGE SWING (GB: SWING, TEACHER, SWING) (1938). A musical spoof of college customs. *Sc:* Walter De Leon, Francis Martin, Frederick Hazlitt Brennan (story by Brennan, idea by Ted Lesser). *Ph:* Victor Milner. *Art Dir:* Hans Dreier, Ernst Fegte. *Ed:* LeRoy Stone. *Mus:* Boris Moross. *With* George Burns (*George Jonas*), Gracie Allen (*Gracie Alden*), Martha Raye (*Mabel*), Bob Hope (*Bub Brady*), Edward Everett Horton (*Hubert Dash*), Florence George, Ben Blue, Betty Grable, Jackie Coogan, John Payne, Cecil Cunningham, Robert Cummings, E. C. Ennis, The Slate Brothers, Jerry Colonna, Charles Colonna, Charles Trowbridge, Jerry Bergen, Tully Marshall, Edward Le Saint. *Prod:* Adolph Zukor, Lewis Gensler for Paramount. 85m.

ST. LOUIS BLUES (1939). A Broadway star deserts her tyrannical manager and joins a show-boat troupe. *Sc:* John C. Moffitt, Malcom Stuart Boylan (story by William Rankin, Eleanor Griffin, adapted by Frederick Hazlitt Brennan). *Ph:* Theodor Sparkhul. *Art Dir:* Hans Dreier. *Ed:* William Shea. *Mus:* Frank Loesser. *With* Dorothy Lamour (*Norma Malone*), Lloyd Nolan (*Dave Guerney*), Tito Guizar (*Ramos*), Jerome Cowan (*Ivar De Brett*), Jessie Ralph (*Aunt Tibbie*), Maxine Sullivan, Mary Parker, Cliff Nazarro, William Frawley, The Hall Johnson Choir. *Prod:* Jeff Lazarus for Paramount. 87m.

THE ROARING TWENTIES (1939). Prohibition saga with Cagney and Bogart in rival mobs fighting one another whilst both trying to outwit the D.A., who was a boyhood chum. *Sc:* Jerry Wald, Richard Macaulay, Robert Rossen (story by Mark Hellinger). *Ph:* Ernest Haller. *Art Dir:* Max Parker. *Ed:* Jack Killifer. *Mus:* Leo Forbstein. *With* James Cagney (*Eddie Bartlett*), Humphrey Bogart (*George Hally*), Gladys George (*Panama Smith*), Jeffrey Lynn (*Lloyd Hart*), Frank McHugh (*Danny Green*), Paul Kelly, Ed Keane, Elizabeth Risdon, Joe Sawyer, Joseph Crehan, George Meeker, John Hamilton, Robert Elliot, Eddie Chandler, Max Wagner, Vera Lewis. *Prod:* Mark Hellinger, Hal B. Wallis for Warner Bros. 106m.

DARK COMMAND (1940). Action-packed Western about one man standing up against Quantrill's Raiders during their post Civil War binge of terror. *Sc:* Grover Jones, Lionel Houser, F. Hugh Herbert (novel by W. R. Burnett). *Ph:* Jack Marta. *Art Dir:* John Victor MacKay. *Ed:* Murray Seldeen. *Mus:* Victor Young. *With* John Wayne (*Bob Setton*), Claire Trevor (*Marie McCloud*), Walter Pidgeon (*William Quantrill*), Roy Rogers (*Fletch McCloud*), George Hayes (*Doc Grunch*), Porter Hall, Marjorie Main, Trevor Bardette, Raymond Walburn, Joe Sawyer, J. Farrell MacDonald, Helen MacKellar. *Prod:* Sol C. Siegel for Republic Pictures. 93m.

THEY DRIVE BY NIGHT (GB: ROAD TO FRISCO) (1940). Drama of competition in the trucking business leading to violence and murder. *Sc:* Jerry Wald, Richard Macaulay (novel by A. E. Bezzerides). *Ph:* Arthur Edeson. *Art Dir:* John Hughes. *Ed:* Thomas Richards. *Mus:* Andre Deutsch. *With* Ann Sheridan (*Cassie Hartley*), Humphrey Bogart (*Paul Fabrini*), George Raft (*Joe Fabrini*), Ida Lupino (*Lana Olsen*), Alan Hale (*Ed Olsen*), Gale Page, Roscoe Karnes, John Litel, Charles Halton, George Tobias, Henry O'Neill, Joyce Compton, Matt McHugh, John Hamilton, Paul Hurst, John Ridgeley, George Lloyd, Pedro Regas, William Haade, Norman Willis, Joe Devlin, Vera Lewis, Dick Wessell, Frank Faylen, Charles Wilson, Eddie Acuff. *Prod:* Hal B. Wallis for Warner Bros. *Assoc. Prod:* Mark Hellinger. 97m.

HIGH SIERRA (1941). Disillusioned with freedom, a former big time gangster plans one last job, but is hounded to death in the High Sierras. *Sc:* John Huston, W. R. Burnett (novel by W. R. Burnett). *Ph:* Tony Gaudio. *Art Dir:* Ted Smith. *Ed:* Jack Killifer. *Mus:* Adolph Deutsch. *With* Humphrey Bogart (*Roy Earle*), Ida Lupino (*Marie*), Alan Curtis (*Babe*), Arthur Kennedy (*Red*), Joan Leslie (*Velma*), Henry Hull, Henry Travers, Elizabeth Risdon, Jerome Cowan, Minna Gombell, Barton MacLane, Cornel Wilde, Donald MacBride, Paul Harvey, Isabel Jewell, Willie Best, Spencer Charters, Louis Jean Heydt, John Eldredge, Sam Hayes, Clancy Cooper, George Meeker, Robert Strange, Zero. *Prod:* Jack L. Warner, Hal B. Wallis for Warner Bros. 110m.

THE STRAWBERRY BLONDE (1941). James Cagney as a dentist hopelessly in love with a married woman (whose husband he hates) and ignoring his true love. Re-make of a 1933 Gary Cooper film. *Sc:* Julius J. Epstein, Philip G. Epstein (play by James Hagan). *Ph:* James Wong Howe. *Art Dir:* Robert Haas. *Ed:* William Holmes. *Mus:* Heinz Roemheld. *With* James Cagney (*Biff Grimes*), Olivia De Havilland (*Amy Lind*), Rita Hayworth (*Virginia Brush*), Jack Carson (*Hugo Barnstead*), Alan Hale (*Old Man Grimes*), George Tobias, Una O'Connor, George Reeves, George Humbert, Lucile Fairbanks, Edward McNamara, Russell Hicks, Dick Wessel, Nell Lynd, Herbert Heywood. *Prod:* Jack L. Warner, Hal B. Wallis for Warner Bros. *Assoc. Prod:* William Cagney. 99m. Previous version *One Sunday Afternoon* (1933, Stephen Roberts), and later musical re-make *One Sunday Afternoon* (1948, Raoul Walsh).

MANPOWER (1941). Two high tension wire repairers fight over Marlene Dietrich in this action drama. *Sc:* Richard Macaulay, Jerry Wald. *Ph:* Ernest Haller. *Art Dir:* Max Parker. *Ed:* Ralph Dawson. *Mus:* Adolph Deutsch. *With* Edward G. Robinson (*Hank MacHenry*), George Raft (*Johnny Marshall*), Marlene Dietrich (*Fay Duval*), Alan Hale (*Jumbo Wells*), Frank McHugh (*Omaha*), Eve Arden, Barton MacLane, Ward Bond, Walter Catlett, Egon Brecher, Joyce Compton, Lucia Carroll, Barbara Pepper, Dorothy Appleby, Joseph Crehan, Ben Walden, Cliff Clark, Faye Emerson, Anthony Quinn, Carl Harbaugh, Barbara Land, Isabel Withers, James Flavin, Chester Clute, Nella Walker, Harry Holman, Beal Wong, Murray Alper, Dick Wessel, Jane Randolph and Lynn Baggett. *Prod:* Hal B. Wallis for Warner Bros. 104m.

A drunken Edward G. Robinson toasts Marlene Dietrich and George Raft in Walsh's MANPOWER

THEY DIED WITH THEIR BOOTS ON (1941). A sympathetic portrayal of General George Armstrong Custer and his last stand with the Seventh Cavalry at Little Big Horn. *Sc:* Wally Kline, Aeneas MacKenzie. *Ph:* Bert Glennon. *Art Dir:* John Hughes. *Ed:* William Holmes. *Mus:* Max Steiner. *With* Errol Flynn (*George Armstrong Custer*), Olivia De Havilland (*Elizabeth Bacon*), Ned Sharp (*Arthur Kennedy*), Charley Grapewin (*California Joe*), Gene Lockhart (*Samuel Bacon, Esq.*), Anthony Quinn, Stanley Ridges, John Litel, Walter Hampden, Sydney Greenstreet, Regis Toomey, Hattie McDaniel, George P. Huntley Jnr., Frank Wilcox, Ian MacDonald, Frank Ferguson, Joe Sawyer, Lane Chandler, Gig Young (Byron Barr), Rene Riano, John Ridgeley, Ray Teal, Eleanor Parker, Irving Bacon, Chuck Hamilton, Minor Watson, Selmar Jackson. *Prod:* Hal B. Wallis for Warner Bros. *Assoc. Prod:* Robert Fellows. 140m.

Errol Flynn (centre) and Joe Sawyer (right) report to Frank Wilcox as the cadets prepare for action in THEY DIED WITH THEIR BOOTS ON

DESPERATE JOURNEY (1942). Entertaining espionage drama with Flynn leading a group of men behind enemy lines. *Sc:* Arthur T. Horman. *Ph:* Bert Glennon. *Art Dir:* Carl Jules Weyl. *Ed:* Rudi Fehr. *Mus:* Max Steiner. *With* Errol Flynn (*Lieut. Terence Forbes*), Ronald Reagan (*Johnny Hammond*), Nancy Coleman (*Kaethe Brahms*), Raymond Massey (*Major Otto Baumeister*), Alan Hale (*Sgt. Kirk Edwards*), Arthur Kennedy, Sig Ruman, Patrick O'Moore, Ronald Sinclair, Louis Arco, Charles Irwin, Richard Fraser, Lester Matthews, Robert O. Davis, Walter Brooke, Harry Lewis, Don Phillips, Henry Victor, Bruce Lester, Ilka Gruning, Albert Basserman, Else Basserman, Felix Basch. *Prod:* Hal B. Wallis for Warner Bros. 107m.

GENTLEMAN JIM (1942). The story of the World Heavyweight Boxing Champion. *Sc:* Vincent Laurence, Horace McCoy (based on the life of James J. Corbett). *Ph:* Sid Hickox. *Art Dir:* Ted Smith. *Ed:* Jack Killifer.. *Mus:* Heinz Roemheld. *With* Errol Flynn (*James J. Corbett*), Alexis Smith (*Victoria Ware*), Jack Carson (*Walter Lowrie*), Alan Hale

(*Pat Corbett*), John Loder (*Clinton De-Witt*), William Frawley, Minor Watson, Ward Bond, Madeleine LeBeau, Rhys Williams, Arthur Shields, Dorothy Vaughan, James Flavin, Pat Flaherty, Wallis Clark, Marilyn Phillips, Art Foster, Edwin Stanley, Henry O'Hara, Frank Mayo, Carl Harbaugh, Fred Kelsey, Sammy Stein, Lon McAllister. *Prod:* Robert Buckner for Warner Bros. 104m.

BACKGROUND TO DANGER (1943). Minor espionage melodrama with intrigue and counterplots as Lorre and Greenstreet meet as opponents in Turkey. *Sc:* W. R. Burnett, Hugh Cummings (from Eric Ambler novel). *Ph:* Tony Gaudio. *Art Dir:* Hugh Reticker, Casey Roberts. *Ed:* Jack Killifer. *Mus:* Frederick Hollander. *With* George Raft (*Joe Barton*), Sydney Greenstreet (*Colonel Robinson*), Peter Lorre (*Zaleshoff*), Brenda Marshall (*Tamara*), Osa Massen, Kurt Katch, Daniel Ocko, Frank Puglia, Turhan Bey, Pedro de Cordoba, Willard Robertson. *Prod:* Jerry Wald for Warner Bros. 80m.

NORTHERN PURSUIT (1943). German-born Mountie Errol Flynn foils a Nazi attempt to destroy vital targets in Canada. *Sc:* Frank Gruber, Alvah Bessie, Hugh Cummings (story by Leslie T. White). *Ph:* Sid Hickox. *Art Dir:* Leo K. Kuter, Casey Roberts. *Ed:* Jack Killifer. *Montage:* Don Siegel. *Mus:* Adolph Deutsch. *With* Errol Flynn (*Steve Wagner*), Julie Bishop (*Laura McBain*), Helmut Dantine (*Hugo von Keller*), John Ridgeley (*Jim Austen*), Gene Lockhart (*Ernst*), Tom Tully, Bernard Nedell, Warren Douglas, Monte Blue, Tom Fadden, Alec Craig, Rose Higgins, Richard Alden, John Royce, Joe Herrera, Carl Harbaugh, Jack Lambert. *Prod:* Jack Chertok for Warner Bros. 94m.

UNCERTAIN GLORY (1944). Flynn as a French criminal who turns into a patriotic saboteur willing to die for his country. *Sc:* Laszlo Vadnay, Max Brand (story by Joe May, Laszlo Vadnay). *Ph:* Sid Hickox. *Art Dir:* Robert Haas, Walter Tilford. *Ed:* George Amy. *Mus:* Adolph Deutsch. *With* Errol Flynn (*Jean Picard*), Paul Lukas (*Marcel Bonet*), Jean Sullivan (*Marianne*), Lucille Watson (*Madame Maret*), Faye Emerson (*Louise*), James Flavin, Douglas Dumbrille, Dennis Hoey, Sheldon Leonard, Odette Myrtil, Francis Pierlot, Wallis Clark, Victor Kilian, Ivan Triesault, Van Antwerp, Art Smith, Carl Harbaugh, Mary Servess, Charles La Torre, Pedro de Cordoba, Bobby Walberg, Erskine Sanford, Felix Basch, Joel Friedkin. *Prod:* Robert Buckner for Warner Bros. 102m.

OBJECTIVE BURMA (1945). Controversial war story about a paratroop mission in Burma; a good film in its own right in spite of British protests at distortion of the American war record in Burma. *Sc:* Ranald MacDougall and Lester Cole (story by Alvah Bessie). *Ph:* James Wong Howe. *Art Dir:* Ted Smith, Jack McConaghy. *Ed:* George Amy. *Mus:* Franz Waxman. *With* Errol Flynn (*Capt. Nelson*), William Prince (*Lieut. Jacobs*), James Brown (*Sgt. Treacy*), Warner Anderson (*Colonel Carter*), George Tobias (*Gabby Gordon*), Henry Hull, John Alvin, Stephen Richards (Mark Stevens), Dick Erdman, Anthony Caruso, Hugh Beaumont, John Whitney, Joel Allen, Buddy Yarus, Frank Tang, William Hudson, Rod Red Wing, Asit Koomar, Kit Carson, John Sheridan, Lester Matthews. *Prod:* Jerry Wald for Warner Bros. 142m.

SALTY O'ROURKE (1945). Racetrack drama about gamblers and crooked jockeys. *Sc:* Milton Holmes. *Ph:* Theodor Sparkhul. *Art Dir:* Hans Dreier, Haldane Douglas, John McNeil. *Ed:* William Shea. *Mus:* Robert Emmet Dolan. With Alan Ladd (*Salty O'Rourke*), Gail Russell (*Barbara Brooks*), Stanley Clements (*Johnny Cate Stanley*), William Demarest (*Smitty*), Bruce Cabot (*Doc Baxter*), Spring Byington, Darryl Hickman, Rex Williams, Don Zelaya, Marjorie Woodworth, David Clyde, Lester Matthews, Jean Willes. Prod: E. D. Leshin for Paramount. 100m.

THE HORN BLOWS AT MIDNIGHT (1945). Screwball comedy with Jack Benny as an angel of doom sent to earth to sound his trumpet. *Sc:* Sam Hellman, James V. Kern (idea by Aubrey Wisberg). *Ph:* Sid Hickox. *Art Dir:* Hugh Reticker, Clarence Steensen. *Ed:* Irene Morra. *Mus:* Franz Waxman. *With* Jack Benny (*The Angel Athanael*), Alexis Smith (*Elizabeth*), Dolores Moran (*Fran*), Allyn Joslyn (*Osidro*), Reginald Gardiner (*Archie Dexter*), Guy Kibbee, John Alexander, Franklin Pangborn, Margaret Dumont, Bobby Blake, Ethel Griffies, Isobel Elsom, James Burke, Harry Morgan, Monte Blue, Jack J. Ford, Emma Dunn, Paul Harvey, Truman Bradley, Mike Mazurki, John Brown, Murray Alper, Pat O'Moore, Harry Rosenthal. *Prod:* Mark Hellinger for Warner Bros. 80m.

THE MAN I LOVE (1946). Singer on a visit home becomes involved with a nightclub owner. *Sc:* Catherine Turney, Jo Pagano (novel by Maritta Wolff). *Ph:* Sid Hickox. *Art Dir:* Stanley Fleischer, Eddie Edwards. *Ed:* Owen Marks. *Mus:* Max Steiner. *With* Ida Lupino (*Petey Brown*), Robert Alda (*Nicky Toresca*), Andrea King (*Sally Otis*), Martha Vickers (*Virginia Brown*), Bruce Bennett (*Sam Thomas*), Alan Hale, Dolores Moran, John Ridgely, Don McGuire, Warren Douglas, Craig Stevens, James Dobbs, William Edmunds, Patrick Griffin. *Prod:* Arnold Albert for Warner Bros. 96m.

PURSUED (1947). The first "psychological" Western dealing with a Spanish-American war veteran hunting down his father's killer. *Sc:* Niven Busch. *Ph:* James Wong Howe. *Art Dir:* Ted Smith, Jack McConaghy. *Ed:* Christian Nyby. *Mus:* Max Steiner. *With* Robert Mitchum (*Jeb Rand*), Teresa Wright (*Thorley Callum*), Judith Anderson (*Medora Callum*), Dean Jagger (*Grant Callum*), Alan Hale (*Jake Dingle*), John Rodney, Harry Carey Jnr., Clifton Young, Ernest Severn, Charles Bates, Peggy Miller, Elmer Ellingwood. Jack Montgomery, Norman Jolley, Lane Chandler, Ian MacDonald, Tom D'Andrea, Ian Wolfe, Tom Fadden and Virginia Brissac. *Prod:* Milton Sperling for United States Pictures. 101m.

CHEYENNE (1947). Gambler hired to capture a notorious outlaw becomes involved with the outlaw's wife. Alternative title for U.S. TV is THE WYOMING KID. *Sc:* Alan Le May, Thames Williamson (novel by Paul I. Wellman). *Ph:* Sid Hickox. *Art Dir:* Ted Smith, Jack McConaghy. *Ed:* Christian Nyby. *Mus:* Max Steiner. *With* Dennis Morgan (*James Wylie*), Jane Wyman (*Ann Kincaid*), Janis Paige (*Emily Carson*), Bruce Bennett (*Ed Landers*), Arthur Kennedy (*Sundance Kid*), Alan Hale, John Ridgly, Barton MacLane, Tom Tyler, Bob Steele, John Campion, John

Errol Flynn and Ann Sheridan aid Thomas Mitchell after a treacherous attack in SILVER RIVER

Alvin, Monte Blue, Ann O'Neal, Tom Fadden, Britt Wood. *Prod:* Robert Buckner for Warner Bros. 100m.

SILVER RIVER (1948). Errol Flynn Western with Flynn in an unsympathetic role as a power-hungry rancher who alienates his pals through his grasping schemes. *Sc:* Stephen Longstreet, Harriet Frank Jnr. (novel by Longstreet). *Ph:* Sid Hickox. *Art Dir:* Ted Smith, William G. Wallace. *Ed:* Alan Crosland Jnr. *Mus:* Max Steiner. *With* Errol Flynn (*Mike McComb*), Ann Sheridan (*Georgia Moore*), Thomas Mitchell (*John Plato Beck*), Bruce Bennett (*Stanley Moore*), Tom D'Andrea (*"Pistol" Porter*), Barton MacLane, Monte Blue, Jonathan Hale, Alan Bridge, Art Baker, Arthur Space, Joseph Crehan. *Prod:* Owen Crump for Warner Bros. 110m.

FIGHTER SQUADRON (1948). Trite war drama picturing the aerial and ground conflict of men under pressure. *Sc:* Seton I. Miller, Martin Rackin. *Ph:* Sid Hickox, Wilfred M. Cline. *Art Dir:* Ted Smith, Lyle B. Reifsnider. *Ed:* Christian Nyby. *Mus:* Max Steiner. *With* Edmond O'Brien (*Major Ed Hardin*), Robert Stack (*Capt. Stu Hamilton*), John Rodney (*Col. Bill Brickley*), Tom D'Andrea (*Sgt. Dolan*), Henry Hull (*Gen. Mike McCready*), James Holden, Walter Reed, Sheppard Strudwick, Arthur Space, Jack Larsen, William McLean, Mickey McCardle, Rock Hudson. *Prod:* Seton I. Miller for Warner Bros. 96m.

ONE SUNDAY AFTERNOON (1948). Musical version of *The Strawberry Blonde* (1941), with Dennis Morgan in the James Cagney role as the dentist in love with a hard-boiled married dame, ignoring the genuine affection of his previous girl friend. *Sc:* Robert L. Richards (play by James Hagan). *Ph:* Sid Hickox, Wilfred M. Cline. *Art Dir:* Anton Grot, Fred M. McLean. *Ed:* Christian Nyby. *Mus:* Ralph Blane (arranged by David Buttolph). *With* Dennis Morgan (*Biff Grimes*), Dorothy Malone (*Amy Lind*), Janis Paige (*Virginia Brush*), Don DeFore (*Hugo Barnstead*), Ben Blue (*Nick*), Oscar O'Shea, Alan Hale Jnr., George Neise. *Prod:* Jerry Wald for Warner Bros. Technicolor. 90m. Made in 1933, as *One Sunday Afternoon* (*d.* Stephen Roberts) and in 1941 as *The Strawberry Blonde* (*d.* Raoul Walsh), both non-musical.

COLORADO TERRITORY (1949). Bad man McCrea escapes from prison but is forced to make a last stand in a valley with his faithful girl. *Sc:* John Twist, Edmund H. North (based on novel

"High Sierra" by W. R. Burnett). *Ph:* Sid Hickox. *Art Dir:* Ted Smith, Fred M. McLean. *Ed:* Owen Marks. *Mus:* David Buttolph. *With* Joel McCrea (*Wes McQueen*), Virginia Mayo (*Colorado Carson*), Dorothy Malone (*Julie Ann*), Henry Hull (*Winslow*), John Archer (*Reno Blake*), James Mitchell, Morris Ankrum, Basil Ruysdael, Frank Puglia, Ian Wolfe, Harry Woods, Houseley Stevenson, Victor Kilian, Oliver Blake. *Prod:* Anthony Veiller for Warner Bros. 94m. Previously made as *High Sierra* (1941, Raoul Walsh); later re-made as *I Died a Thousand Times* (1955, Stuart Heisler).

WHITE HEAT (1949). Classic case history of a ruthless, insane killer strongly played by Cagney, with powerful Freudian overtones. *Sc:* Ivan Goff, Ben Roberts (story by Virginia Kellogg). *Ph:* Sid Hickox. *Art Dir:* Edward Carrere, Fred M. McLean. *Ed:* Owen Marks. *Mus:* Max Steiner. *With* James Cagney (*Cody Jarrett*), Virginia Mayo (*Verna*), Edmond O'Brien (*Hank Fallon/Vic Pardo*), Margaret Wycherly (*Ma Jarrett*), Steve Cochran (*"Big Ed" Somers*), John Archer, Wally Cassell, Mickey Knox, Ian MacDonald, Fred Clark, Pat Collins, Paul Guilfoyle, Fred Cobey, Ford Rainey, Robert Osterloh. *Prod:* Louis F. Edelman for Warner Bros. 114m.

ALONG THE GREAT DIVIDE (1951). Western drama concerning the pursuit and capture of an escaped criminal in the desert. *Sc:* Walter Doniger, Lewis Meltzer (novel by Doniger). *Ph:* Sid Hickox. *Art Dir:* Edward Carrere, G. W. Berntsen. *Ed:* Thomas Reilly. *Mus:* David Buttolph. *With* Kirk Douglas (*Ken Merrick*), Virginia Mayo (*Ann Keith*), John Agar (*Billy Shear*), Walter Brennan (*Pop Keith*), Ray Teal (*Lou Gray*), Hugh Sanders, Morris Ankrum, James Anderson, Charles Meredith, Clem Survey. *Prod:* Anthony Veiller for Warner Bros. 88m.

CAPTAIN HORATIO HORNBLOWER (1951). Adaptation of C. S. Forester's novel about the naval victories and loves of the British sea captain during the Napoleonic wars. *Sc:* Ivan Goff, Ben Roberts, Aeneas MacKenzie (novel by C. S. Forester). *Ph:* Guy Green. *Art Dir:* Tom Morahan. *Ed:* Jack Harris. *Mus:* Robert Farnan. *With* Gregory Peck (*Captain Horatio Hornblower*), Virginia Mayo (*Lady Barbara Wellesley*), Robert Beatty (*Lieut. William Bush*), Terence Morgan (*Lieut. Gerard*), Moultrie Kelsall (*Lieut. Crystal*), James Kenney, James Robertson Justice, Richard Hearne, Michael Dolan, Sam Kydd, Stanley Baker, Richard Johnson, Howard Connell, Raymond Sherry, Jack Stewart, Stuart Pearless, Russell Waters, Alex Mango, Alan Tilvern, John Witty, Ingeborg Wells, Christopher Lee, Alexander Davion, Julio Monterde, Miguel Delgado, Derek Sydney, Michael Mellinger, Denis O'Dea, P. Knyaston Reeves, Basil Bartlett, Anthony Marlowe, Ronald Adam, Anthony Forwood, Michael Goodliffe, Eugene Deckers, Amy Veness, Arthur Gomez, Patrick Young, Andre Belhomme, Gavin Dyer, George Rodriguez, Robert Cawdron, Howard Lang. *Prod:* Gerry Mitchell for Warner Bros. Technicolor. 117m.

DISTANT DRUMS (1951). Western about a Seminole Indian uprising in the Florida swamp-lands. *Sc:* Niven Busch, Martin Rackin (story by Busch). *Ph:* Sid Hickox. *Art Dir:* Douglas Bacon,

William Wallace. *Ed:* Folmar Blangsted. *Mus:* Max Steiner. *With* Gary Cooper (*Capt. Quincey Wyatt*), Mari Aldon (*Judy Beckett*), Richard Webb (*Lieut. Richard Tufts*), Ray Teal (*Pte. Mohair*), Arthur Hunnicutt (*Monk*), George Walsh, Robert Barrat, Clancy Cooper. *Prod:* Milton Sperling for United States Pictures, Technicolor. 101m.

GLORY ALLEY (1952). A returning soldier tries to pick up the traces with an old girl friend in New Orleans. *Sc:* Art Cohn. *Ph:* William Daniels. *Art Dir:* Cedric Gibbons, M. Brown. *Ed:* Gene Ruggiero. *Mus:* George Stoll. *With* Ralph Meeker (*Socks Barbarrosa*), Leslie Caron (*Angela Evans*), Kurt Kasznar (*Gus Evans*), Gilbert Roland (*Peppi Donato*), Louis Armstrong (*Shadow Johnson*), John Indrisano, Pat Goldin, Mickey Little, Dick Simmons, Jack Teagarden, Dan Seymour, John McIntire, Pat Valentino, David MacMahon, George Garver, Larry J. Gates. *Prod:* Nicholas Nayfack for M-G-M. 79m.

THE WORLD IN HIS ARMS (1952). Brawling drama about fur traders bringing their cargoes safely to San Francisco in the days of sailing ships. *Sc:* Borden Chase (novel by Rex Beach). *Ph:* Russell Metty. *Art Dir:* Bernard Herzbrun, Alexander Golitzen. *Ed:* Frank Gross. *Mus:* Frank Skinner. *With* Gregory Peck (*Jonathan Clark*), Ann Blyth (*Countess Maria Selanova*), Anthony Quinn (*The Portugese*), John McIntire (*Deacon*), Andrea King (*Mamie*), Carl Esmond, Eugeneie Leontovich, Sig Ruman, Hans Conreid, Bryan Forbes, Rhys Williams, Bill Radovich, Gregory Gaye, Henry Kulky. *Prod:* Aaron Rosenberg for Universal. Technicolor. 104m.

THE LAWLESS BREED (1952). Whitewashed adventures of John Wesley Hardin. *Sc:* Bernard Gordon (story by William Alland). *Ph:* Irving Glassberg. *Art Dir:* Bernard Herzbrun, Richard Riedel, Russell A. Gausman, Oliver Emert. *Ed:* Frank Gross. *Mus:* Joseph Gershenson. *With* Rock Hudson (*John Wesley Hardin*), Julia Adams (*Rosie*), Mary Castle (*Jane Brown*), John McIntire (*J. G. Hardin; John Clements*), Hugh O'Brien (*Ike Hanley*), Race Gentry, Dennis Weaver, Forrest Lewis, Lee Van Cleef, Tom Fadden, Richard Garland, Glenn Strange, Michael Ansara, Bobbie Hay, Bob Anderson, Stephen Chase, William Pullen. *Prod:* William Alland for Universal. Colour. 83m.

BLACKBEARD THE PIRATE (1952). An attractive girl is held to ransom while Blackbeard the Pirate seeks a hidden fortune. *Sc:* Alan Le May (story by De Vallon Scott). *Ph:* William E. Snyder. *Art Dir:* Albert S. D'Agostino, Jack Okey, Darrell Silvers, John Sturtevant. *Ed:* Ralph Dawson. *Mus:* Victor Young. *With* Robert Newton (*Blackbeard*), Linda Darnell (*Edwina*), William Bendix (*Worley*), Keith Andes (*Maynard*), Torin Thatcher (*Morgan*), Irene Ryan, Alan Mowbray, Richard Egan, Skelton Knaggs, Dick Wessel, Anthony Caruso, Jack Lambert, Clint Dorrington, Tom Humphreys, Noel Drayton, Pat Flaherty. *Prod:* Edmund Grainger for RKO. Technicolor. 98m.

SEA DEVILS (1953). Yet another nautical drama starring Rock Hudson. *Sc:* Borden Chase (loosely based on novel by Victor Hugo). *Ph:* Wilkie Cooper. *Art Dir:* Wilfred Shingleton. *Ed:* John Seabourne. *Mus:* Richard Addinsell. *With*

Rock Hudson (*Gilliatt*), Yvonne De Carlo (*Odette*), Maxwell Reed (*Rantaine*), Denis O'Dea (*Lethierry*), Michael Goodliffe (*Ragan*), Bryan Forbes, Keith Pryott, Rene Poirer, Laurie Taylor, Reed de Rouen, Jacques Brunius, Michael Mulcaster, Gerard Oury, Ivor Barnard, Arthur Wontner. *Prod:* David E. Rose for Coronado Productions. Technicolor. 90m.

A LION IS IN THE STREETS (1953). Drama about the rise of a backwoods politician. *Sc:* Luther Davis (novel by Adria Locke Langley). *Ph:* Harry Stradling. *Art Dir:* Wiard Ihnen. *Ed:* George Amy. *Mus:* Franz Waxman. *With* James Cagney (*Hank Martin*), Barbara Hale (*Verity Wade*), Anne Francis (*Flamingo*), Warner Anderson (*Jules Bolduc*), John McIntire (*Jeb Brown*), James Millican, Mickey Simpson, Sara Haden, Ellen Corby, Jeanne Cagney, Lon Chaney Jnr., Frank McHugh, Larry Keating, Onslow Stevens. *Prod:* William Cagney for Warner Bros. Technicolor. 88m.

GUN FURY (1953). Rock Hudson pursues a lusty gunslinger who has kidnapped his *fiancée*. *Sc:* Roy Huggins, Ivan Wallace (novel by Kathleen B. Roberts and George Granger). *Ph:* Lester H. White. *Art Dir:* Ross Bellah, James Crowe. *Ed:* James Sweeney, Jerome Thomas. *Mus:* Mischa Bakaleinikoff. *With* Rock Hudson (*Ben Warren*), Donna Reed (*Jennifer Ballard*), Phil Carey (*Frank Slater*), Roberta Haynes (*Estella Morales*), Leo Gordon (*Jess Burgess*), Lee Marvin, Neville Brand, Ray Thomas, Robert Herron, Phil Rawlins, Forrest Lewis, John Cason, Don Carlos, Pat Hogan, Mel Welles, Post Park. *Prod:* Lewis J. Rachmil for Columbia. Technicolor. 83m.

SASKATCHEWAN (GB: O'ROURKE OF THE ROYAL MOUNTED) (1954). Mountie tries to quash a movement across the border by the Sioux Indians. *Sc:* Gil Doud. *Ph:* John Seitz. *Art Dir:* Bernard Herzbrun, Richard H. Riedel. *Ed:* Frank Gross. *Mus:* Joseph Gershenson. *With* Alan Ladd (*O'Rourke*), Shelley Winters (*Grace Markey*), Robert Douglas (*Inspector Benton*), J. Carrol Naish (*Batoche*), Hugh O'Brian (*Carl Smith*), Richard Long, Jay Silverheels, Lowell Gilmore, Antonio Moreno, George J. Lewis, Frank Chase, Anthony Caruso, John Cason, Henry Wills. *Prod:* Aaron Rosenberg for Universal. Technicolor. 87m.

BATTLE CRY (1955). Adaptation of Leon Uris's best-selling novel about the Marines, incorporating their romantic lives as did *The Naked and the Dead* (1957). *Sc:* Leon M. Uris (from own novel). *Ph:* Sid Hickox. *Art Dir:* John Beckman, William Wallace. *Ed:* William Ziegler. *Mus:* Max Steiner. *With* Van Heflin (*Major Huxley*), Aldo Ray (*Andy*), Mona Freeman (*Kathy*), Nancy Olson (*Pat*), James Whitmore (*Sergeant Mac*), Raymond Massey (*General Snips*), Tab Hunter, Dorothy Malone, Anne Francis, William Campbell, John Lupton, L. Q. Jones, Perry Lopez, Fess Parker, Jonas Applegarth, Tommy Cook, Felix Noriego, Susan Morrow, Carleton Young, Rhys Williams, Allyn McLerie, Gregory Walcott, Frank Ferguson, Sarah Selby, Willis Bouchey. *Prod:* Warner Bros. Warnercolor. CinemaScope. 149m.

THE TALL MEN (1955). Jane Russell comes between Gable and Ryan on a hazardous cattle drive. *Sc:* Sidney Boehm,

A kittenish Jane Russell distracts Clark Gable from his meat in Walsh's THE TALL MEN

Frank Nugent (novel by Clay Fisher). *Ph:* Leo Tover. *Art Dir:* Lyle R. Wheeler, Mark-Lee Kirk, Walter M. Scott, Chester Bayhi. *Ed:* Louis Loeffler. *Mus:* Victor Young. *With* Clark Gable (*Ben Allison*), Jane Russell (*Nella Turner*), Robert Ryan (*Nathan Stark*), Cameron Mitchell (*Clint Allison*), Juan Garcia (*Luis*), Harry Shannon, Emile Meyer, Steven Darrell, Will Wright, Robert Adler, J. Lewis Smith, Russell Simpson, Mae Marsh, Gertrude Graner, Tom Wilson, Tom Fadden, Dan White, Argentina Brunetti, Doris Kemper, Post Park, Carl Harbaugh. *Prod:* William Bacher and William B. Hawks for 20th Century-Fox. De Luxe Color. Cinema-Scope. 121m.

THE REVOLT OF MAMIE STOVER (1956). Drama essaying the machinations of an opportunistic dance hall hostess in Honolulu prior to and during Pearl Harbor. *Sc:* Sidney Boehm (novel by William Bradford Huie). *Ph:* Leo Tover. *Art Dir:* Lyle Wheeler, Mark-Lee Kirk, Walter M. Scott, Chester Bayhi. *Ed:* Louis Loeffler. *Mus:* Hugo Friedhofer. *With* Jane Russell (*Mamie Stover*), Richard Egan (*Jim*), Joan Leslie (*Annalee*), Agnes Moorehead (*Bertha Parchman*), Georgia Curtright (*Jackie*), Michael Pate, John Halloran, Naida Lani, Dorothy Gordon, Irene Bolton, Max Reid, Claire James, Margia Dean, Jack Mather, Anita Dane, Boyd 'Red' Morgan, Richard Coogan, Alan Reed, Eddie Firestone, Jean Willes, Leon Lontoc, Kathy Marlow, Merry Townsend, Sally Jo Todd, Margarita Camacho, Richard Collier, Carl Harbaugh, Mary Lou Clifford and Eugenia Paul. *Prod:* Buddy Adler for 20th Century-Fox. Eastmancolor De Luxe. CinemaScope. 93m.

THE KING AND FOUR QUEENS (1956). Comedy-drama with Gable battling with four beautiful women and their gun-toting mother-in-law for a prize of $100,000 in gold. *Sc:* Margaret Fitts, Richard Alan Simmons (story by Fitts). *Ph:* Lucien Ballard. *Art Dir:* Wiard Ihnen. *Ed:* David Brotherton (supervised by Louis Loeffler). *Mus:* Alex North. *With* Clark Gable (*Dan Kehoe*), Eleanor Parker (*Sabina*), Jo Van Fleet (*Ma MacDade*), Jean Willes (*Ruby*), Barbara Nichols (*Birdie*), Sara Shane (*Oralie*), Roy Roberts, Arthur Shields, Jay C. Flippen. *Prod:* David Hempstead for United Artists. Eastmancolor De Luxe. Cinema-Scope. 84m.

BAND OF ANGELS (1957). Gable as a Southern gentleman who marries a half-breed just prior to the Civil War. *Sc:* John Twist, Ivan Goff, Ben Roberts (novel by Robert Penn Warren). *Ph:* Lucien Ballard. *Art. Dir:* Franz Bachelin, William Wallace. *Ed:* Folmar Blangsted. *Mus:* Max Steiner. *With* Clark Gable (*Hamish Bond*), Yvonne De Carlo (*Amantha Starr*), Sidney Poitier (*Rau-ru*), Efrem Zimbalist Jnr. (*Ethan Sears*), Patrick Knowles (*Charles de Marigny*), Rex Reason, Torin Thatcher, Andrea King, Ray Teal, Russ Evans, Carolle Drake, Raymond Bailey, Tommie Moore, William Forrest, Noreen Corcoran. *Prod:* (None credited) Warner Bros. Warnercolor. Warnerscope. 126m.

THE NAKED AND THE DEAD (1958). Version of Norman Mailer's best seller highlighting the conflict between officers and men during combat in the Pacific. *Sc:* Denis and Terry Sanders (novel by Norman Mailer). *Ph:* Joseph La Schelle. *Art Dir:* William L. Kuehl. *Ed:* Arthur P. Schmidt. *Mus:* Bernard Herrmann. *With* Raymond Massey (*General Cummings*), Aldo Ray (*Sgt. Croft*), Cliff Robertson (*Lieut. Hearn*), Lili St-Cyr (*Lily*), Barbara Nichol (*Mildred*), William Campbell, Richard Jaeckel, James Best, Joey Bishop, Jerry Paris, Robert Gist, L. Q. Jones, Larry Sterling, Jerry Barclay, Edward Gregson, Casey Adams, John Berardino, Greg Roman, Henry Armago, Edward McNally. *Prod:* Paul Gregory for RKO. Technicolor. RKOscope. 135m.

THE SHERIFF OF FRACTURED JAW (1958). British comedy Western with More as a singularly unsuccessful English inventor who goes West to sell guns, and ends up taming a town with the aid of friendly Indians. *Sc:* Arthur Dales (story by Jacob Hay). *Ph:* Otto Heller. *Art Dir:* Bernard Robinson. *Ed:* John Shirley. *Mus:* Robert Farnon. *With* Kenneth More (*Jonathan Tibbs*), Jayne Mansfield (*Kate*), Henry Hull (*Masters*), William Campbell (*Keeno*), Bruce Cabot (*Jack*), Robert Morley, Ronald Squire, David Horne, Eynon Evans, Sidney James, Donald Stewart, Reed de Rouen, Clancy Cooper, Charles Irwin, Gordon Tanner, Tucker McGuire, Nick Brady, Jack Lester, Nicholas Stuart, Sheldon Lawrence, Susan Denny, Charles Farrell, Chief Jonas Applegarth, Deputy Chief Buffalo, Larry Taylor. *Prod:* Daniel M. Angel for 20th Century-Fox. Eastmancolor De Luxe. CinemaScope. 110m.

A PRIVATE'S AFFAIR (1959). Services comedy with music which serves mainly as a showcase of some of the younger Fox contract stars. *Sc:* Winston Miller (story by Ray Livingston Murphy). *Ph:* Charles G. Clarke. *Art Dir:* Lyle Wheeler, Walter M. Simonds, Walter M. Scott, Stuart A. Reiss. *Ed:* Dorothy Spencer.

A PRIVATE'S AFFAIR, Walsh's last film about the services, was a comedy, featuring (left to right) Robert Burton, Jim Backus, Barry Coe, Gary Crosby, and Sal Mineo

Mus: Cyril Mockridge. *With* Sal Mineo (*Luigi Maresi*), Christine Carrere (*Marie*), Barry Coe (*Jerry Morgan*), Barbara Eden (*Katey*), Gary Crosby (*Mike*), Terry Moore, Jim Backus, Jessie Royce Landis, Robert Burton, Alan Hewitt, Robert Denver, Tige Andrews, Ray Montgomery, Rudolph Anders, Debbie Joyce, Robert Montgomery Jnr., Dick Whittinghill, Emerson Treacy, Maida Severn, Carlyle Mitchell. *Prod:* David Weisbart for 20th Century-Fox. De Luxe color. CinemaScope. 92m.

ESTHER AND THE KING (Italy: ESTHER E IL RE) (1960). Biblical drama about an ambitious Judean maiden who marries a Persian King, and tries to stop his persecution of her people. *Sc:* Raoul Walsh, Michael Elkins. *Ph:* Mario Bava. *Art Dir:* G. Giovanni, Massimo Tavazzi. *Ed:* Jerry Webb. *Mus:* Francesco Lavagnino, Roberto Nicolosi. *With* Richard Egan (*Assuerus*), Joan Collins (*Esther*), Denis O'Dea (*Mardochee*), Sergio Fantoni (*Haman*), Rick Battaglia (*Simon*), Renato Baldini, Folco Lulli, Gabriele Tinti, Rosalba Neri, Daniella Rocca, Robert Buchanan. *Prod:* Raoul Walsh for 20th Century-Fox/Galatea. Eastmancolor De Luxe. CinemaScope. 110m.

MARINES, LET'S GO (1961). Walsh produced, directed and wrote the story of this Services comedy, again using a thin plot as a showcase for 20th Century-Fox contractees. *Sc:* John Twist (story by Raoul Walsh). *Ph:* Lucien Ballard. *Art Dir:* Jack Martin Smith, Alfred Ybarra. *Ed:* Robert Simpson. *Mus:* Irving Gertz. *With* Tom Tryon (*Skip Roth*), David Hedison (*Dave Chatfields*), Tom Reese (*McCaffrey*), Linda Hutchins (*Grace Blake*), William Tyler (*Russ Waller*), Barbara Stuart, David Brandon, Steve Baylor, Adoree Evans, Hideo Inamura, Vince Williams, Fumiyo Fupimoto, Henry Okawa. *Prod:* Raoul Walsh for 20th Century-Fox. De Luxe Color. CinemaScope. 103m.

A DISTANT TRUMPET (1964). Personal conflicts come to the boil at a cavalry outpost as an Indian attack threatens. *Sc:* John Twist (novel by Paul Horgan). *Ph:* William Clothier. *Art Dir:* William Campbell. *Ed:* David Wages. *Mus:* Max Steiner. *With* Troy Donahue (*Second Lieut. Matthew Hazard*), Suzanne Pleschette (*Kitty Mainwaring*), James Gregory (*General Alexander Quait*), Diane McBain (*Laura Greenleaf*), William Reynolds (*Lieut. Mainwaring*), Claude Akins, Kent Smith, Judson Pratt, Bartlett Robinson, Bobby Bare, Richard X. Slattery, Guy Eltsosis, Larry Ward, Mary Patton, Russell Johnson, Lane Bradford. *Prod:* William H. Wright for Warner Bros. Technicolor. Panavision. 116m.

Walsh is also known to have been involved with the following films:

SAN ANTONIO (1945). Elaborate Flynn Western casting him as a rancher who becomes involved with a singer, employed by his long-time enemy. *Dir:* David Butler. *Sc:* Alan Le May, W. R. Burnett. *Ph:* Bert Glennon. *Art Dir:* Ted Smith. *Ed:* Irene Morra. *Mus:* Max Steiner. *With* Errol Flynn (*Clay Hardin*), Alexis Smith (*Jeanne Starr*), S. Z. Sacall (*Sacha*), Victor Francen (*Legare*), Paul Kelly (*Roy Stuart*), John Litel, Robert Shayne, John Alvin, Monte Blue, Robert Barratt, Pedro De Cordoba, Tom Tyler, Chris-Pin Martin, Charles Stevens, Poodles

Hanneford, Doodles Weaver, Dan White, Ray Spiker, Hap Winters, Harry Cording, Chalky Williams, Wallis Clark, Bill Steels, Allen E. Smith, Howard Hill, Arnold Kent. *Prod:* Robert Buckner for Warner Bros. Technicolor. 111m.

STALLION ROAD (1947). Romantic drama set against a background of California stud farms. *Dir:* James V. Kern. *Sc:* Stephen Longstreet (from his novel). *Ph:* Arthur Edeson. *Art Dir:* Stanley Fleischer, Clarence Steensen. *Ed:* David Weisbart. *Mus:* Frederick Hollander. *With* Ronald Reagan (*Larry Hanarahan*), Alexis Smith(*Rory Teller*), Zachary Scott (*Steve Purcell*), Patti Brady (*Chris Teller*), Harry Davenport, Angela Greene, Frank Puglia, Ralph Byrd, Peggy Knudsen, Lloyd Corrigan, Fernando Alvarado, Matthew Boulton, Oscar O'Shea. *Prod:* Alex Gottlieb for Warner Bros. 97m.

MURDER INC. (GB:) THE ENFORCER) (1951). Bogart as a dedicated assistant District Attorney who persistently builds up a case against Murder Inc. *Dir:* Bretaigne Windust. *Sc:* Martin Rackin. *Ph:* Robert Burks. *Art Dir:* Charles H. Clarke. *Ed:* Fred Allen. *Mus:* David Buttolph. *With* Humphrey Bogart (*Martin Ferguson*), Ted De Corsia (*"Big Babe" Lazich*), Everett Sloane (*Albert Mendoza*), Roy Roberts (*Capt. Frank Nelson*), Lawrence Tolan (*Duke Malloy*), King Donovan, Patricia Joiner, Don Beddoe, Susan Cabot, John Kellog, Jack Lambert, Mario Siletti, John Maxwell, Ralph Dunn and Benny Burt, Bob Steele, Zero Mostel, Tito Vuolo, Adelaide Klein. *Prod:* Milton Sperling for United States Pictures. 87m.

Some sources also credit Walsh as assisting in the production of *Come September* (1961, Robert Mulligan).

Intolerance (1916, D. W. Griffith). Walsh worked as an assistant director.

Helen of Troy (1955, Robert Wise). Walsh worked as second unit director.

Below: Walsh (with eye patch) examines a miniature set, and (right) Kirk Douglas with Virginia Mayo in a characteristic scene from THE GREAT DIVIDE

An Appreciation of Henry Hathaway

Henry Hathaway was born on March 13, 1898, in Sacramento, California, but his family moved almost immediately to San Francisco; his mother Jean was a stage actress, and his father Rhoady a theatrical manager, so the young boy grew up in the world of show business.

By rights, he is the Marquis Henri Leopold de Fiennes. The title is inherited from his grandfather, who was commissioned by the King of the Belgians to acquire the Sandwich Islands (in Hawaii) for his country. Failing to do so, and ashamed to return home, he travelled to San Francisco where he established himself as a lawyer in 1850. Soon afterwards he married, and his wife bore him a son, Rhoady, who grew up to become a theatrical manager. Rhoady took his wife's maiden name of Hathaway, and allowed her to pursue her career as a stage actress, with their son Henry being born during a stint in Sacramento. Family contacts led to his becoming a child actor with the American film company in 1908, where he became a *protégé* of the director Allan Dwan. Twenty-three-year-old Dwan had entered the industry by writing and selling a screenplay to Essanay, thereafter moving to the American Film Company as a scenarist, scenario editor and director at their studio in San Diego. Exceptionally prolific in his output, Dwan made over four hundred one and two reel films for the Company in the period 1908–1912. Filming along the Mexican border with a stock company including J. Warren Kerrigan and Wallace Reid, he shot a film a day, five days a week. Thus as a child actor, Hathaway first picked up the smatterings of Western lore, which he was to develop as one of his greatest assets professionally in later years. Unfortunately, due to the absence of any detailed credits for films of this decade, it is not possible to name any of Hathaway's appearances, although at least 239 of the 400 odd titles are known. In 1912 Hathaway moved behind the cameras for a spell as a property boy at Universal, leaving

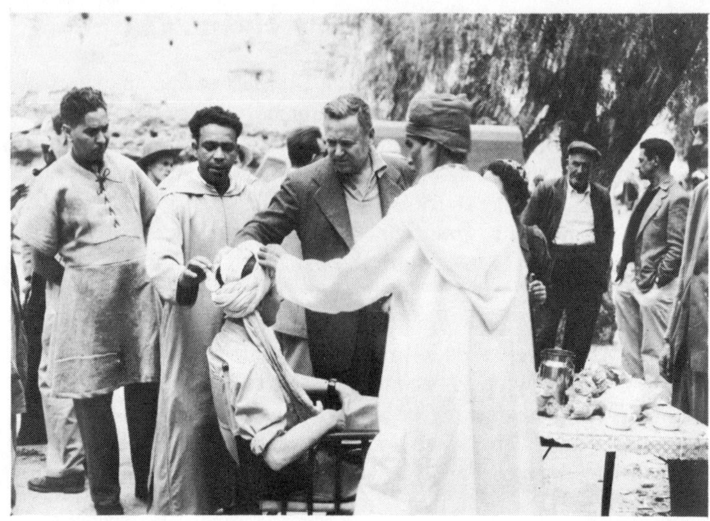

Hathaway checking costumes before shooting a sequence for THE BLACK ROSE

school in order to do so. By 1917 he had also furthered his acting career, playing a number of juvenile roles.

America's entry into the First World War put an end to his acting ambitions, and he became a gunnery instructor at Fort Wingfield School, San Francisco for the duration of the war. He returned to Hollywood in 1921 as a property man for producer/director Frank Lloyd, having failed to make his mark in the world of high finance with the Morris Audit Company, for whom he worked immediately following his Army discharge in 1919. Lloyd made his reputation from his consistently successful adaptations of the literary classics such as *A Tale of Two Cities* (1917), and some of his preoccupation passed on to Hathaway. This was nurtured and flowered under the inspiration of Paul Bern, for whom Hathaway functioned as an assistant director. Bern encouraged him to read widely in order to complete his education, as well as firing Hathaway's passion for travel by encouraging him to travel to India, where he spent nine months collecting material for a documentary on pilgrimages. The project fell through but the experience resulted in his later being assigned *The Lives of a Bengal Lancer* (1935), which was his first popular success as a director.

Gary Cooper questions a captive, watched by Sir C. Aubrey Smith (far left) and Franchot Tone (far right) in Hathaway's THE LIVES OF A BENGAL LANCER

In his capacity as an assistant director, Hathaway also worked briefly for Sam Goldwyn before moving to Paramount, where he worked in close association with Josef von Sternberg and Victor Fleming. The latter association was particularly fruitful as he recalled in a recent interview: "Fleming never had a story conference without me, never went to the front office without me, never did any casting without me, not because he needed to do that but for me to learn. Fleming wasn't a joking man . . . he was a very serious, demanding man and very positive in what he wanted to get, and most of his leading men were patterned after his own behaviour, he was a real tough man. I think there was more of Fleming in Gable at the end than there was Gable in Gable. I think that Gable really mimicked Victor Fleming and became that kind of a man on the screen.

"With Fleming I did *The Virginian*. I did all those early Westerns, all of the Zane Greys, the ones I did over again. I mostly learned from them how to handle people. I would take a script home and think. Now what would I tell these people to do to make the scene, how would I start it, where would be the climax, how would I get out of it, how do I get rid of the people, where would I do it—in front of the fire or on the couch, what would I do? And I'd make up my mind, and I'd make a lot of notes and then I'd see what they did. Entirely different! But you learn." ("Focus on Film." No. 7, 1971.)

Fleming's influence is particularly notable in several areas of Hathaway's work; firstly in the consistency of performances in all his films, and secondly in the composition of the images in his films. His screen is seldom empty, but on the other hand it is never overcrowded so that there is little attempt to assault the audience on a visual level, unless the image is conceived as a shock cut or zoom which is justified in its context. At the same time the close attention to detail within the frame is relevant to both the characterisation and narrative development. For instance in 1927, Hathaway worked as Fleming's assistant on *Mantrap,* an outdoor romantic drama starring Ernest Torrence, Clara Bow and Percy Marmont, adapted from a novel by Sinclair Lewis. It is set in a log hut community in the Canadian Rockies during the early years of the Twentieth century. An aging storekeeper (Torrence) takes off his apron and goes down to Minneapolis for the first time since 1903 on hearing that "ankles ain't the half of what the girls are showin' now." He buys a wife (Bow), who finds life in the wilds unbearable and runs off with a handsome young trapper (Marmont). Nine years after *Mantrap,* Hathaway directed *The Trail of the Lonesome Pine;* it was his second *major* assignment, and the first 'A' budget Western in the three colour process. As such it does make certain concessions in terms of images filmed purely for colour effect, but a close examination of the opening scene and the content of the plot outline contain both Fleming's influence and indications of Hathaway's later development.

It is set in a backwoods log hut community where "old woods, old ways and old codes live unchanged." The introduction classifies the inhabitants as people whose hatred and feuds were their patriotism, and quaint customs their religion. The prologue, set in the early years of the Twentieth century, opens with the camera panning across a blue mountain valley, picking out figures in the rocks firing at a log cabin. Cutting down to the occupants, it establishes that the father and two sons are pinned down under fire in an outhouse, while the pregnant wife is about to deliver another child in the house. The elder son restrains the father as he tries to break cover and run to the house, but their concern is diverted as the younger boy falls after returning a shot at their attackers. He is unhurt, merely knocked back by the impact of his gun-shot. The cries of a baby confirm that mother and child are both alive. Hathaway cuts to the interior of the cabin where the mother (Beulah Bondi) cradles the new-born baby, a girl, in her arms praying, "Give her the strength to be good, Lord, but don't let her carry the burden of fear.

Oh, the killing, the killing! Why has it got to be?" The image fades to a panning shot down a single pine tree on a hill, and the superimposed title: "Today." The plot revolves around the inter-family feud which is finally settled through the intervention of a young mining engineer (Fred MacMurray), who has fallen in love with the girl (Sylvia Sidney). She is as unhappy with her environment as the Clara Bow character in *Mantrap,* and longs to escape to the excitement of city life.

Thus the film fits as much into the "folk/myth" category as that of the Western; other Hathaway films in this tradition are *Go West Young Man* (1936) with movie star Mae West making an unscheduled stopover in a hick town; *The Shepherd of the Hills* (1941) which is reputed to be the best of the "mountain feud" films, and was Hathaway's first picture with John Wayne, and *Home in Indiana* (1944), a small town drama about young love and harness racing. Hathaway's career has embraced most types of Hollywood films including Westerns (his first eight films, mostly starring Randolph Scott and based on Zane Grey stories)—*Rawhide, Garden of Evil, From Hell to Texas/Manhunt, North to Alaska,* episodes of *How the West Was Won, The Sons of Katie Elder, Nevada Smith, Five Card Stud, True Grit,* and *Shootout;* crime/gangster films—*Johnny Apollo, The Dark Corner, Kiss of Death, Call Northside 777,* and *Seven Thieves.* His melodramas include *Peter Ibbetson, Now and Forever, 14 Hours, Niagara, The Racers/Such Men Are Dangerous, The Bottom of the Bottle/Beyond the River, 23 Paces to Baker Street, Woman Obsessed,* and *Circus World/The Magnificent Showman* (also romantic with a Western circus setting); his comedies consist of *The Witching Hour, Go West Young Man, You're in the Navy Now/U.S.S. Tea Kettle,* and *North to Alaska.* War/service films include *Come On Marines, The Lives of a Bengal Lancer, The Real Glory, Sundown, Ten Gentlemen from West Point, Wing and a Prayer, You're in the Navy Now/U.S.S. Tea Kettle, The Desert Fox/*

One of Hathaway's gentle jibes at the mountain folk as the Tulliver family receive their first-ever telegram in THE TRAIL OF THE LONESOME PINE. Left to right: Fred Stone, Henry Fonda, Sylvia Sidney, and Beulah Bondi

Rommel—Desert Fox, and *Raid on Rommel;* while spy films include *13 Rue Madeleine* and *Diplomatic Courier* as well as straight action dramas like *China Girl, Down to the Sea in Ships, Prince Valiant* (costume), *Legend of the Lost,* and *The Last Safari.*

★ ★ ★

By no means a stylist in his own right, Hathaway is an accomplished technician, and has often turned negligible material into a capable film. But his career constitutes more than just an aptitude for freshening well-used staple items. It cannot be merely coincidental that he was selected to direct the first three-colour Western;

that he was entrusted with the direction of Gary Cooper—a major star at the time—in three consecutive films, one of which, *Peter Ibbetson,* must have constituted a definite box-office risk since it was a romantic fantasy; that he directed the first of Twentieth Century-Fox's semi-documentary features, *The House on 92nd Street* (1945) and later followed this up with one of the best examples of this trend, which he had initiated, *Call Northside 777.* His work in the field can be seen in retrospect to be less intense than that of Kazan [*Boomerang,* 1947]; Dassin [*Brute Force,* 1947] or Keighley [*The Street with No Name,* 1948], while his technique is matched only by Dassin's *The Naked City* (1948). No special thematic thread marks his work; yet a number of disparate ideas can be discerned in many of his films. The motivation of revenge plays an important role in *The Trail of the Lonesome Pine, Kiss of Death, The Black Rose, Prince Valiant, From Hell to Texas/Manhunt, Nevada Smith, The Sons of Katie Elder, True Grit,* and *Shootout.* This is often linked with the disruption of a family, especially in the three films made between 1966–69, with Steve McQueen tracking down the three murderers of his mother and father; John Wayne, Dean Martin, Earl Holliman and Michael Anderson clearing the name of their dead parents; and Kim Darby chasing his father's killer. The young often have to prove their manhood—for example, Anderson in *The Sons of Katie Elder* or Richard Cromwell in *The Lives of a Bengal Lancer,* or in the case of Kim Darby in *True Grit,* a girl must assume the role of her dead parent. An older, more experienced man usually aids or gives advice to the more impetuous youngsters (*cf.* Cooper in *The Lives of a Bengal Lancer,* Jack Hawkins in *The Black Rose,* Brian Keith in *Nevada Smith,* or John Wayne in *True Grit*). Frequently, as in the films of Sam Fuller, the price of this education or assistance is death. Women play a larger role in the urban dramas, normally being confined to the background as a conventional love interest, with certain exceptions such as Hathaway's films with Susan

Hathaway directing Frances Dee in a scene from SOULS AT SEA

Hayward (*Rawhide; White Witch Doctor,* and *Woman Obsessed*); Marilyn Monroe (*Niagara*) and Kim Darby (*True Grit*). In these particular cases, the women concerned provide the motivation through their innocence or feelings of guilt; yet they all share the screen time with heroes who become involved in their problems. In general his women appear to have less need than the menfolk to play out morally dubious motivations.

A callousness in the hero often leads to an ambiguous climax, characterised by a burst of violent action that resolves *without* the hero kissing the heroine in the fadeout. When this is reversed, as in *The Black Rose,* it appears patently false, and could possibly have been inserted on the insistence of the studio concerned. Hathaway has never attempted to conceal the compromises and concessions made on his films, notably those made while he was under contract to Twentieth Century-Fox. A tally of his work shows that he worked with Randolph Scott eight times; Gary Cooper appeared on seven occasions; John Wayne on six; Tyrone Power on five; Richard Widmark on four; and he has also worked with George Raft, Edward G. Robinson, Joseph Cotten, Stewart Granger, Gregory Peck and Shirley Temple. This list is indicative of his liking for action films, but does not necessarily take into account the scope of his range.

For instance, *14 Hours,* one of the very few of his films which has a factual basis, concerns an unbalanced man (Richard Basehart) threatening to jump off a building. In its visual "casualness" it resembles *Call Northside 777* (both are photographed by Joseph MacDonald). It opens at dawn as a traffic cop (Paul Douglas) is walking to work; high above him in a hotel a waiter brings Basehart breakfast, fumbles in his pocket for change, looking up to find Basehart gone—onto the balcony ledge. An irritable cop (Howard Da Silva) brings two psychiatrists to the scene, but Basehart will talk only to Douglas, who is not very happy with his role as "nursemaid."

A crowd gathers, disturbing Basehart ("They only want to see me jump"), as do his whining, wheedling mother (Agnes Moorehead) and alcoholic father (Robert Keith). Attempts to pull him into the room or to hook him with a rope fail, and Douglas begins to feel sorry for him, further angering the police. They call his *fiancée* (Barbara Bel Geddes) to the scene, but she cannot persuade him to go back into the room. Finally, under cover of the dusk, the police move a net in place several floors below the ledge, and Basehart is rescued after the sudden shock of a spotlight, played directly on his face, causes him to fall.

The climax is the main departure from the factual basis since the man died in the real incident; and there is further falsification in the addition of romance, as two lovers are reunited in the watching crowd. Hathaway has admitted that the ending was altered in accordance with the wishes of a Twentieth Century-Fox executive, Spyros Skouras:

"The day *14 Hours* was shown in New York with the proper—suicide—end to it, Skouras's daughter jumped out of the eighth storey window of a hospital she was in and committed suicide. He saw the picture. He said, 'Put it away, I don't want anybody ever to see it. Hide it, tear it up.' So we just let it sit for about a month and didn't say anything about it. Then we took it out again, and said, well, what about it and he said, 'I'll never release it, never. It'll never be released as long as I have anything to do with 20th Century.' So Darryl [Zanuck] got the idea, 'Let's save him, we have to do something with the picture.' So we made that unsatisfactory ending. I shouldn't have done it. I should have said, 'To hell with you, then we don't show the picture.'" ("Focus on Film." No. 7, 1971.)

Accepting this, Hathaway's use of incidentals to create tension successfully plays down the more hysterical aspects of John Paxton's script, which employs the methods of the subject that it is attacking —sensationalism. Visual effects such as traffic jams or the spotlight blinding Basehart, causing him to fall as he hits out at the light, and a shot of the police rig reflected in the window of a lawyer's office across the street, are blended in with sick jokes such as, "Look out, he's gonna fall right on top of you!" (Crowd to photographer), or remarks like, "So what is it? Advertising?" or, "They always die for the morning papers." The parents' dialogue is blatantly hysterical or neurotic, as indicated by an exchange between mother and policeman, played in a bug-eyed ham style: "Son, you don't want to do

Paul Douglas as the traffic cop in Hathaway's FOURTEEN HOURS

this to ME! Lady, you gotta talk to him, he LOVES you!" The point is far better made by the performance of the father, unnerved by his son's taunts after he has apologised for delaying the St. Patrick's Day Parade: "You're scared to look down, aren't you?" as he deliberately drops a cigarette and watches its progress with a faint smile. Another example of the sensationalistic script is reflected in the attitude of the cab-drivers, who exchange bets as to the exact time Basehart will jump, abandoning work entirely as each deadline approaches.

Four other directors, including Howard Hawks, had turned the film down before Hathaway was signed to direct, suggesting it was quite definitely a studio assignment rather than a subject of personal choice, although certain aspects must have appealed to him as compensation for the pedestrian and hysterical elements of the script, and I would suggest that they were the relationship which is established between the would-be suicide and the older traffic policeman (a variation of a consistent Hathaway theme), as well as the disillusionment and resentment that Basehart feels toward his parents, which prompts his act as a form of revenge. Since high-tension thrillers were not Hathaway's *forte,* and as he was again working with a favourite cameraman, it is to be expected that he would underplay the visual aspects of the story in keeping with the general stylistic drabness matching both the mood of the story, and, as in *Call Northside 777,* adding symbolical notes of reference to its development.

★ ★ ★

In John Ford's films, violence is seen as a threat to the peace of the community, which, unless it is stemmed by law and order or channelled by military service, leads to anarchy. Thus Wyatt Earp is civilised by Clementine Carter in *My Darling Clementine* (1946), while Ethan Edwards is visually isolated from the community by the establishing and concluding shots of the film because he is motivated by violence in *The Searchers* (1956). Hathaway is far more ambiguous. Tyrone Power in *The Black Rose,* Victor Mature in *Kiss of Death* and Steve McQueen in *Nevada Smith* all regain self-respect through violent actions, while James Cagney in *13 Rue Madeleine,* Gary Cooper in *The Lives of a Bengal Lancer* and Jack Hawkins in *The Black Rose* die as heroes in violent situations. Only one instance springs to mind of a Hathaway hero rejecting violence as a solution, and that is in *The Trail of the Lonesome Pine* when Fred Stone persuades Fred MacMurray to let the death of his girl friend's brother go unavenged in the interests of peace in the community.

An apparent paradox is created by his supposed disdain for any multiplicity of dialogue, yet if this was total he would not have made so many urban films. The answer lies in his long apprenticeship in the silent cinema, from which he acquired much of his visual sense and in the quality of understatement which he applied so well to his work in the latter half of the Forties. *The Dark Corner* is a typical example; a tightly constructed suspense film which utilises all the iconographic data of the crime thriller: the tough private eye with an adoring, wise-cracking secretary finds himself involved in a complicated plot of violence and mayhem which he manages to solve in the nick of time after he has been neatly framed for murder. There is a strong emphasis on location work and a notable car chase in which the hero steals a taxi containing evidence. The police pursue him hotly, until he evades them by driving the taxi to its home base vanishing amongst twenty other taxis! A nice eye for detail includes a child who gives the hero vital information about the movement of a villain, because the latter has frightened her and she subsequently spies on him whenever he is in the building, or the quick, knowing leer on a milkman's face as a hand takes the morning paper from under Lucille Ball's arm while she talks to him through a half-opened door.

The script bears a strong resemblance to that of *Laura* (1944), showing a portrait of the utmost corrosiveness under the veneer of elegant sophistication and tasteful *décor* of the art world, even to the point of Clifton Webb's repeating his role as an insanely jealous guardian of the Perfect Woman—in this case his wife. Where the film differs from Otto Preminger's is in the dual development of the plot so that the audience is kept one step ahead of the hero, whose toughness is shown to be a mask. He begins to fall apart under the pressure, seeking solace in drink until his secretary pulls him together, but even then he is quick to lose heart ("I feel all dead inside. I'm backed up in a dark corner and I don't know who is

Perplexity shows on both Gary Cooper and Jack Webb as they examine the engines of the "Tea Kettle" in YOU'RE IN THE NAVY NOW

hitting me"). Hathaway keeps a tight rein on his mainly small-time cast, and succeeds in making a very plausible film.

While *The Dark Corner* was very much a film of its time, a certain nostalgia can be found in other Hathaway works; most notably in the films set in the backwoods as well as *The Witching Hour, Down to the Sea in Ships* and *You're in the Navy Now*. The two former films had previously been made in the silent era; *You're in the Navy Now* (which was originally released as *U.S.S. Tea Kettle* but withdrawn and re-issued under the new title some months later although there appeared to be no extra footage or re-editing incorporated in the latter version) was light in tone and was more suited to the style of comedy in the Thirties with its decisive moral code and division of uncomplicated characters as well as a mistrust of specialised development.

Naval Reserve Captain Harkness (Gary Cooper) is assigned to an old tub much to his wife's scorn, and he in turn is jealous of her success in the "Waves." His crusty bosun is horrified to find that Cooper is just "another ninety day wonder," and becomes a major source of comedy as he suffers the indignities and mishaps caused by his Captain's lack of experience. Cooper's problems mount as the film progresses since he is unable to retain any self respect, foiled both by his lack of experience and the low morale of the crew. The bosun, unlike other secondary Hathaway heroes, cannot find any quality or talent in Cooper to admire or develop. Eventually, when Cooper enters the crew for a boxing tournament to improve morale and relaxes sufficiently to allow the men to lay a side bet for the honour of the ship, he begins to win over the bosun. But by then he has discovered that the crew have been rigging the times on some test trials—a familiar Cooper comedy situation: that of a simple, honest man faced by corruption on all sides.

His efforts to expose the fraud go unheeded; the crew win the boxing match but the final time trial ends in disaster culminating in Cooper facing a court-martial during which he vigorously attacks Naval concern with specialists over and above the interests of the common man.

★ ★ ★

Hathaway had a great respect for Gary Cooper as an actor, having worked as an assistant director on many of his films before coming to direct him, and this respect is reflected in the natural ease of Cooper's performances in his work for Hathaway. He was not always as fluent in obtaining good work from other star performers like Van Johnson and Tyrone Power. On the surface there would appear to be very little to link *23 Paces to Baker Street, The Black Rose* and *Brigham Young, Frontiersman.* The first is a contemporary thriller, based on a Philip MacDonald story; the second film is set in the reign of Edward I; and the last is based on Louis Bromfield's story of the famous Mormon leader.

23 Paces to Baker Street is not one of Hathaway's best works by any means. The plot is far-fetched and contrived, relying on coincidences such as a girl remembering a particular perfume scent after an interval of three years, and obvious aids like Jean (Vera Miles) knowing Philip's theory about the crimes before he has explained it to her; while the hero's dialogue is mostly a series of *clichés* referring to his embitterment at his blindness. The action revolves around a blind playwright, Philip Hannon (Van Johnson) stumbling on a kidnap plot, meeting total disbelief from the police, but alerting the kidnapper, who plans to kill him. Flashes of quality appear, as in the reconstruction of a phone-booth murder, using blanks, shot entirely in close-ups; the scene in which the kidnapper leads Johnson into a demolished building, leaving him precariously balanced on a dangerous ledge, or the climactic night search in Regent's Park which leads Hannon to the villainess, who confronts him in his flat but is outwitted by his use of multiple tape-recordings that upset her concentration, and enable him to push her off his balcony. The camerawork of Milton Krasner is the complete opposite of MacDonald's style with a dazzling display of tricks in urban exteriors including two 270° pans—once crossing Hungerford Bridge and the other in Regent's Park as well as a number of well-composed overhead shots on a spiral staircase.

The recurrent motif of the hero's guilt complex (for once legitimate considering the circumstances in which he has accepted responsibility for a person's death) and his lack of confidence in his own abilities link the film very strongly with the other two mentioned. In the same light, the traffic policeman in *14 Hours* lacks confidence in his ability to save Basehart, while Harkness is motivated initially by a feeling of great inferiority to his wife in *You're in the Navy Now.* The films starring Tyrone Power have another common factor in that, although he was a major star, he is often absent from the screen for some considerable footage; seen in order of release they also offer a portrait of his talent broadening with experience.

Brigham Young, which was written by Lamarr Trotti and photographed by Arthur Miller, both of whom had worked with John Ford, is essentially a pioneering epic in the Fordian vein, although Hathaway himself underrates it as a studio assignment. Great care was given to the visual composition and lighting, as Hathaway confirms, and the sparse dialogue—in comparison with other works of this nature—stresses the importance of the imagery. Less concerned with the religious aspects (although a parallel is drawn between Moses and Brigham Young, while the character portrayed by John Carradine physically resembles a Biblical Old Testament figure), the emphasis lies more squarely on community and historical development. The film opens with a denunciation of press sensationalism as the camera zooms in to a sign announcing a wolf hunt, with the Mormons substituting for the wolves. Anarchy erupts, but Brigham Young (Dean Jagger) stops Mormon retaliation. A young girl, Zina Webb (Linda Darnell), loses both her parents and her faith in a disturbing image, cutting away from the body of her father to a burning Bible. The Mormons face a split in leadership between Angus Duncan (Brian Donlevy) in favour of compromise, and Joseph Smith (Vincent Price) who favours sticking to their principles. Town bigotry is rife ("What's the difference between a white man and a Mormon? Don't know—'bout 50 wives, I guess"), and Smith is put on trial on some trumped-up charges. Young defends him eloquently, putting the case that the Mormons were and always have been victims; telling of his lake-side conversion by Smith following an accidental meeting, and quoting legal and historical precedents for the trial. He is met with a stunned silence in court before the jury pass a unanimous death sentence on Smith. A lynch mob completes the job, and Duncan claims leadership of the Mormons, having previously shown himself to be in league secretly with crooked businessmen in the town.

Brigham Young, at this stage, bears a resemblance to the young Lincoln in John Ford's film, made the previous year. He is humble in origin, educated, dignified and able to communicate with all manner of folk by using his backwood charm. Unlike Lincoln, he is unable to halt a lynch mob with his oratory skill, and as the film progresses he constantly expresses doubt as to his right to lead. He is ordered to leave by the Army ("Funny thing that major taking it for granted. Why doesn't the Lord tell me I am leader?"), after clashing with Duncan over what he considers the latter's material interests in leading. Duncan later joins Young's party after he finds the townsmen equally willing to carry out reprisals on his business interests. They move across an ice-packed lake (The Red Sea?) with their band playing to raise the general spirits. But, like the ship's crew in *You're in the Navy Now,* they have little faith in their leader as soon as they are faced with adversity—the sign of their homes burning behind them. Zina Webb travels with a young friend of Young's named Jonathan Kent (Tyrone Power), but they do not join in the general back-biting about Young, preferring to talk about the Christian sense of love, and the hatred incurred by the Mormons wherever they travel.

It is odd that Hathaway almost disowns the film since it is clearly one of his more committed works, committed in the sense that he presents the film with sufficient atmosphere to suggest that his theme of the persecution of a minority for their beliefs is genuinely felt. It is certainly more subjective than the coldly observed "message" films of his contemporary, Mervyn LeRoy, and it is unusual for a director to place secondary value on the romantic angle (involving two major stars like Ty Power and Linda Darnell who were both top Fox properties at the time), unless he is committed to his theme.

Admittedly, his probing of ideological freedom is watered down by the failure to face up to the moral implications of the Mormon belief in polygamy, although this may have been imposed by the regulations of the Censor's office. Yet he encompasses all the main events in Young's life in a vivid canvas, following the migration to the West which was to culminate in the foundation of Salt Lake City, ending the film with an excitingly constructed montage as gulls descend from an empty sky to destroy the crickets that threaten the tiny Mormon crops. These events are consistently related to the bigotry and intolerance that the Mormons encounter, and to Young's self doubts about his worth as a leader.

Like Harkness, Young finds that the public defence of his actions and the honesty of his examination of his credentials results in a justification of his integrity. Justification and vindication of integrity are prime motivating forces for many Hathaway heroes and heroines, yet the attainment of these goals often turns into a Pyrrhic victory since the pursuit has completely occupied their existence and has worn them into a shell so that they find little to celebrate. Tyrone Power in *The Black Rose* is an exception, although his achievement, as I mentioned earlier, seems false.

★ ★ ★

The Black Rose is curiously structured in three segments, beginning and ending in England at the time of the Norman/Saxon hostilities, with the central section taking place in the Far East. It was one of the first American productions to be filmed on location after the Second World War, being shot largely in North Africa. For an epic type of costume picture it is unusual in both length—ninety minutes—and in that it contains no key battle scenes. All battles are represented by columns of troops on the march (3 or 4 shots) cutting away into the march away from the ruins of a burning city. The influence of legend is especially evident, as is the extremely "jingoistic" patriotism of the Jack Hawkins character, who is elevated from the advisory capacity of the older man in the normal Hathaway hierarchy to the status of joint hero (as is Gary Cooper in *The Lives of a Bengal Lancer,* the comparison being further linked by the fact that both die in the climactic action of the respective films). The story bears a strong resemblance to such classical literature as "The Travels of Marco Polo" in that it centres around similar adventures of dual heroes; but it carries undertones of two thematic ideas which, unfortunately, are not totally developed.

Cecile Aubrey puts up a spirited fight against Jack Hawkins in Hathaway's THE BLACK ROSE

the film recalled in the "London Magazine" at the time of shooting: "Hathaway seems to be everywhere at once, and does not recognise that the impossible exists, or that there are 120 degrees of sunshine! He drives on, possessed with a fury of direction. Everyone curses, but everyone gets on with the job and the picture is made. We trek hundreds of miles with all our tents and camels and gear, north, south, east and west, and Hathaway always seems to be there."

Hathaway's penchant for location work had been instrumental in his selection as director of *The House on 92nd Street.* The producer, Louis De Rochemont, bore Hathaway's experience in mind when selling Darryl F. Zanuck on the programme of semi-documentary crime films; he convinced Zanuck that this type of film was ideal for postwar audiences because of the factual or apparently factual basis of the material created with the assistance of official bodies such as the Federal Bureau of Investigation. The F.B.I. for instance not only supplied material for the stories, but in the case of *The House on 92nd Street,* they also supplied actual footage of Fifth Column agents at work—material which had been secretly filmed by their own agents, and that had been top secret information during the War.

All Hathaway's films for De Rochemont, and also *The Black Rose,* provide outstanding examples of Hathaway's style, or rather the only consistent effects that recur in a chronological sequence of Hathaway films: they all contain outstanding second unit work (normally shot by a specialist or an assistant with a few exceptions including Hathaway and Don Siegel), while most of their dialogue sequences are structured around the compositional basis of the medium two-shot. Also, with the exception of *The Black Rose,* they reflect a mature approach to camera placement and integral use of locations. In his earlier works such as *The Lives of a Bengal Lancer* or *The Trail of the Lonesome Pine,* he had shown less precise concern for camera values by placing more emphasis on the spectacle of the image being

Firstly, that of racial conflict between the Normans and the Saxons, a conflict that is directly responsible for both men leaving England in search of better fortune elsewhere. The liberal attitude of the King, who would give his throne to see an end to the conflict, and the prospect of a united England are passed over like red herrings. Secondly, the differing attitude towards power and conquest which causes them to split up and travel opposite roads, results in a film in which the hero who survives is an unpleasant character. While, on the one hand, he refuses to become involved in domestic quarrels, he reveals that his apparent patriotism—in this case his strong stance against the Normans—is in fact secondary to his desire for power through possessions. When he is disinherited by means of trickery, he leaves England to explore the East and make a name for himself so that in the terms of a Peckinpah, he can "enter his house justified."

His companion's skill as an archer brings them to the attention of an ambitious war-lord, Bayan of the Thousand Eyes (Orson Welles). Bayan finds Walter (Tyrone Power) both a willing opponent at chess, and an ambitious aide with a good knowledge of military strategy. They join forces, but Tristram cannot stomach the savagery of Bayan's ways, so Walter helps him escape—only to meet him again in another battle. After Tristram's death, Walter returns to England, having fulfilled his destiny in a determinedly Fascist manner. He receives recognition for discoveries that are not of his own making; relies on the power and protection of a war-lord to further his interests and ends up getting the girl whom he has constantly abused and cynically mistreated.

Hathaway and Welles did not see eye to eye during the making of the film, possibly because the latter saw that Hathaway was driving too hard for scenic accomplishment at the expense of the story. Always an extremely hard task-master on the set, Hathaway excelled himself on *The Black Rose* as an electrician who worked on filmed than on the composition or cohesion of the image; but by the time he made *The Shepherd of the Hills* he had started to implement the lessons of his experience in silent films. He made greater use of landscapes as an integral part of the film, and his violence in both *The Shepherd of the Hills* and *Ten Gentlemen from West Point* took on a new punch and realistic brutality (as in the "drag" illustration, and a vicious lacrosse game) that derived from a keener visual awareness.

★ ★ ★

Another unsavoury Hathaway hero, reflecting the interest of the director's moral tones in the nastier sides of the human personality, is Nick Bianco (Victor Mature) in *Kiss of Death.* It comes as no surprise to find him idealising a gangster, as was common practice in the early days of the gangster films before the censorship code cracked down on the habit; it also provides yet another example of Hathaway's greater concern for the way in which his material is presented as opposed to the *subject* matter. Mature's role embodied his qualities of appeal—animal magnetism and sensuality—which had been put to off-beat use by von Sternberg in *The Shanghai Gesture* (1941) in which he was required to play a male Marlene Dietrich (!)—as well as affording him a meaty acting role. John Ford, Jules Dassin and Robert Siodmak also capitalised on Mature's appeal during the Forties by giving him roles that enabled him to extend his limited range, but in the Fifties he became a caricature of his own image in progressively poorer parts. Richard Widmark, who made his *début* in *Kiss of Death,* also took some time to live down the image of the insane, giggling, mentally unstable killer he portrayed in the film.

Kiss of Death tells the story of Nick Bianco, a small-time thug, who is caught during a Christmas Eve robbery (which an off-screen narrator claims he has undertaken so that his child can have a decent present). Sentenced to twenty years, he at first refuses to listen to the offer of a lighter sentence if he becomes an informer. The Assistant D.A., D'Angelo (Brian Donlevy) is a patient man, and he bides his time. Bianco's wife commits suicide; a friend, Lettie (Coleen Gray), reveals that the dead woman had been two-timing Nick with a gangster named Rizzio, prior to Nick's incarceration, and that as a result his two children have been sent to an orphanage. Rizzio is the man D'Angelo wants Nick to finger, so he obliges, but is then told to perform the same service with Tommy Udo (Richard Widmark) before his debt to society is paid. He co-operates, but Udo is not convicted. Udo finds out that Nick ratted on him, and ignores Nick's pleas, terrorising him, Lettie and the children until Nick, in desperation, tips off D'Angelo that he is setting himself up as live bait to lure Udo. Unarmed, Nick is mown down, but Udo is caught and convicted, while Nick recovers in hospital.

Tension is rivetingly created and sustained from the opening sequence, aided by some very effective location photography by Norbert Brodine (another Hathaway regular) with a strong emphasis on low-key interior lighting to evoke mood. Widmark became an overnight star on the strength of his performance, and Mature was equally competent. The flaws in the film amount to the strong sentimentalisation of the Bianco character, introduced by Lettie's sympathetic off-screen narration at the start; to a particularly banal scene in which Bianco and D'Angelo exchange snaps of their children, with D'Angelo commenting, "No guy could have kids like that and be a crook"; and to a peculiar decision made by Twentieth Century-Fox at the time of the film's release, and never since explained, to cut out all the footage involving Bianco's wife (Patricia Morison), which tends to obscure the plot development.

When talking about the film, Hathaway concentrates on the technical aspects, especially those involved in shooting the exteriors and the opening sequence of the robbery carried out on the thirty-second floor of a skyscraper, with the robbers descending in a slow lift that constantly stops to pick up more passengers, thus increasing their chances of their being apprehended as the alarm is sounded.

"The main drawbacks were crowd control, preventing spectators mingling with actors—we used fifty cops. Identification too posed problems. Usually we made but little attempt to block out incidental secondary noises when dialogue was being recorded. If distant children were shouting or dogs were barking afar off, we went ahead, so that as in real street life noise noises and other background sounds were recorded very naturally, with the close-to-camera conversation of the principals, with most realistic effect. Transportation of our equipment was one of our great problems. It took a carload of equipment weighing forty tons to make *Kiss of Death;* six large trucks were in constant use to move us to one of the seventy-six different sets used in the film's making.

"Unlike studio shooting we had to transport the equipment above ground level—i.e. the opening shots in the Chrysler building thirty to forty stories up. We also carried over two miles of special cable to cope with shooting in moving elevators. Our studio engineers provided us with a special sound recording outfit, weighing nearly a ton, but built in fourteen separate sections to aid quick moves. Portable gasoline generators were used to give current for lighting. The lift shots were taken with Norbert Brodine wedged in the lift shaft corner with a 16mm camera—hand-operated; a special steel and leather harness held both him and the camera, which was loaded with colour film transferred in process to 35mm black-and-white to retain the quality of clarity of the images. No overhead lighting was used, and the zoom lens was employed to great effect, saving trucking." (Quoted from publicity handout for *Kiss of Death.*)

The same attention to mechanical detail was evident on-screen in *Call Northside 777*, where the visual effects of operative telephoto apparatus, lie detecting machines and linotypes were vital facets

James Stewart (left) watches the reunion of wrongly convicted Richard Conte with his family in CALL NORTHSIDE 777. E. G. Marshall at right

of the narrative development. The role of the newspaper industry was positive as opposed to the negative examples in films discussed in previous films, with a particularly credible atmosphere created in the newspaper offices, blending the more exciting moments with the humdrum and the tedium. Lee J. Cobb's performance as a crusading news editor, prepared to follow a hunch to stick on the trail of justice with no concrete evidence, in the face of police and political barriers, and that of James Stewart, his cynical chief reporter, totally convince as characters as opposed to star performers. This in spite of Stewart using all the familiar stops in his range; head lowered and thrust forward in determination, open mouth, hands held low and stiff, with his voice deliberately flattened—a carefully established image of homespun simplicity and rugged worth.

He responds cynically at first to his assignment of answering an advertisement offering a large reward for information about a killing which took place some eleven years earlier. But he becomes more interested when he finds that the mother of a man, sentenced for his part in a robbery during which a policeman was killed, has scrubbed floors for the eleven years to save up the reward money in an attempt to clear her son's name. He visits the son, Frank Wiecek (Richard Conte), in prison, and publishes a few articles. No response is forthcoming so he prepares to drop the case, but his editor insists he keep digging, and his wife encourages him by pointing out that he has aroused some public interest and thus it is his duty to continue. His attitude turns from one of uncertainty to a passionate belief in Wiecek's innocence. The film ends with this innocence being proved at the eleventh hour through a discrepancy in the evidence regarding the time of arrest and booking, during which period a female witness who positively identified him, was shown to have seen him at police headquarters. Most of the clues that the reporter uncovers are reasonable, but it would seem to be just too coincidental that the lawyer who originally defended Wiecek was a drunk.

★ ★ ★

In the context of a number of Hathaway's films, people in positions of responsibility are often vulnerable, or have blind spots which lead to the endangering of many lives. A typical example of this is in *The Real Glory*, where the acting commanding officer, Captain Hartley (Reginald Owen) has been seriously hurt in an assassination attempt. He appears to recover from his wounds, but conceals the fact that he is slowly going blind, and in these circumstances his judgement is severely affected. This leads to a series of confrontations with the hero, Dr. Canavan (Gary Cooper). Cooper is the most closely drawn of a trio of hero figures—a structure favoured by Hathaway (e.g. *The Lives of a Bengal Lancer* and *The Sons of Katie Elder*)—comprising himself, McCool (David Niven) and Larsen (Broderick Crawford). They are both professional soldiers of fortune; McCool comes from an Irish family which has been represented at every great historical battle for centuries, while Larsen is a giant, rather stupid Swede who enjoys growing orchids when he is not fighting. Since they are professional soldiers, they cannot oppose Captain Hartley on humanitarian grounds as may Canavan, but they are still eligible for the respect of the colonel's daughter, Linda (Andrea Leeds), who falls in love with Canavan. Her romantic presence definitely intrudes in the last third of the film on what is basically a "Boy's Own" adventure yarn about the Philippines. The isolation of life as a professional soldier is seen to breed anarchic personalities, and a humanising element is necessary to contain this growth as in the military films of John Ford (e.g. *Fort Apache*) but since *The Real Glory* is a Sam Goldwyn production the stress is on entertainment, so that the point is not expanded upon.

The plot concerns the situation that arises when the American Army evacuates, leaving a few white officers to train the native levies to fight for their own independence. The hostile Moros create a crisis by attempting to kill these officers in order to draw the Filipinos into unwise forays. Although the emphasis is on action, certain subtle touches in the script deserve mention. The fear and uncertainty of the natives is stressed by the juxtaposition of two key scenes: the first being the despair at the sight of the last boat leaving, voiced by the Catholic priest in conversation with the retiring commander, "We who are about to die salute you." The gladiators of Roman times who used this salute had an even chance of survival, but the natives do not, as is shown by a movement of the camera away from the priest to the end of a jetty.

Diane Varsi displays the stubbornness of the Hathaway heroine in MANHUNT, to the amusement of Chill Wills (centre) and Don Murray (right)

A shaven head appears as a huge half-naked Moro swordsman levers himself on to the jetty; the natives flee in terror as he makes a fanatic, desperate charge at his victim—the commanding officer—unhindered by a hail of bullets. As Canavan remarks to Captain Hartley later in the film, "Drill is not enough. Fear is what has to be conquered." Rudy Maté admirably conveys the isolation of the defenceless town, underlining the basis of this fear as well as setting the scene for the vividly staged action scenes which include an ambush, a river being diverted by dynamite, and the final Moro assault on the garrison, employing tree catapults to hurl men and missiles into the skirmish. Discipline takes priority over common sense. Thus Canavan is confined to quarters for experimenting with methods to frighten Moro prisoners, such as threatening to violate their religion by burying them in pig skins, but in any case Canavan is an exception to the general run of Hathaway hero figures in that he possesses common sense in the first place.

The confrontation between discipline and common sense appeared again in *Manhunt,* but here the shrewdness of the hero, Tod Lohman (Don Murray), amounted more to a native cunning since he was too naïve, lacking the experience and assurance of a Canavan. The film opens with Tod stampeding a herd of horses, and badly injuring one of his pursuers in the process. He later outwits the injured man's brother, Tom Boyd (Dennis Hopper), who stays on his tail, but not before Tom has killed Tod's mount. Tod claims he did not kill Tom's brother ("I'm running to prevent killing"); old man Boyd (R. G. Armstrong) berates his son for killing the horse, and for stupidly allowing Tod to wound him ("The only time I went alone was when I did not have any money to hire guns"). Justifying his proposal to track down Tod and murder him ("That saddle tramp has come close to washing my mark out"), he enlists a posse of five men to pursue the fugitive into the desert. Like most patriarchs, he is blind to the faults of his sons, preferring to term them high spirits.

Meanwhile Tod has been surprised at a waterhole by a friendly rancher, Amos Bradley (Chill Wills) and his daughter Juanita (Diane Varsi); they share their food without trying to pry into his business. Tod is embarrassed by Juanita's total frankness and unconventionality—she pointedly tells him he needs a bath, and when he decides to take a midnight dip (clear moonlight) he finds her doing likewise, unashamed of her nudity and quite determined to watch him take his bath! He gives her details of the vendetta between him and the Boyd family, which started with a fight over a girl, resulting in the death of a Boyd son. In return Bradley obliges with a short history of Hunter Boyd ("A powerful wicked man with a queer sense of justice, all his own"). Tod continues his story about his dead mother who gave him a dowry of a Bible and a photo of herself, and of his father who deserted (Juanita: "If you want to find him and give him a hand you *must* be stupid!"). As Tod is talking, Hunter Boyd rides up quietly. He offers Tod a chance: a saddle, a horse and four hours' start because he feels that the family owe him a horse. Tod goes on alone in spite of Juanita's pleas, and kills Boyd's top gun, Carmody (John Larch), burying him but sparing his horse even though it will help to give him away.

He meets a wily trader, Jake Leffertfinger (Jay C. Flippen), who offers him a ride on his wagon. Soon they are being shadowed by Tom Boyd and a henchman; a confrontation is foiled by an Indian attack in which the Boyd men are wiped out. Jake saves his and Tod's life by giving them horses, and deposits Tod in the nearest town, advising him to solve his problems by resorting to plain, cold-blooded murder ("Convictions must fit the time and place"). Hunter Boyd arrives in town, but news of his mission has preceded him, so he gets a cold shoulder. He learns of the death of the Boyd son, trampled by the horses, just before he encounters Tod in the bar. Tod escapes, finding refuge with the Bradleys. He discovers that his father, whom he has long been seeking, died recently in a nearby mission; unable to overcome the hostility of the local people Hunter Boyd resorts to violence in order to draw Tod into open conflict by arranging for gunmen to raid the Bradley ranch and wound Amos Bradley seriously. Tod has no choice: "Like the man said, there's a time and a place."

Tod wounds Tom, pinning him down under fire, also aiming at the Boyd ammunition dump with the desired effect. He kills the last remaining hired gun, who is trying to shoot him from behind. Tom, acting on Hunter Boyd's verbal instructions, shoots down a chandelier in the room in which he is hiding. In so doing, he sets himself alight. Tod, braving Hunter's fire, knocks Tom into a trough and douses the flames, for which Hunter spares his life: "I gave you your life because you saved my last son." Lohman: "I'll grant that but have no doubt you'll go to hell!"

In hindsight, *Manhunt* provides a mirror image of *Nevada Smith* with which it shares a deep involvement in personal responsibility, revenge and family disruption, while on merit it is the better film, thanks to tighter construction, able performances and the competent inter-action of duty and respect shown by the characters towards one another. The tight construction was a welcome return to form for Hathaway since his career had been in the doldrums in the Fifties. He had begun the decade evenly with *Rawhide, You're in the Navy Now* and *14 Hours*; *Rommel–the Desert Fox* was a brave subject to film only a few years after the Second World War, and *Diplomatic Courier* was a neat thriller with semi-documentary overtones (the latter is also one of Hathaway's favourite films):

"*Diplomatic Courier* is a film I like very much, and it was another experience. I had made many pictures outside. The picture took place in Europe and went on all over. I made it on the stage, I never left the stage. The second unit shot the scene with Tyrone Power on the Trocadero. It was an action picture, automobiles chasing each other, and they showed this thing all over the industry. As soon as a guy wanted to go to Europe they said, 'Get *Diplomatic Courier*, show the son-of-a-bitch the picture–it was made on the stage.' All the stuff on the street, everything, was shot with transparencies, like the Trocadero scene." ("Focus on Film." No. 7, 1971.)

But after this film, Hathaway's work declined rapidly, due partly to poor scripts, and partly to the general slump in the industry. The star system was dying, but Twentieth Century-Fox were loath to face the facts, and continued to churn out star vehicles, many of which were shot in CinemaScope. Cameramen and directors share a dislike of the process, and few of the early Fox Scope films stand up well to the passage of time. This internal crisis at the studio proved beneficial to men like Samuel Fuller, who claims he was given *Pick-up on South Street* and *Hell and High Water* by the studio simply because they wanted a fall guy to experiment with the process, and to carry the can if the experiments flopped.

★ ★ ★

Just prior to making *Manhunt,* Hathaway had invested his own money in an independent vehicle for John Wayne and Sophia Loren entitled *Legend of the Lost*; but it had a weak script which was swamped by a mass of attractive but repetitive images, and it proved a disaster both artistically and financially. However he returned to form with three of his four remaining films for Fox. After several independent stints, he signed a five picture contract with Paramount, personally producing two of the films, while Hal Wallis produced the rest. Two of these works rank with his best films; the first being *The Last Safari,* which was based on a novel by Gerald Hanley and filmed on location in Africa with Hathaway using a second unit under the direction of Dick Talmadge. Jack Hawkins, who was recovering from his throat operation, also played a part in the production as an assistant to Hathaway. The film was a solid, unpretentious, professional work, evoking a number of the director's favourite thematic threads.

Professional hunter Miles Gilchrist (Stewart Granger) walks out on a brash young American's safari after a near fatal accident with a rhino, later letting off steam about the changing face of Africa and the gutlessness of the younger generation. The young man, Casey, refuses no for an answer when Gilchrist turns down his request to accompany him on a last safari—in search of a rogue elephant that has killed Gilchrist's best friend. Gilchrist is motivated by guilt, but gradually his narrow-mindedness is worn down by his partner's persistence. After a variety of adventures that involve brushes with the police and a savage tribe, they locate the herd of elephants. But at the last moment Gilchrist finds himself unable to kill his prey. He has however taught the young man humility, while at the same time he has regained his self-respect. The film is beautifully composed in mellow colours, although the effect is marred by the over-insertion of processed animal stock shots. Performances are good, and the film is enlivened by Johnny Dankworth's score—a change for Hathaway in that the music in his films seldom attracts attention.

The second film, *True Grit,* won an Oscar for John Wayne, giving him one of the best roles of his career. Wayne's Rooster Cogburn was a character built around the actor's right-wing personality, but the portrait was softened by a mixture of sentiment and a good natured humour, guying the character's advancing age. For John Ford, Wayne has moved from a stubborn young hero (*Stagecoach*), through the cavalry trilogy (*Rio Grande, Fort Apache* and *She Wore a Yellow Ribbon*) in which his roles became increasingly hard-bitten anarchic men into the obsession and insanity of Ethan Edwards (*The Searchers*) before finally being seen as a tragic hero in *The Man Who Shot Liberty Valance.* In his films for Howard Hawks the progression has been more rapid. Hathaway's films with Wayne have encompassed some of the qualities stressed by Ford and Hawks without, until *True Grit,* particularly developing them. The image of Wayne as a character of violence around whom whole films are built and projected so incensed Dennis Hopper that, after working with him on Hathaway's *The Sons of Katie Elder,* he began a project which has emerged as *The Last Movie* (1971) in protest against this type of image projection.

Hathaway is a personal friend of Wayne, and speaks highly of him: "There are two kinds of actors. There's the kind that are natural-born-for-what-they-are actors. John Wayne is a natural-born strong man, he just looks, he's strong. Cooper was a gentle man but strong. They're born with these kind of things—Henry Fonda and Jimmy Stewart are born with it, it's nothing they learned in school or from the stage or experience, except that they learned to have confidence. Now there's other actors that learn techniques . . . but the best actor's the one that's naturally qualified to do it." ("Focus on Film." No. 7, 1971.)

True Grit is based on a novel by Charles Portis, and the screenplay by Marguerite Roberts is undoubtedly the most literate work that Hathaway has filmed in his entire career. The whole film is earmarked with a quality of solid, unpretentious professionalism; as well as Hathaway and Wayne, the producer Hal B. Wallis and the cameraman Lucien Ballard were seasoned veterans of the old Hollywood. Ballard did not work on any Western films until the Fifties, but has the distinction of filming the two key Westerns of the Sixties: Sam Peckinpah's *Ride the High Country* (GB: *Guns in the Afternoon*) and Tom Gries's *Will Penny* (1968). In *True Grit,* he extends his use of mellow autumnal landscapes into a whole seasonal range of images crucial to the narrative development.

The script literally transferred complete segments of the novel's dialogue to the screen and the frequent wit and unfamiliar turn of phrase gave a new freshness to the situation. Yet Hathaway chose to change the emphasis of the Portis novel by incorporating the contrast between the main characters but lending greater emphasis to the developing sense of affection between them. In lesser hands, it could easily have resulted in a minor film revolving around the conflict between age and experience at the expense of the literate dialogue.

Again the film is enriched by the observation of a number of small details. Mattie, the young heroine, as played by Kim Darby, displays a combination of adult earnestness and sense of purpose with a prim childishness. Soon after the film begins she arrives in town, searching for a man who killed her father. She is told that everybody

Kim Darby fires on her father's killer (Jeff Corey) as he stands over the body of Glen Campbell, whom he has seriously injured in Hathaway's TRUE GRIT

is watching the public hanging in the square; Hathaway invests the scene with some dignity by the introduction of an old hymn, "Amazing Grace," but his main concern is to present the event through Mattie's eyes as a child. Peanut sellers move through the crowd, children play nearby on the swings and a nosey woman points out the hanging judge to Mattie who is grimly watching the proceedings. She confronts the sheriff who evades his job by protesting he cannot enter Indian territory, but he gives her the names of several lawmen who would, including Rooster Cogburn ("Fear don't enter into his thinking"). Mattie's shrewdness and her ability to deal with adults in their own terms has been established through her experience in keeping the ranch accounts, and her clear diction and prim spirit give her a tone of authority.

These qualities help in her first confrontation with Cogburn outside the court ("They tell me you're a man with true grit?"). He is amused as she casts down her eyes while he swigs whisky, and kids her ("I'm givin' you my kid's rate for doing the job!" Mattie: "I'm not paying for your whisky." Rooster: "I don't buy that . . . I confiscate it!") A deal is eventually made, and a young Texas Ranger who is hunting the killer on another charge joins the manhunt with them.

Hathaway uses the journey to celebrate traditional Western imagery: he holds riders in long shot before vast, autumn-tinted forests, lovingly details a river crossing and accelerates the film into top gear with a stunningly photographed attack on an outlaw stronghold. At the same time, he makes the most of the chance to flesh out the characterisations with a running banter between the crusty Wayne and the cocksure Ranger about the merits and demerits of Texas, while Mattie pierces the older man's armour by making him talk about his past as an outlaw, his marriage and a son ("He didn't like me anyway"), and his attitude to his present semi-legitimate bounty-hunting job ("We had a good court–until the lawyers came!").

The attack on the outlaw cabin also reveals Rooster's real motive for taking Mattie's offer. He is motivated by a sense of professional pride because the killer they are seeking is riding with a gang headed by Ned Pepper. Pepper is the only man ever to escape capture or death at Rooster's hands. Hathaway draws a strong parallel between the two men: both are ruthless, but careful planners and neither look for trouble. Yet when confronted with Mattie, Pepper is amusingly unable to cope with verbal onslaughts while Rooster develops a reciprocal affection for the girl.

An incident during the attack is typical of Hathaway's consummate skill in changing the mood of a scene from comedy to stark violence in one dramatic movement. One of the outlaws is wounded (Rooster: "Sit right still so it don't bleed so much. Talk! If not you'll lose your leg or your life as we're not going back to the doc's. That's right. I *am* getting at you!"). Another outlaw has been given a turkey to pluck (an accidental victim of the Ranger's inaccuracy with a scatter-gun), but when his wounded companion begins to talk, he turns his chopper on the man's fingers. Rooster shoots him, but as he falls, he stabs the stool-pigeon who in turn stabs him as both fall to the ground. Rooster's sympathy is brutally frank: "I can't do a thing for you, boy; your partner's killed you, and I've done for him."

Aggression flares between the three central figures over the Civil War, but Mattie keeps Rooster in hand until he takes to the bottle and launches a virulent attack on women, upsetting Mattie who goes for a swim, only to fall into the hands of her father's killer. This new development provides Hathaway with an opportunity to present the classic image of Wayne confronting four outlaws in a glen, charging like a knight, reins in teeth with a gun and a repeating rifle blazing in each hand. He kills three men, but (in a nice touch indicating his age) he is trapped under his dead horse and the Ranger has to help him finish off Ned Pepper.

The film might have ended here, but in typical Hathaway tradition Cogburn kills off one of his heroes—the young Ranger—in a gallant effort to save Mattie's life after she has fallen into a pit of rattlesnakes. Rooster rides his horse to death, eventually carrying Mattie to safety on his back.

Months later in winter time, Mattie takes Rooster to see her pa's grave. The snow-covered background is used by Hathaway to underline the inevitability of death and the fallibility of Rooster, which he comes to accept at long last as Mattie waives aside his protests ("Someday I'll be here beside my pa. I'd like you to rest beside me, Rooster"). A wealth of tradition, the good humour and parody of the film and of the Wayne character itself are frozen in the end title image.

It could have been a fitting climax to a long career, but incredibly Hathaway works steadily on. He helped out his old friend George Seaton by shooting part of *Airport* (1969), while Seaton was ill, and has subsequently shot *Raid on Rommel* and *Shootout*. At the time of writing he is preparing another film which will further extend a career of admittedly variable quality but undeniably polished finish.

Russian agents search an unconscious Tyrone Power's apartment in Hathaway's DIPLOMATIC COURIER. Left to right: Lawrence Dobkin, Stefan Schnabel, Tyrone Power

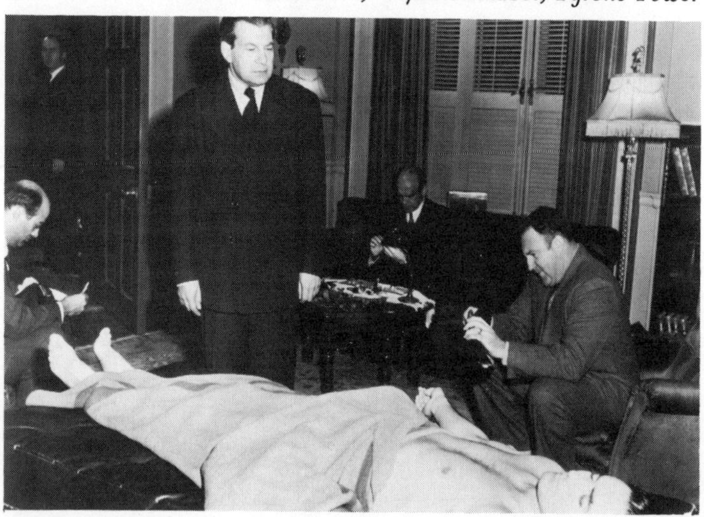

HENRY HATHAWAY Filmography

Actor between 1908–1917 mainly in Westerns for Allan Dwan.

Assistant Director:
Hathaway is know to have worked in this capacity between 1919–1933 with Paul Bern, Victor Fleming, Frank Lloyd and Joseph von Sternberg as director, and also in a number of films starring Gary Cooper. His known credits include:
THE SPOILERS (1923, Lambert Hillyer).
TO THE LAST MAN (1923, Victor Fleming).
THE HERITAGE OF THE DESERT (1924), Irving Willat).
BORDER LEGION (1924, William K. Howard).
THE THUNDERING HERD (1925, William K. Howard).
WILD HORSE MESA (1925, George B. Seitz).
BACHELOR BRIDES (1926, William K. Howard).
MANTRAP (1926, Victor Fleming).
MAN OF THE FOREST (1926, John Waters).
HULA (1927, Victor Fleming).
UNDERWORLD (1927, Josef von Sternberg).
THE LAST COMMAND (1928, Josef von Sternberg).
UNDER THE TONTO RIM (1928, Herman C. Raymaker).
THE SHOPWORN ANGEL (1928, Richard Wallace).
SUNSET PASS (1929, Otto Brower).
WOLF SONG (1929, Victor Fleming).
THUNDERBOLT (1929, Josef von Sternberg).
THE VIRGINIAN (1929, Victor Fleming).
SEVEN DAYS LEAVE (GB: *MEDALS*) (1930, Richard Wallace).
THE TEXAN (1930, John Cromwell).
THE SPOILERS (1930, Edwin Carewe, David Burton).
MOROCCO (1930, Josef von Sternberg).
SHANGHAI EXPRESS (1932, Josef von Sternberg).

Hathaway was the director of all the following films, and also producer where indicated. Historian William K. Everson has reported that the Zane Grey Westerns used stock footage from the earlier versions. It is not possible to establish complete lists of Hathaway's work as a child player and assistant director.

HERITAGE OF THE DESERT (1932). Hero outwits a claim jumper in Western drama. *Sc:* Harold Shumate, Frank Partos (the novel by Zane Grey). *Ph:* Archie Stout. *Art Dir:* Earl Hedrick. *With* Randolph Scott (*Jack Hare*), Sally Blane (*Judy*), J. Farrell MacDonald (*Adam Naab*), David Landau (*Judson Holderness*), Gordon Wescott, Guinn Williams, Vince Barnett. *Prod:* Paramount. 63m. Silent version 1924 (*Dir:* Irvin Willat); re-made 1939 (*Dir:* Leslie Selander).

WILD HORSE MESA (1932). Wild horse tamer clashes with a villain who has discredited his brother. *Sc:* Harold Shumate, Frank Howard Clark (the novel by Zane Grey). *Ph:* Arthur Todd. *Art. Dir:* Earl Hedrick. *With* Randolph Scott (*Chane Weymer*), Sally Blane (*Sandy Melberne*), Fred Kohler (*Rand*), Lucille LaVerne (*Ma Melberne*), James Bush, Charles Grapewin, Jim Thorpe, George

F. Hayes, Buddy Roosevelt, E. H. Calvert. *Prod:* Paramount. 61m. Silent version 1925 (*Dir:* George B. Seitz); re-made 1947 (*Dir:* Wallace A. Grissell).

UNDER THE TONTO RIM (1933). Slow-witted cowboy finds his manhood and wins the boss's daughter. *Sc:* Jack Cunningham, Gerald Geraghty (the novel by Zane Grey). *Ph:* Archie Stout. *Art Dir:* Earl Hedrick. *With* Stuart Erwin (*Tonto Duley*), Fred Kohler (*Murther*), Fuzzy Knight (*Porky*), Verna Hillie (*Nina Weston*), John Lodge (*Joe Gilbert*), George Barbier, Patricia Farley, Edwin J. Brody, Marion Burdell, Allan Garcia. *Prod:* Paramount. 63m. Silent version 1928 (*Dir:* Herman C. Raymaker); re-made 1947 (*Dir:* Lew Landers).

SUNSET PASS (1933). Government agents uncover a gang of rustlers. *Sc:* Jack Cunningham, Gerald Geraghty (the novel by Zane Grey). *Ph:* Archie Stout. *Art Dir:* Earl Hedrick. *With* Randolph Scott (*Ash Preston*), Tom Keene (*Jack Rock*), Kathleen Burke (*Jane Preston*), Harry Carey (*John Hesbitt*), Noah Beery (*Marshall Blake*), Leila Bennett, Fuzzy Knight, Kent Taylor, George Barbier, Vince Barnett, Patricia Farley, Charles Middleton, Tom London, Christian J. Frank, Frank Beal, Al Bridge, Bob Kortman, James Mason. *Prod:* Paramount. 64m. Silent version 1929 (*Dir:* Otto Brower); re-made 1946 (*Dir:* William Berke).

MAN OF THE FOREST (1933). Romantic Western highlighted by a fight between a crooked sheriff and a lion. *Sc:* Jack Cunningham, Harold Shumate (the novel by Zane Grey). *Ph:* Ben Reynolds. *Art Dir:* Earl Hedrick. *With* Randolph Scott (*Brett Dale*), Verna Hillie (*Alice Gaynor*), Harry Carey (*Jim Gaynor*), Noah Beery (*Clint Beasley*), Barton MacLane (*Mulvey*), Buster Crabbe (*Yegg*), Guinn Williams, Vince Barnett, Blanche Frederici, Tempe Piggott, Frank McGlynn, Jr., Tom Kennedy, Duke Lee, Frank Kelly. *Prod:* Paramount. 59m. Silent version 1926 (*Dir:* John Waters).

TO THE LAST MAN (1933). A Western family feud is healed by young love. *Sc:* Jack Cunningham (the novel by Zane Grey). *Ph:* Ben Reynolds. *Art Dir:* Earl Hedrick. *With* Randolph Scott (*Lynn Hayden*), Jack LaRue (*Jim Daggs*), Esther Ralston (*Ellen Colby*), Buster Crabbe (*Billy Hayden*), Noah Beery (*Jed Colby*), Barton MacLane, Muriel Kirkland, Fuzzy Knight, Gail Patrick, Egon Brecher, James Eagles, Eugene Besserer, Harlan Knight, Shirley Temple. *Prod:* Paramount. 61m. Silent version 1923 (*Dir:* Victor Fleming).

THE THUNDERING HERD (1933). Action-packed Western about buffalo hunters and marauding Indians. *Sc:* Jack Cunningham, Mary Flannery (the novel by Zane Grey). *Ph:* Ben Reynolds. *Art Dir:* Earl Hedrick. *With* Randolph Scott (*Tom Doane*), Judith Allen (*Millie Fayre*), Noah Berry (*Randall Jett*), Harry Carey (*Clark Sprague*), Blanche Frederici, Raymond Hatton, Barton MacLane, Monte Blue, Al Bridge, Dick Rush, Frank Rice, Charles McMurphy, Buck Connors. *Prod:* Paramount. 62m. Silent version 1925 (*Dir:* William K. Howard).

THE LAST ROUND-UP (1934). Chivalry in a gang of rustlers leads to the boss sacrificing his life for two young lovers. *Sc:* Jack Cunningham (novel *The Border Legion* by Zane Grey). *Ph:* Archie Stout. *Art Dir:* Earl Hedrick. *With* Randolph

Scott (*Jim Cleve*), Barbara Fritchie (*Joan Randall*), Fred Kohler (*Sam Gulden*), Monte Blue (*Jack Kells*), Fuzzy Knight, Richard Carle, Frank Rice, Barton MacLane, Charles Middleton, Dick Rush, Bob Miles, Jim Corbett, Buck Connors, Jack M. Holmes, James Mason, Sam Allen, Ben Corbett, Jim Corey. *Prod:* Paramount. 61m. Silent versions in 1919 (*Dir:* T. Hayes Hunter) and 1924 (*Dir:* William K. Howard); sound re-makes in 1930 (*Dir:* Otto Brower, Edwin H. Knopf) and 1940 (*Dir:* Joseph Kane)—all under title *The Border Legion.*

COME ON MARINES! (1934). Comedy-drama highlighted by the rescue of some ship-wrecked children who turn out to be glamorous American girls. *Sc:* Byron Morgan, Joel Sayre (a Philip Wylie story). *Ph:* Ben Reynolds. *Ed:* James Smith. *Art Dir:* Earl Hedrick. *Mus:* Ralph Rainger. *With* Richard Arlen (*Lucky Davis*), Ida Lupino (*Esther Smith-Hamilton*), Roscoe Karns (*Spud McGurke*), Toby Wing (*Dolly*), Grace Bradley (*Jo-Jo La Verne*), Virginia Hammond, Gwenllian Gill, Clara Lou (Ann) Sheridan, Lona Andre, Leo Shalzel, Fuzzy Knight, Julian Madison, Monte Blue, Pat Flaherty, Edmund Breeze, Jean Chatborn, Jennifer Gray, Kay McCoy, Mary Blackwood, Colin Tapley, Yancey Lane, Eldred Tidbury, Gil Berry, Roger Gray. *Prod:* Albert Lewis for Paramount. 70m.

THE WITCHING HOUR (1934). Drama about the relationship of thought transference and mysticism to love. *Sc:* Anthony Veiller (adaptation by Salisbury Field of the play by Augustus Thomas). *Ph:* Ben Reynolds. *Ed:* Jack Dennis. *Art Dir:* Earl Hedrick. *With* Sir Guy Standing (*Martin Prentice*), Tom Brown (*Clay Thorne*), John Halliday (*Jack Brookfield*), Judith Allen (*Nancy Brookfield*), Olive Tell (*Mrs. Thorne*), William Frawley, Richard Carle, Rolf Harolde, Purnell Pratt, Frank Sheridan, John Larkin, Selmar Jackson, Howard Lang, George Webb, Robert Littlefield. *Prod:* Bayard Veiller for Paramount. 69m. Silent version in 1921 (*Dir:* William D. Taylor).

NOW AND FOREVER (1934). Comedy-drama about the reformation of a jewel thief by a little girl. *Sc:* Vincent Lawrence, Sylvia Thalberg (a story by Jack Kirkland, Melville Barker). *Ph:* Harry Fischbeck. *Art Dir:* Hans Dreier, Robert Usher. *Ed:* Ellsworth Hoagland. *Mus:* Harry Revel, Mack Gordon. *With* Gary Cooper (*Jerry Day*), Shirley Temple (*Penelope Day*), Carole Lombard (*Toni Day*), Sir Guy Standing (*Felix Evans*), Charlotte Granville (*Mrs. Crane*), Gilbert Emery, Egon Brecher, Henry Kolker, Tetsu Komai, Jameson Thomas, George Webb, Akim Tamiroff, Richard Loo, Ronnie Crosby, Sam Harris, Grace Hale, Look Chan, Buster Phelps, Ynez Seabury. *Prod:* Louis D. Lighton for Paramount. 81m.

THE LIVES OF A BENGAL LANCER (1935). Adventure as the Lancers put down an uprising on the Indian frontier. *Sc:* Waldemar Young, John Balderston (adaptation by William Slavens McNutt, Grover Jones, Achmed Abdullah of a novel by Francis Yeats-Brown). *Ph:* Charles Lang. *Art Dir:* Hans Dreier, Roland Anderson. *Ed:* Ellsworth Hoagland. *Mus:* Milan Roder. *With* Gary Cooper (*Lieut. McGregor*), Franchot Tone (*Lieut. Forsythe*), Richard Cromwell (*Lieut. Stone*), Sir Guy Standing (*Colonel Stone*), Sir C. Aubrey Smith (*Major*

Noah Beery distracts a smug Jack La Rue in TO THE LAST MAN, with Gail Patrick looking on

Hamilton) Monte Blue (*Hamzulla Kahn*), Douglas Dumbrille (*Mohammed Kahn*), Kathleen Burke (*Tania*), Colin Tapley, Akim Tamiroff, Jameson Thomas, Noble Johnson, Rollo Lloyd, J. Carrol Naish, Lumsden Hare, Charles Stevens, Leonid Kinskey, Eddie Das, James Warwick, Boswan Singh, Abdul Hassan, Clive Morgan, George Regas, Major Sam Harris, Carli Taylor, Ram Singh, James Bell, General Konnikoff, F. A. Armenta, Claude King, Reginald Sheffield, Ray Cooper, Lya Lys. *Prod:* Louis D. Lighton for Paramount. 109m. Indian location footage shot by Ernest B. Schoedsack.

PETER IBBETSON (1935). Romantic fantasy in which a condemned man relives his relationship with his sweetheart. *Sc:* Constance Collier, Vincent Lawrence, Waldemar Young, John Meehan, Edwin Justus Mayer (a novel by George Du Maurier and play by Nathaniel Raphael). *Ph:* Charles Lang. *Art Dir:* Hans Dreier, Robert Usher. *Ed:* Stuart Heisler. *Mus:* Ernest Toch. *With* Gary Cooper (*Peter Ibbetson*), Ann Harding (*Mary, Duchess of Towers*), John Halliday (*Duke of Towers*), Ida Lupino (*Agnes*), Douglas Dumbrille (*Colonel Forsythe*), Virginia Weidler (*Mimsie*), Dickie Moore, Doris Lloyd, Christian Rub, Gilbert Emery, Elsa Buchanan, Donald Meek, Leonid Kinskey. *Prod:* Louis D. Lighton for Paramount. 85m. Earlier version (George Fitzmaurice, 1921) was released in U.S. as *Forever* but as *Peter Ibbetson* in Europe.

THE TRAIL OF THE LONESOME PINE (1936). Tale of a young engineer who walks into the middle of a long-standing mountain family feud. *Sc:* Grover Jones (adaptation by Harvey Thew and Horace McCoy of the novel by John Fox, Jr.). *Ph:* Robert C. Bruce and W. Howard Greene. *Art Dir:* Hans Dreier. *Ed:* Robert Bischoff. *Mus:* Boris Morros. *With* Fred MacMurray (*Jack Hale*), Henry Fonda (*Dave Tolliver*), Sylvia Sidney (*June Tolliver*), Spanky McFarland (*Buddy Tolliver*), Nigel Bruce (*Thurber*), Fuzzy Knight, Ricca Allen, Margaret Armstrong, Powell Clayton, George Ernest, Frank McGlynn, Jnr., Samuel S. Hinds, Alan Baxter, Ed LeSaint, Hank Bell, Fred Burns, Bud Gerry, Richard Carle, Jim Welch, John Beck, William McCormick, Bob Kortman, Yakima Canutt, Fred Stone, Beulah Bondi, Robert Barrat and Henry Kleinbach. *Prod:* Walter Wanger for Paramount. 102m. The first three-colour "outdoors" picture. Previous versions 1916 (*Dir:* Cecil B. DeMille) and 1923 (*Dir:* Charles Maigne).

GO WEST, YOUNG MAN (1936).

Comedy of movie queen's romantic adventures in the sticks. *Sc:* Mae West (play "Personal Appearance" by Lawrence Riley). *Ph:* Karl Struss. *Art Dir:* Earl Hedrick. *Ed:* Ray Curtis. *Music:* George Stoll. *With* Mae West (*Mavis Arden*), Randolph Scott (*Bud Norton*), Warren William (*Morgan*), Isabel Jewell (*Gladys*), Alice Brady (*Mrs. Struthers*), Lyle Talbot (*Francis X. Harrigan*), Elizabeth Patterson (*Aunt Kate*), Margaret Perry, Etienne Girardot, Maynard Holmes, Jack LaRue, Alice Ardell, Robert Baiko, Nicodemus, G. P. Hartley, Jr., Xavier Cugat and his orchestra. *Prod:* Emmanuel Cohen for Paramount. 82m.

SOULS AT SEA (1937). Skullduggery aboard a sailing ship. *Sc:* Grover Jones, Dale Van Every (additional scenes by Richard Talmadge) (a story by Ted Lesser). *Ph:* Charles Lang, Merritt Gerstad. *Art Dir:* Hans Dreier, Roland Anderson. *Ed:* Ellsworth Hoagland. *Mus:* W. Frank Harling, Milan Roder. *With* Gary Cooper (*Nuggin' Taylor*), George Raft (*Powdah*), Frances Dee (*Margaret Tarryton*), Henry Wilcoxon (*Lieut. Tarryton*), Harry Carey (*Captain*), Olympe Bradna (*Babsie*), Robert Cummings (*George Martin*), Porter Hall, Paul Fix, Virginia Weidler, George Zucco, Joseph Schildkraut, Gilbert Emery, Lucien Littlefield, Tully Marshall, Monte Blue, Stanley Fields, Lon McAllister, Luana Walters, Fay Holden, Clyde Cook, Rollo Lloyd, Wilson Berge, Eugene Borden, Lee Shumway, Ethel Clayton, Jane Weir, Davison Clark, Harvey Clark, William Stack, Charles Middleton, Olaf Hytten, Forrester Harvey, Robert Barratt, Constantine Romanoff, Agnes Ayres, Lina Basquette, Pauline Haddon, Lowell Drew, Paul Stanton, Leslie Francis, Margaret Daggett, Lil Bean, Betty Lorraine, Alan Ladd. *Prod:* Paramount. 87m.

George Raft greets Louise Platt, with John Barrymore, Dorothy Lamour and Lynn Overman in attendance, in SPAWN OF THE NORTH

SPAWN OF THE NORTH (1938). Russian pirates undermine the salmon fishing industry, and break up a friendship. *Sc:* Talbot Jennings, Jules Furthman (and, uncredited, Dale Van Every) (a story by Barrett Willoughby). *Ph:* Charles Lang, Jr. *Ed:* Ellsworth Hoagland. *Mus:* Dimitri Tiomkin. *With* George Raft (*Tyler Dawson*), Henry Fonda (*Jim Kimmerlee*), Dorothy Lamour (*Nicky Duval*), Louise Platt (*Diane*), John Barrymore (*Windy Turlon*), Akim Tamiroff (*Red Skain*), Richard Ung, Lynne Overman, Fuzzy Knight, Vladimir Sokoloff Alex Woloshin, Duncan Renaldo, Archie Twitchell, Henry Brandon, Wade Boteler, Michio Ito, Lee Shumway, Stanley Andrews, Guy Usher, Egon Brecher, Harvey Clark, Galan Galt, Monte Blue, Irving Bacon, Ray Middleton, Rollo Lloyd, John Wray, Eddie Marr,

Aida Kutzenoff, Frank Puglia, Leonid Snegoff, Edmund Elton, Arthur Aylesworth. *Prod:* Albert Lewin for Paramount. 110m. Re-made 1954 as *Alaska Seas* (*Dir:* Jerry Hopper).

THE REAL GLORY (1939). Three soldiers of fortune take part in a campaign to put down a terrorist uprising in the Philippines. *Sc:* Jo Swerling, Robert Presnell (a story by Charles L. Clifford). *Ph:* Rudolph Mate. *Art Dir:* James Basevi. *Ed:* Daniel Mandell. *Mus:* Alfred Newman. *With* Gary Cooper (*Doctor Canavan*), Andrea Leeds (*Linda Hartley*), Broderick Crawford (*Lieut. Larson*), David Niven (*Lieut. McCool*), Reginald Owen (*Captain Hartley*), Kay Johnson (*Mrs. Manning*), Russell Hicks (*Captain Manning*), Vladimir Sokoloff, Nick Shaid, Benny Inocencio, Charles Waldron, Rudy Robles, Tetsu Komai, Roy Gordon, Henry Kolker, Fritz Leiber, Bob Naihe, George Kaluna, Caiya Amboli, Luke Chan, Elvira Rios, John Villasin, Charles Stevens, Martin Wilkins, Karen Sorrell, Satini Puailoa, Kalu Sonkur, Soledad Jiminez, Locio Villegas, Elmo Lincoln. *Prod:* Samuel Goldwyn for Goldwyn/United Artists. 95m.

JOHNNY APOLLO (1940). Gangster melodrama with college graduate choosing crime as a career. *Sc:* Philip Dunne, Rowland Brown (story by Samuel G. Engel and Hal Long). *Ph:* Arthur Miller. *Mus:* Lionel Newman. *With* Tyrone Power (*Bob Cain*), Lloyd Nolan (*Mickey Dwyer*), Marc Lawrence (*Bates*), Dorothy Lamour (*Lucky DuBarry*), Edward Arnold (*Robert Cain, Snr.*), Charles Grapewin (*Judge Emmett T. Brennan*), Lionel Atwill, Russell Hicks, Jonathan Hale, Harry Rosenthal, Fuzzy Knight, Selmar Jackson, Charles Lane, John Hamilton, Charles Trowbridge, Eddie Marr, William Pawley, Eric Wilton, Gary Breckner, Harry Tyler, George Irving, Anthony Caruso, Stanley Andrews, Wally Albright. *Prod:* Darryl F. Zanuck, Harry Joe Brown for 20th Century-Fox. 93m.

BRIGHAM YOUNG—FRONTIERSMAN (1940). Fictionalised part-biography of the Mormon leader who founded Salt Lake City. *Sc:* Lamar Trotti (a story by Louis Bromfield). *Ph:* Arthur Miller. *Art Dir:* William Darling, Maurice Ransford. *Ed:* Robert Bischoff. *Mus:* Alfred Newman. *With* Dean Jagger (*Brigham Young*), Brian Donlevy (*Angus Duncan*), Tyrone Power (*Jonathan Kent*), Linda Darnell (*Zina Webb*), Mary Astor (*Mary Ann Young*), John Carradine (*Porter Rockwell*), Jane Darwell (*Eliza Kent*), Jean Rogers (*Clara Young*), Vincent Price (*Joseph Smith*), Moroni Olsen, Willard Robertson, Marc Lawrence, Dickie Jones, Stanley Andrews, Arthur Aylesworth, Frank Thomas, Selmar Jackson, Fuzzy Knight, Frederick Burton, Chief Big Tree, Davidson Clark, Claire Du Brey, Tully Marshall, Dick Rich, Ralph Dunn, Edwin Maxwell, Edmund McDonald, George Melford. *Prod:* Kenneth MacGowan for 20th Century-Fox. 114m.

THE SHEPHERD OF THE HILLS (1941). Drama of mountain family feuding in the Ozarks. *Sc:* Grover Jones, Stuart Anthony (the novel by Harold Bell Wright). *Ph:* Charles Lang, Jr., W. Howard Greene. *Art Dir:* Hans Dreier, Roland Anderson. *Ed:* Ellsworth Hoagland. *Mus:* Gerard Carbonara. *With* John Wayne (*Young Matt*), Betty Field (*Sammy Lane*), Harry Carey (*Daniel Howitt*),

Old pals John Wayne and Ward Bond appear to be on opposite sides in Hathaway's SHEPHERD OF THE HILLS

Beulah Bondi (*Aunt Mollie*), James Barton (*Old Matt*), Tom Fadden, Samuel S. Hinds, Marjorie Main, Marc Lawrence, Ward Bond, John Qualen, Fuzzy Knight, Olin Howland, Dorothy Adams, Fern Emmett, Vivita Campbell. *Prod:* Jack Moss for Paramount. 98m. Technicolor. Earlier versions 1919 (*d* Wright) and 1927 (*d* Albert S. Rogell).

SUNDOWN (1941). Jungle girl aids the British in foiling a Nazi take-over bid in Africa. *Sc:* Barré Lyndon (adaptation by Charles G. Booth of a story by Barré Lyndon). *Ph:* Charles Lang, Jr. *Art Dir:* Alexander Golitzen. *Ed:* Dorothy Spencer. *Mus:* Miklos Rozsa. *With* Gene Tierney (*Zia*), George Sanders (*Major Coombes*), Bruce Cabot (*Crawford*), Harey Carey (*Dewey*), Joseph Calleia (*Pallini*), Sir Cedric Hardwicke (*Bishop*), Gilbert Emery, Jeni LeGon, Emmett Smith, Reginald Gardner, Marc Lawrence, Ivan Browning, Dorothy Dandridge, Horace Walker, Edward Das, Prince Maelupe, Hassan Said, Wesley Gale, Jester Hairston, Gustas Nero, Woody Strode, Al Duval, Kenny Washington, Walter Knox, Tetsu Komai, William Broodes, William Dunn, Frederick Clark, Darby Jones, Blue Washington, Frank Clark, Lawrence Lamarr, George Lincoln, St. Luke's Choristers. *Prod:* Walter Wanger for United Artists. 90m.

TEN GENTLEMEN FROM WEST POINT (1942). Fictional drama about the start of the formation of the U.S.M.A. at West Point. *Sc:* Richard Maibaum (additional dialogue by George Seaton) (story by Malvin Wald). *Ph:* Leon Shamroy. *Art Dir:* Richard Day, Nathan Juran. *Ed:* James B. Clark. *Mus:* Alfred Newman. *With* George Montgomery (*Dawson*), Laird Cregar (*Major Sam Carter*), Maureen O'Hara (*Carol Bainbridge*), John Sutton (*Howard Shelton*), John Sheppard (*Henry Clay*), Ward Bond (*Scully*), Victor Francen, Harry Davenport, Douglas Dumbrille, Ralph Byrd, Joe Brown, Jr., David Bacon, Esther Dale, Richard Dunn, Louis Jean Heydt, Stanley Andrews, Edna Mae Jones, James Flavin, Charles Trowbridge, Morris Ankrum, Tully Marshall, Edwin Maxwell, Edward Fielding, Selmar Jackson, Noble Johnson, Eddie Dunn, George Holmes, Frank Ferguson, Dick Winslow, Blake Edwards, John Meredith, Anthony Marsh, Dick Hogan, Roger Kirby, Gordon Wynne, Gene Garrick, Stanley Parlam, Malcolm McTaggart, Gene Rizzi, Herbert Patterson, John Whitney, Tom Neal, Max Cole, John Hartley, William Kersen, Dan Peters. *Prod:* Ben Hecht for 20th Century-Fox. 102m.

CHINA GIRL (1942). Adventure story

about an American newsreel photographer working in the Orient in 1941. *Sc:* Ben Hecht (a story by Melville Crossman). *Ph:* Lee Garmes. *Art Dir:* James Basevi, Chester Gore. *Ed:* Harmon Jones. *Mus:* Hugo Friedhofer. *With* George Montgomery (*Johnny Williams*), Gene Tierney (*Miss Young*), Lynn Bari (*Captain Fifi*), Alan Baxter (*Jones*), Victor McLaglen (*Major Bull Weed*), Sig Ruman (*Jarubi*), Myron McCormick, Bobby Blake, Ann Pennington, Philip Ahn, Allen Jung, Tom Neal, Chester Gahn, Paul Fung, Mal Chand Mehra, Beal Wong, Olie Chan, Kam Tong. *Prod:* Ben Hecht for 20th Century-Fox. 95m.

HOME IN INDIANA (1944). Small-town Americana about harness racing and young love. *Sc:* Winston Miller (magazine story "The Phantom Filly" by George Agnew Chamberlain). *Ph:* Edward Cronjager. *Art Dir:* James Basevi, Chester Gore. *Ed:* Harmon Jones. *Mus:* Hugo Friedhofer. *With* Lon McAllister (*Sparke*), Walter Brennan (*J.P.–Thunderbolt*), Jeanne Crain (*Char*), June Haver (*Cri-Cri*), Charlotte Greenwood (*Penny*), Ward Bond (*Jed Bruce*), Charles Dingle (*Godaw Boole*), Robert Condon, Charles Surgau, Willie Best, George Reed, Tom Dugan, Noble Chissell, Walter Baldwin, George Cleveland, Arthur Aylesworth, Libby Taylor, Roger Imhof, Sam McDaniel, Matt McHugh, Eddy Waller, Billy Mitchell, Emmett Smith. *Prod:* Andre Daven for 20th Century-Fox. 103m. Technicolor. Remade 1957 as *April Love* (*Dir:* Henry Levin).

WING AND A PRAYER (1944). Action drama of Navy carrier pilots and wartime heroism. *Sc:* Jerome Cady (and Mortimer Braus, uncredited). *Ph:* Glen MacWilliams. *Art Dir:* Lyle Wheeler, Lewis Creber. *Ed:* J. Watson Webb. *Mus:* Hugo Friedhofer. *With* Don Ameche (*Bingo Harper*), Dana Andrews (*Moulton*), Sir Cedric Hardwicke (*The Admiral*), William Eythe (*Oscar Scott*), Charles Bickford (*Captain Waddell*), Kevin O'Shea (*Cookie*), Richard Jaeckel, Henry Morgan, Glenn Langan, Renny McEvoy, Robert Bailey, Reed Hadley, Ray Teal, George Matthews, B. S. Pully, Dave Willock, Murray Alper, John Miles, Charles Lane, Irving Bacon, Joe Haworth, Charles Trowbridge, Matt McHugh, Charles Smith, Larry Thompson, Billy Lechner, John Kelly. *Prod:* William A. Bacher, Walter Morosco for 20th Century-Fox. 97m.

NOB HILL (1945). Romantic drama in which a saloon owner wins a blue-blooded socialite, on his own terms, in turn of the century San Francisco. *Sc:* Norman Reilly Raine, Wanda Tuchock (a story by Elenore Griffin). *Ph:* Edward Cronjager. *Art Dir:* Lyle Wheeler, Russell Spencer. *Ed:* Harmon Jones. *Mus:* Emil Newman, Charles Henderson. *With* George Raft (*Tony Angel*), Joan Bennett (*Harriet Carruthers*), Vivian Blaine (*Sally Templeton*), Peggy Ann Garner (*Katie Flanagan*), Alan Reed (*Dapper Jack Harrigan*), B. S. Pully, Emil Coleman, Edgar Barrier, George Anderson, Joe Smith, Charles Dale, Don Costello, J. Farrell MacDonald, Joseph J. Greene, The Three Swifts, William Haade, Mike Mazurki, George E. Stone, George Blagoi, Veda Ann Borg, George McKay, Beal Wong, George T. Lee, Robert Grieg, Charles Cane, Helen O'Hara, Dorothy Ford, Arthur Loft, Nestor Paiva, Chick

Chandler, Paul Everton, Anita Bolster, Otto Reischow, Jane Jones, Bugo Berg, Rory Calhoun, Harry Shannon, Russell Hicks. *Prod:* Andre Daven for 20th Century-Fox. 95m. Technicolor.

THE HOUSE ON 92nd STREET (1945). Semidocumentary spy thriller, which initiated a cycle of films in this style. *Sc:* Barré Lyndon, Charles G. Booth, John Monks, Jr. (a story by Charles G. Booth). *Ph:* Norbert Brodine. *Art Dir:* Lyle Wheeler, Lewis Creber. *Ed:* Harmon Jones. *Mus. Dir:* Emil Newman. *With* William Eythe (*Bill Dietrich*), Lloyd Nolan (*Inspector George A. Briggs*), Signe Hasso (*Elsa Gebhardt*), Gene Lockhart (*Charles Ogden Roper*), Leo G. Carroll (*Colonel Hammersohn*), Lydia St. Clair, William Post, Jr., Harry Bellaver, Bruno Wick, Harro Meller, Charles Wagenheim, John McKee, Alfred Linder, Renee Carson, Salo Douday, Elisabeth Neumann, Alfred Zeisler, E. G. Marshall, Reed Hadley (*narrator*), Paul Ford. *Prod:* Louis de Rochemont for 20th Century-Fox. 88m.

THE DARK CORNER (1946). Drama about a detective who is framed for murder. *Sc:* Jay Dratler, Bernard Schoenfeld (a story by Leo Rosten). *Ph:* Joseph MacDonald. *Art Dir:* James Basevi, Leland Fuller. *Ed:* J. Watson Webb. *Mus:* Cyril Mockridge. *With* Mark Stevens (*Bradford Galt*), Lucille Ball (*Kathleen*), Clifton Webb (*Cathcart*), Kurt Kreuger (*Tony Jardine*), William Bendix (*White Suit*), Constance Collier (*Mrs. Kingsley*), Cathy Downs, Reed Hadley, Molly Lamont, John Goldsworthy, Forbes Murray, Regina Wallace, Charles Wagenheim, Eddie Heywood and his Orchestra, Ellen Corby, John Russell. *Prod:* Fred Kohlmar for 20th Century-Fox. 99m.

Lucille Ball with a troubled Mark Stevens in Hathaway's THE DARK CORNER

13 RUE MADELEINE (1946). Semidocumentary tribute to the work of the O.S.S. in the Second World War. *Sc:* John Monks, Jr., Sy Bartlett. *Ph:* Norbet Brodine. *Art Dir:* James Basevi, Maurice Ransford. *Ed:* Harmon Jones. *Mus:* Alfred Newman. *With* James Cagney (*Bob Sharkey*), Annabella (*Suzanne de Beaumont*), Richard Conte (*Bill O'Connell*), Frank Latimore (*Jeff Lassiter*), Melville Cooper (*Pappy Simpson*), Sam Jaffe, Marcel Rousseau, Walter Abel, Richard Gordon, E. G. Marshall, Blanche Yurka, Alfred Linder, Ben Low, Horace MacMahon, James Craven, Karl Malden, Red Buttons, Reed Hadley (*narrator*). *Prod:* Louis de Rochemont for 20th Century-Fox. 95m.

KISS OF DEATH (1947). Crime drama. *Sc:* Charles Lederer, Ben Hecht (a story by Eleazar Lipsky). *Ph:* Norbert Brodine. *Art Dir:* Lyle Wheeler, Leland Fuler.

Ed: J. Watson Webb. *Mus:* David Buttolph. *With* Victor Mature (*Nick Bianco*), Richard Widmark (*Tommy Udo*), Coleen Gray (*Nick's girl*), Brian Donlevy (*Assistant D.A.*), Taylor Holmes, Howard Smith, Karl Malden, Anthony Ross, J. Scott Smart, Mildred Dunnock, Millard Mitchell, Temple Texas, Henry Brandon, Harry Bellaver, Robert Keith, Patricia Morison (cut out of British print). *Prod:* Fred Kohlmar for 20th Century-Fox. 90m. Re-made at Fox in 1958 (Gordon Douglas) as *The Fiend Who Walked the West.*

CALL NORTHSIDE 777 (1948). Semi-documentary drama about a persistent crime reporter clearing a young Pole of a wrongful conviction. *Sc:* Jerome Cady, Jay Dratler (articles by James P. McGuire, adapted by Leonard Hoffman, Quentin Reynolds). *Ph:* Joseph MacDonald. *Art Dir:* Lyle Wheeler, Mark-Lee Kirk. *Ed:* J. Watson Webb. *Mus:* Alfred Newman. *With* James Stewart (*McNeal*), Richard Conte (*Frank Wiecek*), Lee J. Cobb (*Brian Kelly*), Helen Walker (*Laura McNeal*), Betty Garde (*Wanda Skutnik*), Kasia Orzaewski (*Tillie*), Jeanne de Bergh (*Helen Wiecek-Rayska*), Howard Smith, Moroni Olsen, John McIntire, Paul Harvey, Samuel S. Hinds, J. M. Kerrigan, George Tyne, Dick Bishop, Otto Waldis, Michael Chapin, John Bleifer, Addison Richards, Richard Rober, Eddie Dunn, Percy Helton, Joan Crawley, Charles Lane, E. G. Marshall, Lou Eccles, Norman McKay, William Post, Jr., Lionel Stander, Henry Kulky, Walter Greaza, Tom Bosley, Thelma Ritter (part cut). *Prod:* Otto Lang for 20th Century-Fox. 111m.

DOWN TO THE SEA IN SHIPS (1949). Life on a New England whaling boat seen through the eyes of a young boy. *Sc:* Sy Bartlett, John Lee Mahin (story by Sy Bartlett based on the 1922 version scripted by John L. E. Pell). *Ph:* Joseph MacDonald. *Art Dir:* Lyle Wheeler, Ben Hayne. *Ed:* Dorothy Spencer. *Mus:* Alfred Newman. *With* Richard Widmark (*Dan Lunceford*), Lionel Barrymore (*Captain Bering Joy*), Dean Stockwell (*Jed Joy*), Cecil Kellaway (*Slush Tubbs*), Gene Lockhart (*Andrew Bush*), Berry Kroeger (*Manchester*), John McIntire (*Thatch*), Henry Morgan, Harry Davenport, Paul Harvey, Jay C. Flippen, Fuzzy Knight, Arthur Hohl, Dorothy Adams, Hubert E. Flanagan. *Prod:* Louis D. Lighton for 20th Century-Fox. 120m. Previous version 1922 (*Dir:* Elmer Clifton).

THE BLACK ROSE (1950). Period adventure in which a disinherited Saxon noble becomes a soldier of fortune in Mongolia to regain his self-respect. *Sc:* Talbot Jennings (novel by Thomas B. Costain). *Ph:* Jack Cardiff. *Art Dir:* Paul Sherriff, W. Andrews. *Ed:* Manuel del Campos. *Mus:* Richard Addinsell. *With* Tyrone Power (*Walter of Gurnie*), Orson Welles (*Bayan*), Jack Hawkins (*Tristram, the Bowman*), Cecile Aubry (*Maryam, the Black Rose*), Michael Rennie, Finlay Currie, Herbert Lom, Mary Clare, Alfonso Bedoya, Gibb McLaughlin, James Robertson Justice, Henry Oscar, Laurence Harvey, Bobby Blake. *Prod:* Louis D. Lighton for 20th Century-Fox. 120m. Technicolor.

RAWHIDE (1950). Western suspense drama about a man and woman held prisoner in a remote stagecoach swing station by a band of outlaws. *Sc:* Dudley

Nichols. *Ph:* Milton Krasner. *Art Dir:* Lyle Wheeler, George W. Davis. *Ed:* Robert Simpson. *Mus:* Sol Kaplan. *With* Tyrone Power (*Tom Owens*), Susan Hayward (*Vinnie Holt*), Hugh Marlowe (*Zimmerman*), Dean Jagger (*Yancy*), Edgar Buchanan (*Sam Todd*), Jack Elam (*Tevis*), George Tobias (*Gratz*), Jeff Corey (*Luke Davis*), James Millican, Louis Jean Heydt, William Haade, Milton R. Corey, Ken Tobey, Dan White, Edith Evanson, Walter Sande, Norman Lloyd. *Prod:* Samuel G. Engel for 20th Century-Fox. 86m. Alternative TV title: DESPERATE SIEGE.

YOU'RE IN THE NAVY NOW (Original U.S. title: U.S.S. TEA KETTLE) (1951). Comedy about a group of misfits led by a green officer who are chosen to man a craft fitted with a new steam turbine engine. *Sc:* Richard Murphy (a story by John W. Hazard). *Ph:* Joseph MacDonald. *Art Dir:* Lyle Wheeler, J. Russell Spencer. *Ed:* James B. Clark. *Mus:* Lionel Newman. *With* Gary Cooper (*Lieut. John Harkness*), Jane Greer (*Ellie*), Eddie Albert (*Lieut. Bill Barrow*), Millard Mitchell (*Chief Boatswain's Mate Larrabee*), Harry Von Zell (*Captain Eliot*), John McIntire (*Commander Reynolds*), Ray Collins, Jack Webb, Henry Slate, Ed Begley, Richard Erdman, Harvey Lembeck, Jack Warden, Fay Roope, Charles Tannen, Charles Buchinski (Bronson), Lee Marvin, Damian O'Flynn. *Prod:* Fred Kohlmar for 20th Century-Fox. 93m.

14 HOURS (1951). Drama about the efforts to prevent a mentally disturbed man from jumping off a Manhattan hotel ledge. *Sc:* John Paxton (story "The Man on the Ledge" by Joel Sayre). *Ph:* Joseph MacDonald. *Art Dir:* Lyle Wheeler, George W. Davis. *Ed:* Dorothy Spencer. *Mus:* Alfred Newman. *With* Paul Douglas (*Dunnigan*), Richard Basehart (*Robert Cosick*), Debra Paget (*Ruth*), Barbara Bel Geddes (*Virginia*), Agnes Moorehead (*Mrs. Cosick*), Robert Keith (*Mr. Cosick*), Howard Da Silva (*Lieut. Moskar*), Brad Dexter, Jeffrey Hunter, Martin Gabel, Grace Kelly, Frank Faylen, James Millican, Donald Randolph, Russell Hicks, Frank Taylor, James Warren, Ossie Davis, David Burns, John Randolph, Joyce Van Patten, Brian Keith, Harvey Lembeck, Willard Waterman. *Prod:* Sol C. Siegel for 20th Century-Fox. 92m. Pocket remake MAN ON THE LEDGE (1955, *d* Lewis Allen).

THE DESERT FOX (G.B.:ROMMEL—DESERT FOX) (1951). War drama set behind German lines during the Second World War's African campaign. *Sc:* Nunnally Johnson (from book *Rommel* by Desmond Young). *Ph:* Norbert Brodine. *Art Dir:* Lyle Wheeler, Maurice Ransford. *Ed:* James B. Clark. *Mus:* Daniel Amphitheatrof. *With* James Mason (*Rommel*), Sir Cedric Hardwicke (*Dr. Karl Strolin*), Jessica Tandy (*Frau Rommel*), Luther Adler (*Hitler*), Everett Sloane (*General Bergdorf*), Leo G. Carroll (*Field Marshal Von Rundstedt*), George Macready (*General Fritz Bayerland*), Richard Boone (*Aldinger*), Eduard Franz, Michael Rennie (*Voice*), William Reynolds, Charles Evans, John Hoyt, Walter Kingsford, Don De Leo, Robert Coote, Richard Elmore, John Vosper, Sean McClory, Dan O'Herlihy, Scott Forbes, Victor Wood, Lester Matthews, Mary Carroll, Paul Cavanagh, Lumsden Hare, Jack Baston, John Goldsworthy, Carleton Young, Freeman Lusk. *Prod:* Nunnally Johnson for 20th Century-Fox. 88m.

DIPLOMATIC COURIER (1952). Spy thriller with semi-documentary overtones. *Sc:* Casey Robinson, Liam O'Brien (novel *Sinister Errand* by Peter Cheyney). *Ph:* Lucien Ballard. *Art Dir:* Lyle Wheeler, John De Cuir. *Ed:* James B. Clark. *Mus:* Sol Kaplan. *With* Tyrone Power (*Mike Kells*), Patricia Neal (*Joan Ross*), Karl Malden (*Ernie*), Stephen McNally (*Col. Cagle*), Hildegarde Neff (*Janine*), Stefan Schnabel (*Plator*), James Millican (*Sam Carew*), Herbert Berghoff, Arthur Blake, Helene Stanley, Michael Ansara, Peter Coe, Russ Conway, Lumsden Hare, Lee Marvin, Stuart Randall, Charles Bronson, Mario Siletti. *Prod:* Casey Robinson for 20th Century-Fox. 97m.

O. HENRY'S FULL HOUSE (G.B.: FULL HOUSE) (1952)–episode *The Clarion Call* in which a conscientious detective has to pay back a debt to an old colleague before he can arrest him. *Sc:* Richard Breen (the story by O. Henry). *Ph:* Lucien Ballard. *Art Dir:* Lyle Wheeler, Chester Gore. *Ed:* Nick de Maggio. *Mus:* Alfred Newman. *With* Dale Robertson (*Barney Woods*), Richard Widmark (*Johnny*), Joyce MacKenzie (*Hazel*), Richard Rober (*Chief Detective*). *Prod:* Andre Hakim for 20th Century-Fox. 118m.

NIAGARA (1953). Melodrama of a faithless wife. *Sc:* Charles Brackett, Walter Reisch, Richard Breen. *Ph:* Joseph MacDonald. *Art Dir:* Lyle Wheeler, Maurice Ransford. *Ed:* Barbara McLean. *Mus:* Sol Kaplan. *With* Marilyn Monroe (*Rose Loomis*), Joseph Cotten (*George Loomis*), Jean Peters (*Polly Cutler*), Casey Adams (*Ray Cutler*), Denis O'Dea (*Inspector Starkey*), Richard Allan, Don Wilson, Lurene Tuttle, Russell Collins, Carleton Young, Will Wright, Lester Matthews, Sean McClory, Patrick O'Moore, Harry Carey, Jr. *Prod:* Charles Brackett for 20th Century-Fox. 89m. Technicolor.

WHITE WITCH DOCTOR (1953). Medicine, murder, gold and guilt on an African safari. *Sc:* Ivan Goff, Ben Roberts (novel by Louise A. Stinetorf). *Ph:* Leon Shamroy. *Art Dir:* Lyle Wheeler, Mark-Lee Kirk. *Ed:* James B. Clark. *Mus:* Bernard Herrmann. *With* Robert Mitchum (*Lonnie*), Susan Hayward (*Ellen*), Walter Slezak (*Huysman*), Mashood Ajula, Timothy Carey, Joseph C. Norcisse, Elzie Emanuel, Otis Greene, Charles Gemore, Paul Thompson, Nasman Brown, Myrtle Anderson, Everett Brown, Dorothy Harris. *Prod:* Otto Lang for 20th Century-Fox. 96m. Technicolor.

PRINCE VALIANT (1954). Impetuous young Viking endeavours to regain his father's throne, overthrowing a rebellion against King Arthur in the process. *Sc:* Dudley Nichols (a cartoon strip by Harold Foster). *Ph:* Lucien Ballard. *Art Dir:* Lyle Wheeler, Mark-Lee Kirk. *Ed:* Robert Simpson. *Mus:* Franz Waxman. *With* Robert Wagner (*Prince Valiant*), James Mason (*Sir Brack*), Janet Leigh (*Aleta*), Sterling Hayden (*Sir Gawain*), Debra Paget (*Ilene*), Donald Crisp (*King Aquar*), Victor McLaglen (*Boltar*), Brian Aherne (*King Arthur*), Barry Jones (*King Luke*), Mary Phillips, Howard Wendell, Tom Conway, Sammy Ogg, Robert Adler, Hal Baylor, Neville Brand, John Dierkes, Jarma Lewis, Richard Webb, Carleton Young, Don Megowan, Primo Carnera, Ray Spiker, Fortunio

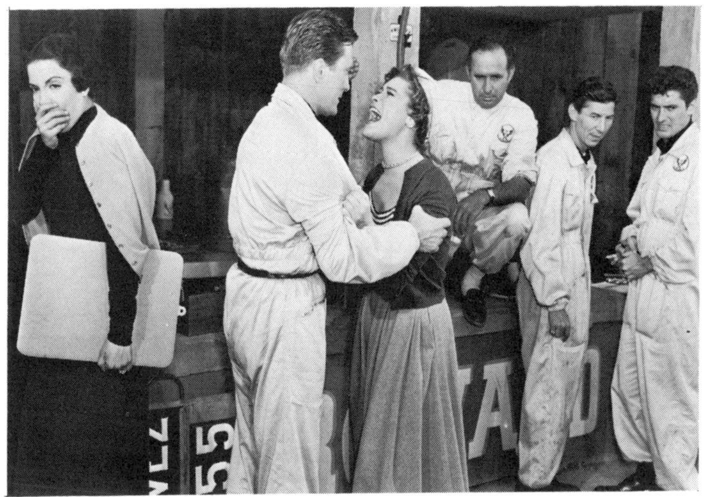

Katy Jurado, Kirk Douglas and the late Bella Darvi in the motor racing drama, SUCH MEN ARE DANGEROUS

Gordian, Percival Vivian, Otto Waldis. *Prod:* Robert L. Jacks for 20th Century-Fox. 100m. Technicolor. CinemaScope.

GARDEN OF EVIL (1954). Western with a woman hiring a group of men to hunt for her missing husband. *Sc:* Frank Fenton (a story by Fred Freiberger and William Tunberg). *Ph:* Milton Krasner, Jorge Stahl, Jr. *Art Dir:* Lyle Wheeler, Edward Fitzgerald. *Ed:* James B. Clark. *Mus:* Bernard Herrmann. *With* Gary Cooper (*Hooker*), Susan Hayward (*Leah Fuller*), Richard Widmark (*Fiske*), Cameron Mitchell (*Luke Daly*), Hugh Marlowe (*John Fuller*), Rita Moreno, Victor Manuel Mendoza, Fernando Wagner, Arturo Soto Rangel, Manuel Donde, Antonio Bribiesca, Salvado Terroba. *Prod:* Charles Brackett for 20th Century-Fox 100m. Technicolor. CinemaScope.

THE RACERS (G.B.: SUCH MEN ARE DANGEROUS) (1954). Racing car melodrama, investigating the life and motivations of the drivers. *Sc:* Charles Kaufman (novel by Hans Ruesch). *Ph:* Joseph MacDonald. *Art Dir:* Lyle Wheeler, George Patrick. *Ed:* James B. Clark. *Mus:* Alex North. *With* Kirk Douglas (*Gino*), Bella Darvi (*Nicole*), Gilbert Roland (*Dell 'Oro*), Lee J. Cobb (*Maglio*), Cesar Romero (*Carlos*), Katy Jurado (*Maria*), Charles Goldner (*Piero*), John Hudson (*Michel Caron*), Agnes Laury, George Dolenz, John Wengraf, Richard Allan, Mel Welles, Norbert Schiller, Francesca de Scaffa, Ina Anders, Stephen Bekassy, Gene D'Arcy, Mike Dergate, Peter Brocco, June McCall, Frank Yaconelli, Gladys Holland, Ben Wright, Carleton Young, James Barrett, Salvador Baganez, Chris Randall, Eddie Le Baron, Anna Cheselka, Joe Vitale, George Givot. *Prod:* Julian Blaustein for 20th Century-Fox. 112m. Colour by De Luxe. CinemaScope.

THE BOTTOM OF THE BOTTLE (G.B.: BEYOND THE RIVER) (1956). Melodrama about an escaped convict hiding out at his brother's house. *Sc:* Sidney Boehm (novel by Georges Simenon). *Ph:* Lee Garmes. *Art Dir:* Lyle Wheeler, Maurice Ransford. *Ed:* David Bretherton. *Mus:* Leigh Harline. *With* Joseph Cotten (*P.M.*), Van Johnson (*Donald Martin*), Ruth Roman (*Nora Martin*), Jack Carson (*Hal Breckenridge*), Margaret Hayes (*Lil Breckenridge*), Bruce Bennett (*Brand*), Brad Dexter (*Stanley Miller*), Peggy Knudsen (*Ellen Miller*), Jim Davis, Nancy Gates, Ted Griffin, Margaret Lindsay, Pedro Gonzalez-Gonzalez, John Lee, Shawn Smith, Ernestine Barrier, Walter Woolf King, Sandy Descher, Kim Charney, Mimi Gibson, Carleton Young, Frances Dominguez, Orlando Beltram, Maria M. Valerani, George Trevino, Joanne Jordan, Lee Gonzalez, George Anderson. *Prod:* Buddy Adler for 20th Century-Fox 88m. Colour by De Luxe. CinemaScope.

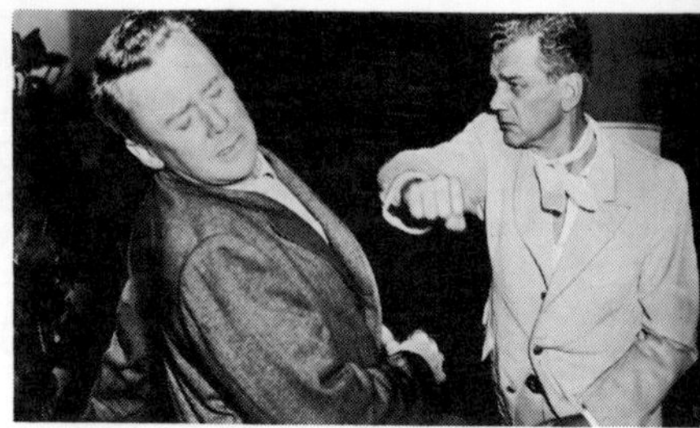

Joseph Cotten tries to knock sense into his criminal brother Van Johnson in BEYOND THE RIVER

23 PACES TO BAKER STREET (1956). A blind man attempts to solve a murder. *Sc:* Nigel Balchin (novel *A Warrant for X* by Philip Macdonald). *Ph:* Milton Krasner. *Art Dir:* Lyle Wheeler, Maurice Ransford. *Ed:* James B. Clark. *Mus:* Leigh Harline. *With* Van Johnson (*Philip Hannon*), Vera Miles (*Jean Lennox*), Patricia Laffan (*Alice MacDonald*), Cecil Parker (*Matthews*), Maurice Denham (*Inspector Gravening*), Liam Redmond (*Mr. Murch*), Estelle Winwood, Isobel Elsom, Martin Benson, A. Cameron Grant, Natalie Norwick, Les Sketchley, Terence De Marney, Queenie Leonard, Charles Keane, Ben Wright, Lucie Lancaster, Ashley Cowan, Fred Griffiths, Reginald Sheffield, Phyllis Montefiore, Arthur Gomez, Janice Kane, Robert Raglan, Howard Lang, Margaret McGrath, Walter Horsbrough, Yorke Sherwood, Charles Stanley, Robin Alalouf, Michael Trubshawe. *Prod:* Henry Ephron for 20th Century-Fox. 103m. Colour by De Luxe. CinemaScope.

LEGEND OF THE LOST (1957). Modern day desert saga. *Sc:* Robert Presnell, Jr., Ben Hecht. *Ph:* Jack Cardiff. *Art Dir:* Alfred Ybarra. *Ed:* Bert Bates. *Mus:* A. F. Lavagnino. *With* John Wayne (*Joe January*), Sophia Loren (*Dita*), Rossano Brazzi (*Paul Bonnard*), Kurt Kaznar (*Prefect Dukas*), Sonia Moser, Angela Portaluri, Ibrahim El Hadish. *Prod:* Henry Hathaway for Batjac Prods./Robert Haggiag/Dear Film Prods. 109m. Technicolor. Technirama.

FROM HELL TO TEXAS (G.B.: MANHUNT) (1958). A young cowboy tries unsuccessfully to stay clear of trouble in the days of the law of the gun. *Sc:* Robert Buckner, Wendell Mayes (novel "The Hell-Bent Kid" by Charles O. Locke). *Ph:* Wilfrid M. Cline. *Art Dir:* Lyle Wheeler, Walter Simonds. *Ed:* Johnny Ehrin. *Mus:* Daniel Amphitheatrof. *With* Don Murray (*Tod Lohman*), Diane Varsi (*Juanita Bradley*), Chill Wills (*Amos Bradley*), Dennis Hopper (*Tom Boyd*), R. G. Armstrong (*Hunter Boyd*), Jay C. Flippen (*Jake Leffertfinger*), Margo (*Mrs. Bradley*), John Larch (*Hal Carmody*), Ken Scott, Rudolfo Acosta, Harry Carey, Jr., Salvador Baguez, Jerry Oddo, Jose Torvay, Malcolm Atterbury. *Prod:* Robert Buckner for 20th Century-Fox. 100m. Colour by De Luxe. CinemaScope.

WOMAN OBSESSED (1959). Romantic drama in which a woman finds love again after her husband is accidentally killed. *Sc:* Sidney Boehm (novel *The Snow Birch* by John Mantley). *Ph:* William C. Mellor. *Art Dir:* Lyle Wheeler, Jack Martin Smith. *Ed:* Robert Simpson. *Mus:* Hugo Friedhofer. *With* Susan Hayward (*Mary*), Stephen Boyd (*Fred Carter*), Arthur Franz (*Tom*), Dennis Holmes (*Robbie*), Ken Scott (*Sergeant LeMoyne*), Theodore Bikel (*Dr. Gibbs*), James Philbrook, Florence MacMichael, Jack Raine, Mary Carroll, Fred Graham, Mike Wally, and Barbara Nichols. *Prod:* Sidney Boehm for 20th Century-Fox. 102m. Colour by De Luxe. CinemaScope.

SEVEN THIEVES (1960). Thriller about a casino robbery. *Sc:* Sidney Boehm (novel *Lions at the Kill* by Max Catto). *Ph:* Sam Leavitt. *Art Dir:* Lyle Wheeler, John De Cuir. *Ed:* Dorothy Spencer. *Mus:* Dominic Frontiere. *With* Edward G. Robinson (*Theo Wilkins*), Rod Steiger (*Paul*), Eli Wallach (*Pancho*), Joan Collins (*Melanie*), Berry Kroeger (*Hugo Baumer*), Alexander Scourby (*Raymond Le May*), Michael Dante (*Louis*), Sebastian Cabot, Marcel Hillaire, Margo Ann Deighton, Alphonse Martell, John Beradino, Jonathan Kidd. *Prod:* Sidney Boehm for 20th Century-Fox. 102m. CinemaScope.

NORTH TO ALASKA (1960). Lusty adventure comedy about prospectors in the Far North. *Sc:* John Lee Mahin, Martin Rackin, Claude Binyon (play "Birthday Gift" by Lazlo Fodor from an idea by John Kafka). *Ph:* Leon Shamroy. *Art Dir:* Duncan Cramer, Jack Martin Smith. *Ed:* Dorothy Spencer. *Mus:* Lionel Newman. *With* John Wayne (*Sam McCord*), Stewart Granger (*George Pratt*), Capucine (*Michelle*), Fabian (*Billy Pratt*), Ernie Kovacs (*Frankie Canon*), Karl Swenson, Mickey Shaughnessy, Joe Sawyer, Kathleen Freeman, John Qualen, Stanley Adams, Stephen Courtleigh, Douglas Dick, Jerry O'Sullivan, Ollie O'Toole, Frank Faylen. *Prod:* Henry Hathaway for 20th Century-Fox. 122m.

Colour by De Luxe. CinemaScope.

HOW THE WEST WAS WON (1962)—Episodes *The Rivers, The Plains, The Outlaws*. The saga of the winning of the West. *Sc:* James R. Webb (suggested by a series in "Life" magazine). *Ph:* William Daniels, Milton Krasner. *Art Dir:* George W. Davis, William Ferrari, Addison Hehr. *Ed:* Harold F. Kress. *Mus:* Alfred Newman. *With* Karl Malden (*Zebulon Prescott*), Agnes Moorehead (*Rebecca Prescott*), Carroll Baker (*Eve Prescott*), Debbie Reynolds (*Lillith Prescott*), James Stewart (*Linus Rawlings*), Brigid Bazlan (*Dora Hawkins*), Walter Brennan (*Colonel Hawkins*) in *The Rivers. With* Debbie Reynolds (*Lillith Prescott*), Gregory Peck (*Cleve Van Valen*), Robert Preston (*Roger Morgan*), Thelma Ritter (*Agatha Clegg*), David Brian (*Van Valen, attorney*) in *The Plains. With* George Peppard (*Zeb Rawlings*), Eli Wallach (*Charley Gant*), Lee J. Cobb (*Lew Ramsay*), Lee Van Cleef, Jay C. Flippen, Carolyn Jones and Mickey Shaughnessy in *The Outlaws. Prod:* Bernard Smith for Cinerama—M-G-M. 162m. Metrocolor. Cinerama.

CIRCUS WORLD (U.S.) or THE MAGNIFICENT SHOWMAN (G.B.) (1964). Circus extravaganza which delves into the private lives of the artistes and owners. *Sc:* Ben Hecht, Julian Halevy, James Edward Grant (a story by Philip Yordan and Nicholas Ray). *Ph:* Jack Hildyard. *2nd unit Ph:* Claude Renoir. *Prod design:* John De Cuir. *Ed:* Dorothy Spencer. *Mus:* Dimitri Tiomkin. *With* John Wayne (*Matt Masters*), Rita Hayworth (*Lili Alfredo*), Claudia Cardinale (*Toni Alfredo*), John Smith (*Steve McCabe*), Lloyd Nolan (*Cap Carson*), Henri Dantes, Wanda Rotha, Katharyna, Kay Walsh, Margaret MacGrath, Miles Malleson, Katherine Kath, Kate Ellison, Moustache, Franz Althoff and his circus. *Prod:* Samuel Bronston for Bronston-Midway. 137m. (U.S.: 135). Technicolor. 70mm. Super Technirama.

THE SONS OF KATIE ELDER (1965). Western built around four sons clearing their dead family's name. *Sc:* William H. Wright, Allan Weiss, Harry Essex (a story by Talbot Jennings). *Ph:* Lucien Ballard. *Art Dir:* Hal Pereira and Walter Tyler. *Ed:* Warren Low. *Mus:* Elmer Bernstein. *With* John Wayne (*John Elder*), Dean Martin (*Tom Elder*), Martha Hyer (*Mary Gordon*), Michael Anderson, Jr. (*Bud Elder*), Earl Holliman (*Matt Elder*), George Kennedy (*Curley*), Jeremy Slate, James Gregory, Paul Fix, Dennis Hopper, Sheldon Allman, John Litel, John Doucette, James Westerfield, Rhys Williams, John Qualen, Rodolfo Acosta, Strother Martin, Percy Helton, Karl Swenson. *Prod:* Hal B. Wallis for Hal Wallis Prod./Paramount. 122m. Technicolor. Panavision.

NEVADA SMITH (1966). Revenge Western with title figure seeking his parents' murderers. *Sc:* John Michael Hayes (suggested by a character in Harold Robbins' novel *The Carpetbaggers*). *Ph:* Lucien Ballard. *Art Dir:* Hal Pereira, Tambi Larsen, Al Roelofs. *Ed:* Frank Bracht. *Mus:* Alfred Newman. *With* Steve McQueen (*Nevada Smith*), Karl Malden (*Tom Fitch*), Suzanne Pleshette (*Pilar*), Brian Keith (*Jonas Cord*), Raf Vallone (*Father Zaccardi*), Janet Margolin (*Neesa*), Arthur Kennedy (*Bill Bowdre*), Howard Da Silva (*Warden*), Pat Hingle (*Big Foot*), Martin Landau (*Jesse Coe*),

Kaz Garas and Stewart Granger discuss their personal experiences of killing in THE LAST SAFARI

Paul Fix, Gene Evans, Josephine Hutchinson, Val Avery, John Doucette, Sheldon Allman, Lyle Bettger, Bert Freed, David McLean, Steve Mitchell, Merritt Bohn, Sandy Kenyon, Ric Roman, John Lawrence, Stanley Adams, John Litel, George Mitchell, Ted de Corsia. *Prod:* Henry Hathaway for Joseph E. Levine/Solar/Paramount. 131m. (G.B.: 120). Technicolor. Panavision.

THE LAST SAFARI (1967). African adventure as an old hunter conquers his obsession on his last safari. *Sc:* John Gay (novel *Gilligan's Last Elephant* by Gerald Hanley). *Ph:* Ted Moore. *Art Dir:* Maurice Fowler. *Ed:* John Bloom. *Mus:* Johnny Dankworth. *With* Stewart Granger (*Miles Gilchrist*), Kaz Garas (*Casey*), Gabriella Licudi (*Grant*), Johnny Sekka (*Janna*), Liam Redmond (*Alec Beaumont*), Eugene Deckers, David Munys, Wilfred Moore, John De Villiers, Jean Parnell, Bill Grant, Labina, Kipkoske, the Masai Wakamba Tribal Dancers. *Prod:* Henry Hathaway for Paramount. 110m. (G.B.: 99). Technicolor.

5 CARD STUD (1968). Detective story in Western setting featuring a religious maniac killer. *Sc:* Marguerite Roberts (a novel by Ray Gaulden). *Ph:* Daniel L. Fapp. *Prod. design:* Walter Tyler. *Ed:* Warren Low. *Mus:* Maurice Jarre. *With* Dean Martin (*Van Morgan*), Robert Mitchum (*Rev. Rudd*), Roddy McDowall (*Nick Evers*), Inger Stevens (*Lily Langford*), Katherine Justice (*Nora Evers*), John Anderson (*Marshal Dana*), Yaphet Kotto, Ruth Springford, Denver Pyle, Bill Fletcher, Whit Bissell, Ted de Corsia, Don Collier, Roy Jenson, Boyd Morgan, George Rowbotham. *Prod:* Hal B. Wallis for Hal Wallis Prod./Paramount. 103m. Technicolor.

TRUE GRIT (1969). Western in which a young girl avenges her father's death with the aid of a one-eyed marshal. *Sc:* Marguerite Roberts (the novel by Charles

The discovery of a mutilated victim in 5 CARD STUD illustrates Hathaway's use of savage imagery in his later works

Portis). *Ph:* Lucien Ballard. *Prod. design:* Walter Tyler. *Ed:* Warren Low. *Mus:* Elmer Bernstein. *With* John Wayne (*Rooster Cogburn*), Kim Darby (*Mattie Ross*), Glen Campbell (*La Boeuf*), Jeremy Slate (*Emmett Quincey*), Robert Duvall (*Ned Pepper*), Dennis Hopper (*Moon*), Strother Martin (*Colonel G. Stonehill*), Jeff Corey (*Tom Chaney*), Alfred Ryder, Ron Soble, John Fiedler, James Westerfield, John Doucette, Donald Woods, Edith Atwater, Carlos Rivas, Isabel Boniface, John Pickard, Elizabeth Harrower, Ken Renard, Jay Ripley, Kenneth Becker, Hank Worden, Myron Healey. *Prod:* Hal B. Wallis for Paramount. 128m. Technicolor.

RAID ON ROMMEL (1971). Wartime adventure (North Africa, 1942) in which a commando mission goes to knock out German guns before the British fleet arrives. *Sc:* Richard Bluel. *Ph:* Earl Rath. *Prod design:* Frank Beetson. *Art Dir:* Alexander Golitzen, Henry Bumstead. *Ed:* Gene Palmer. *Mus:* Hal Monney. *With* Richard Burton (*Foster*), John Colicos (*MacKenzie*), Clinton Greyn (*Major Tarkington*), Danielle De Metz (*Vivi*), Wolfgang Preiss (*Rommel*), Christopher Cary, John Orchard, Brook Williams, Greg Mullavey, Ben Wright, Michael Sevareid, Chris Anders. *Prod:* Harry Tatelman for Universal. Technicolor. 99m. Film re-uses action sequences from *Tobruk* (1967).

SHOOTOUT (1971). Revenge Western in which an ex-convict tracks down his betrayer. *Sc:* Marguerite Roberts (novel *The Lone Cowboy* by Will James). *Ph:* Earl Rath. *Art Dir:* Walter Tyler. *Ed:* Archie Marshek. *Mus:* David Grusin. *With* Gregory Peck (*Clay Lomax*), Pat Quinn (*Juliana*), Robert F. Lyons (*Bobby Jay*), Susan Tyrrell (*Alma*), Jeff Corey (*Trooper*), James Gregory (*Sam Foley*), Rita Gam, Dawn Lyn, Pepe Serna, John Chandler, Paul Fix, Arthur Hunnicutt, Nicholas Beavvy. *Prod:* Hal B. Wallis for Universal. Technicolor. 94m. Re-make of THE LONE COWBOY (1934, *d* Paul Sloane).

ADDENDA

Hathaway made a short in 1937, *Lest We Forget,* in collaboration with Richard Thorpe, E. Mason Hoffer and Harry Loud (possibly as part of a tribute to the late Will Rogers).

Also started and abandoned I LOVE A SOLDIER (1936), later re-worked into HOTEL IMPERIAL (1939, *d* Robert Florey). Shot scenes without credit for RED SKIES OF MONTANA (1952, *d* Joseph Newman) and RAMPAGE (1963, *d* Phil Karlson).

He also began *Of Human Bondage* (1964), replaced temporarily by Bryan Forbes and finally by Ken Hughes; and shot some of *Airport* (1970) while director George Seaton was ill.

(*The assistance of Jean Canham and Robert Holton is gratefully acknowledged*)

Opposite: the lacrosse game as seen in Hathaway's TEN GENTLEMEN FROM WEST POINT, and (below), DOWN TO THE SEA IN SHIPS, one of a series of re-makes of silent films that Hathaway undertook (with Paul Harvey and Harry Davenport)

Index to Names

A2